Partners for Good

Joan Levitt MBE, 1925–2012
An inspiring servant of her community

Partners for Good

Business, Government and the Third Sector

TOM LEVITT

GOWER

Published by
Gower Publishing Limited
Wey Court East
Union Road
Farnham
Surrey, GU9 7PT
England

Ashgate Publishing Company
Suite 420
101 Cherry Street
Burlington,
VT 05401-4405
USA

www.gowerpublishing.com

British Library Cataloguing in Publication Data
Levitt, Tom.
  Partners for good : business, government and the third sector.
  1. Social policy. 2. Nonprofit organizations. 3. Charities.
  4. Voluntarism. 5. Social responsibility of business.
  6. Strategic alliances (Business) 7. Public-private sector
  cooperation.
  I. Title
  361.2'5-dc23

ISBN 9781409434375 (hbk)
ISBN 9781409434382 (ebk)

Library of Congress Cataloging-in-Publication Data
Levitt, Tom.
  Partners for good : business, government and the third sector / by Tom
Levitt.
      p. cm.
  Includes bibliographical references and index.
  ISBN 978-1-4094-3437-5 (hbk) -- ISBN 978-1-4094-3438-2 (ebk)
1. Voluntarism--Great Britain. 2. Social service--Great Britain.
3. Non-governmental organizations--Great Britain. 4. Social responsibility of
business--Great Britain. 5. Associations, institutions, etc.--Great
Britain. I. Title.
  HN400.V64L48 2011
  302'.14--dc23
                                                                    2011045653

Printed and bound in Great Britain by the
MPG Books Group, UK

Contents

List of Figures

List of Tables

About the Author

Tom Levitt has been involved in politics and communities for as long as he can remember. After ten years in local government, in Gloucestershire and then Derbyshire, he became the Member of Parliament for High Peak in the Labour landslide of 1997 where he remained until stepping down in 2010.

During that time he was recognised as a Parliamentary authority on the third sector, spending time chairing both the All Party Group on the Community and Voluntary Sector and the Government's Advisory Body on Third Sector Commissioning. He was a member of the Neuberger Commission on the Future of Volunteering and Chair of the Community Development Foundation.

Between 1998 and 2003, Tom was a trustee of one of Britain's most influential charities, the Royal National Institute for Deaf People (now Action on Hearing Loss).

He was a ministerial aide for eight years, including four with Hilary Benn as Secretary of State for International Development, where he witnessed how business could play a central role in the development of communities. He also had the opportunity to see community development in other parts of the world: in Africa, Asia and the Middle East. He is currently Chair of the UK operation of the development charity, Concern Worldwide, patron of the award winning charity READ International and a trustee of the Work Foundation Alliance.

Prior to Parliament, Tom worked as a science teacher in comprehensive schools and then as a freelance consultant, trainer and writer on access issues for people with sensory impairments.

Today he works as a consultant and writer on cross sector partnerships, showcasing his work online (see www.sector4focus.co.uk). He is a director of the business consultancy Good Measures and has an honorary doctorate from the University of Derby.

Preface

No single sector of the economy has a monopoly on doing good. In the bringing about of positive and qualitative social change the private sector is not as well developed as the public or third sectors – other than in the not insignificant field of creating wealth and jobs. Huge opportunities exist for co-working between sectors today and in the future, not least as a result of the new political, cultural and economic environment in which we find ourselves.

Consider the following dozen facts:

1. Cuts in public spending are highlighting the urgency of the eternal need for charities and voluntary organisations to diversify their income streams.

2. Public responses to the banking and other crises include demands for greater scrutiny of corporate behaviour in the private sector and high expectations of ethical conduct.

3. The business case for tackling climate change has been won as companies find that the green agenda can generate innovation, cost savings and a responsible image. The same arguments in favour of community engagement by business have not yet been universally accepted.

4. Over the last 15 years partnerships between agents of government and voluntary organisations have developed and ground rules have evolved. As a result, many charities and third sector bodies have experienced growing professionalisation which makes them more attractive as partners for business.

5. The qualities that the voluntary sector can bring to a service delivery partnership include personalisation, local flexibility and cost efficiency.

6. The growth of social enterprise has been significant but unless new and attractive forms of investment emerge soon its continued growth will be insufficient to grasp the opportunities that Government policy presents.

7. In Britain there is a willingness to give to, and volunteer for, good causes which is regarded as part of our national character.

8. Companies now running public services find themselves in the same position that local authorities were in 15 years ago – of starting to recognise the benefits of partnership with voluntary sector providers.

9. Employer-based volunteering is not as well developed in this country as it is in the USA.

10. Some excellent practice in business/voluntary sector partnerships can be found in developing countries where the public sector is weak.

11. The economic climate is likely to cause a fall in the number and size of acts of major personal and corporate philanthropy.

12. In today's 'Big Society' it is said that 'we are all in this together'.

This book comes during a fascinating period in our political and economic history. Its timing is also prompted by the publication in November 2010 of the first internationally agreed standard on social responsibility, ISO26000.

The international standard covers six strands of activity and much of its content is already covered by legislation in this country. Where it is not, such as in the Community Involvement and Development strand, there is no means of enforcement, no body of good practice and few established external incentives to take the issue forward. This is where business and charities can work together with the greatest benefit to all concerned.

This story is about these facts in this context; how they interact, how they arose and how they might coalesce in the future.

It will be a fascinating journey.

* * *

I am deeply indebted to many people, companies, charities and institutions who have helped me put this book together, many of whom will not have known they were doing so at the time.

Tom Levitt

London, UK

List of Abbreviations

ACEVO   Association of Chief Executives of Voluntary Organisations
ACF   Association of Charitable Foundations
ADP   Accenture Development Partnerships
AIDS   Acquired Immunity Deficiency Syndrome (see HIV)
AMREF   African Medical Research Foundation
BAA   Business Action on Africa
BABA   British African Business Association
BAH   Business Action on Homelessness
BCtA   Business Call to Action
BFP   Business Fights Poverty
BID   Bargaining for International Development
BIF   Business Innovation Facility
BIS   [Department of] Business, Innovation and Skills
BITC   Business in the Community
BOND   British Overseas NGOs for Development (known now as Bond)
BTCV   British Trust for Conservation Volunteers
CAB   Citizens Advice Bureau
CAF   Charities Aid Foundation
CAFOD   Catholic Agency for Overseas Development
CBI   Confederation of British Industries
CDFI   Community Development Finance Institutions
CEL   Collective Enterprises Ltd
CEO   Chief Executive Officer
CIC   Community Interest Company
CIPFA   Chartered Institute of Public Finance Administration
CITR   Community Investment Tax Relief
CLG   [Department for] Communities and Local Government
CR   Corporate Responsibility
CRI   Corporate Responsibility Index
CSO   Civil Society Organisation

CSHR	Corporate Social Human Resources
CSR	Corporate Social Responsibility
CSV	Creating Shared Value
CVS	Community and Voluntary Sector
CVS	Council for Voluntary Service
DfID	Department for International Development
DOL	Digital Outreach Limited
DSC	Directory of Social Change
DTI	Department for Trade and Industry (now BIS)
DWP	Department for Work & Pensions
EITI	Extractive Industries Transparency Index
ESG	Environmental, Social and [corporate] Governance
ETI	Ethical Trading Initiative
EU	European Union
FSB	Federation of Small Businesses
FSC	Forest Stewardship Council
GAVI	Global Alliance for Vaccination and Immunisation
GRI	Global Reporting Initiative
HIA	Home Improvement Agency
HIV	Human Immunodeficiency Virus (see AIDS)
HR	Human Resources
HMRC	Her Majesty's Revenue and Customs
HSE	Health and Safety Executive
IBLF	International Business Leaders Forum
IDeA	[Local government] Improvement and Development Agency
ILO	International Labor Organisation
INGO	International Non-Governmental Organisation
ISO	International Standards Organisation
LBG	London Benchmarking Group
LGIU	Local Government Information Unit
LLW	London Living Wage
LSP	Local Strategic Partnership
MBA	Master of Business Administration
MDG	Millennium Development Goals
NACVS	National Association of Councils for Voluntary Service (now NAVCA)
NAO	National Audit Office
NAVCA	National Association for Voluntary and Community Action
NCSS	National Council for Social Services (now NCVO)
NCVO	National Council for Voluntary Organisations
NESTA	National Endowment for Science and the Arts

NGO	Non-Governmental Organisation
NHS	National Health Service
OCS	Office for Civil Society (formerly OTS)
ODI	Overseas Development Institute
OECD	Organisation for Economic Co-operation and Development
OTS	Office of the Third Sector (now OCS)
PFI	Private Finance Initiative
PLA	Preschool Learning Alliance
PPP	Public Private Partnership
PRI	Principles of Responsible Investment
RBS	Royal Bank of Scotland (or RBS Group)
RNIB	Royal National Institute of the Blind
RNID	Royal National Institute for Deaf People (now Action on Hearing Loss)
RNLI	Royal National Lifeboat Institute
RoSPA	Royal Society for the Prevention of Accidents
RSPCA	Royal Society for the Prevention of Cruelty to Animals
SCC	Small Charities Coalition
SEUK	Social Enterprise UK
SIB	Social Impact Bond
SME	Small and Medium-sized Enterprise
SPV	Special Purpose Vehicle
SRI	Socially Responsible Investment
SROI	Social Return on Investment
TSR	Total Shareholder Return
TUC	Trade Union Congress
TUPE	Transfer of Undertakings (Protection of Employment) Regulations
UN	United Nations
UNGC	United Nations Global Compact
UNPRI	United Nations Principles of Responsible Investment
USAID	United States Aid
VCS	Voluntary and Community Sector
VSO	Voluntary Service Overseas
WHO	World Health Organisation
WRVS	Women's Royal Voluntary Service
WWF	Worldwide Fund for Nature
YHA	Youth Hostels Association
ZCT	Zurich Community Trust

1

Who Do They Think They Are?

From where he sits, Paul Kennedy can see a wide vista of a fascinating, varied and exciting landscape. There are rolling hills, dangerous cliffs, tempting streams. So much is happening out there, involving so many varied and competing players, that it would be tempting to do nothing other than watch them interacting in this newly discovered territory, the land between the sectors, fascinated: but he cannot. He has work to do.

Running a company is a full time job. Collective Enterprises Limited, CEL, is an established private company which looks after third sector clients, many of whom provide services traditionally associated with the public sector. The landscape that Paul surveys used to have strict territorial demarcation – but no longer. Boundaries have been crossed, blurred, eradicated. Traditional centres still remain in the three kingdoms that make it up – the private, public and third sectors – but thousands have left the safety of their citadels to engage with the strangers from other lands; most that have done this now feel comfortable in having done so and wonder why ever they didn't do it earlier.

Wherever they came from Paul can tell them apart, like a seasoned birdwatcher:

> *It's about risk. In the private sector risk is part of your everyday life. You take risks – with your capital, your marketing, your job – and you know you might lose everything if it goes wrong. But there's always the chance it could go very right, too.*

His relaxed Merseyside accent is at home in the director's chair or the board room.

> *In the public sector you're not so keen on risk. But if it does go wrong, you come into work next day and just carry on. And if you think*

councils, for example, are risk averse well – just look at charities. 'Our charitable status doesn't allow us to take risks with our funds', they say, and they're right.

So how do cross-sector partnerships, co-working, common missions emerge?

I'm not saying you have to change your attitude to risk when you enter into a partnership. There are all sorts of reasons why partnerships might be the right course to take. But you do have to understand your partner's attitude to risk, and you have to take it on board. Without a common understanding of risk no cross-sector partnership can survive.

In this book I seek to explore how cross-sector partnerships, particularly those between UK businesses and third sector organisations, have emerged, developed and become sustainable.

Fifteen years ago business capital and social capital were the twain that never would meet: activists regarded business as a bunch of ruthless, uncaring capitalists whilst business saw the third sector as well-meaning but amateur do-gooders. Charity was something industry did once a year at the Golf Club, at the Chairman's wife's behest, principally to make shareholders and selected members of the workforce feel good. The typical charity worker either had a blue rinse and worked a few hours a week in a charity shop or wore shorts, sandals and a well-meaning smile somewhere in Africa.

How things have changed.

Before we find out how CEL has managed cross-sector partnerships for a generation, let us first define our terms (see Figure 1.1).

Defining the Three Principal Sectors

The 'private sector' is the 'for profit' business sector of registered companies, corporations, multinationals, Small and Medium-sized Enterprises (SMEs) and sole traders. The South African corporate citizenship guru, Professor Mervyn King, reminds us that amongst the 100 largest economies in the world there are more corporates than countries.

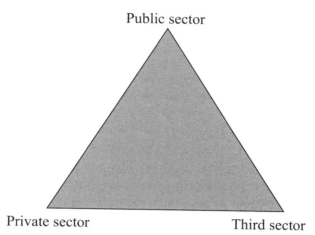

Figure 1.1   The sector triangle

The 'public sector' is that part of the economy which is paid for (largely) from taxation and operated by central or local government, their agents and agencies.

Civil society is what is left.

A small part of civil society is made up of organisations which would not normally be included in the term 'voluntary sector'. They play a peripheral role in the economy but an important one in society: political parties, universities, pressure groups, trade unions and the media. Despite being the preferred term to describe all this by the National Council for Voluntary Organisations (NCVO) and the eponymous Office for Civil Society (OCS) within the Cabinet Office, the term 'civil society' is not widely used in Britain. In international development a healthy civil society is one in which there are academic, political and media freedoms; whilst we take these things for granted they are in short supply in too many places. The United Nations Global Compact (UNGC) defines 'civil society organisations' (CSO) as 'non-governmental and non-profit entities that seek to bring about positive social and environmental change'. It specifically excludes 'academia, labour or municipal organisations' from its definition because they have their own defined channels of engaging with the Compact.

Table 1.1 describes convenient, if not definitive, distinctions between the sectors and their sub-groups: 'X' shows membership and '(X)' a close association.

Table 1.1   A guide to the sectors

	Business	Not for Profit	Voluntary Sector	VCS	Third Sector	Civil Society	Public Sector
Private Business	X						
Social Business	X					X	
Social Enterprise	X	X				X	
Mutuals	X	(X)				X	
Foundations	(X)				X	X	
Charities		X	X	X	X	X	
Volunteers			X	X	X	X	
Community/Faith Groups				X	X	X	
Trade Unions					X	X	
Media						X	
Philanthropists						X	
Exempt Charities		X				X	X
Academia						X	X
Politics						X	X
Local Government						(X)	X
Central Government							X

Civil society is therefore too broad a phrase to describe one of the players in this book. I prefer either 'third sector' which I take to mean the UNGC view of civil society, stripped of its developmental or human rights meaning; or 'voluntary' or 'voluntary and community' sector (VCS). For the purposes of this book VCS, voluntary sector and third sector are roughly synonymous. The reference to 'community sector' reminds us that whilst there are multimillion pound charities, tiny, single purpose community groups also exist in every town and village. These are the 75 per cent of UK's voluntary groups which will not feel the impact of cuts in government spending, claimed the Cabinet Office Minister Francis Maude in January 2011[1] – but only because they receive no government money in the first place. Over half of all registered charities have an income of under £10,000.[2]

'Voluntary' does not simply mean 'made up of volunteers'. If it did, there would be very few large 'voluntary' organisations in this country. The word

---

1   Progress/Res Publica meeting, 14 February 2011 and on BBC Radio 4.
2   Evidence of Dame Suzi Leather, Chair of the Charity Commission, to the Public Affairs Select Committee, 12 July 2007.

'professional' in the sector would be oxymoronic and yet such professionals exist in their thousands. I take 'voluntary' to mean 'providing services which are not statutory; from within the ethos of volunteering'. The 'ethos of volunteering' includes individual volunteers engaged by bodies outside the sector: such as those 'Friends' which provide catering and other services in hospitals.

The number of charities varies over time and depending who is counting, but there are probably between 160,000 and 180,000 of them, sharing a turnover of over £53 billion. Their income and expenditure is listed in Table 1.2. Almost 12,000 were charitable foundations, bodies which exist in law to provide funds from their own capital resources to other bodies or their own charitable arms, often through income earned from an endowment. There could be 300,000 more non-registered voluntary organisations whose turnover is insufficient to require Charity Commission registration or which have chosen not to register for another reason. Across the UK this is roughly one organisation for every 150 people. Charities providing services do so to the value of £35 billion per year, of which £13 billion comes from the state directly and three-quarters comes from contractual delivery, says NCVO.

Table 1.2   Charity income and expenditure, 2009–10 (£ billion)

Income		Expenditure	
Voluntary income	15.19	Fundraising costs	1.71
Trading	4.02	Trading costs	2.13
Investment	3.37	Investment/management	0.34
Charitable activity	29.28	Charitable spending	45.71
Other	1.56	Governance/other	1.59
Total	53.43	Total	51.48

A charity is an organisation which is not for profit, delivers a definable public benefit, is registered with and regulated by the Charity Commission[3] and qualifies for certain benefits under the UK tax system. The vast majority of third sector organisations featured in this book are charities but not all involve volunteers (other than as trustees) or provide public services.

There will therefore be few if any occasions in this book where it is necessary to distinguish between 'charities' and the third or voluntary sector.

---

3   Some charities are regulated by someone other than the Charity Commission. So-called 'exempt charities', such as universities, are usually regulated by the relevant Secretary of State.

Wikipedia tells us that the acronym NGO (Non-Governmental Organisation) is synonymous with CSO, charity, voluntary body, and so on. The World Bank defines NGOs as 'private organisations that pursue activities to relieve suffering, promote the interests of the poor, protect the environment, provide basic social services or undertake community development'. Most if not all NGOs in Britain are charities. The phrase 'NGO' has its widest currency in the international arena dating back to the early days of the United Nations (UN). There are thought to be 40,000 international NGOs (more properly called INGOs) operating today. Many of the major ones are based in the UK or US. My use of the term 'NGO' will be confined to international matters.

There is no such thing as a typical charity. The income of the ten largest British charities is a quarter of that of the top 300 and is growing faster than the rest. In 2007–08 those biggest 300 charities shared an income of £10.1 billion whilst 85 per cent of charities, 150,000 of them, have an income of less than £100,000 each. Of £79 billion of assets held by the sector, over a third (£28.4 billion) is held by the 12,000 foundations. Not every charity with 'foundation' in its name is technically a foundation!

The list is remarkably stable. Of the 50 biggest charities in 1985, 28 were still in the top 50 in 2010 and 45 others were still in the top 350. Of the 50 largest UK companies in 1985 only 15 were still in the top 50 some 25 years later whilst many, unlike the charities, had closed, changed their name or merged beyond recognition. Only five others remained in the top 350 (Mason, 2011). In 1985 the National Trust had the largest charitable income at £70 million and it grew six-fold in 25 years whilst falling to third place; in the corporate sector BP remained top whilst its income grew 16-fold to £119 billion in the same time.

Even amongst the biggest charities there is variety: in 2009 the Royal National Lifeboat Institute (RNLI),[4] since 1824 the principal provider of lifeboat services in this country, had an income of £167 million of which over half was from legacies. The charity held half a billion pounds-worth of assets (over half of which were fixed assets such as property). The Guys and St Thomas' charity had assets of a similar value but its 2009–10 income was only £13.5 million, mostly interest from its investments. Another giant, the international development and disaster relief charity Oxfam, had an income of £318 million against which it spent £294 million. £126 million came from voluntary sources,

---

4 RNLI had the tenth largest income of any charity in 1985, the seventeenth in 2010. Oxfam was in third and fifth place respectively.

£112 million from government sources and £75 million from trading, not least from its High Street charity shops (Smouha, 2011).

Cash donations were the most important source of income for the top 500 fundraising charities in 2009–10 at 30 per cent of income; charitable activities (21 per cent), statutory fees and legacies (both 12 per cent) made up most of the rest (Pharaoh, 2011).

In Britain the third sector has its origins in communities, neighbourhoods and the provision of services complementary to those of the public sector. No other European country has quite the same quantity or quality of third sector as Britain.

INTERNATIONAL COMPARISONS

In France, the third sector was a fairly late developer: not-for-profit associations were actually illegal during the nineteenth century. The legal status of social enterprise – Sociétés Coopératives d'Intérêt Collectif – has only existed for 20 years and they are defined by having multiple types of shareholders rather than their not-for-profit nature. From its origins as a collective of doctors and journalists in France in 1971, Médecins Sans Frontières is their best known charity. It has grown to be a genuinely international organisation working in development and disaster relief, with offices in 19 countries and a multimillion pound turnover, despite getting almost no core funding from any government.

In the German charity environment churches have a relatively larger role than in Britain, in a smaller scene. Street collections are allowed but highly bureaucratic and rare; most charity working is local and fragmented. Red Nose Day exists, hosted in the early days by Boris Becker and Claudia Schiffer, and development is the major area for charitable fundraising. The average German donates €30 a year (mostly older people) or 40 hours voluntary work (mostly younger people).

In the Netherlands, Ireland and Belgium more than 10 per cent of the working population are employed by not-for-profit bodies, the highest figure in the world. They are followed by Israel, USA, Australia and UK. When the last international comparisons were made the lowest proportions of third sector workers in developed countries are found in Eastern Europe (Archambault, 2000).

Britain and other European Union (EU) countries are currently resisting a five-year-old ruling by the EU that donations given by a resident of one EU country to a bona fide charity based in another EU country should be treated for tax purposes as if the gift were given to a charity based in the same country as the donor. The EU argues that the rules on free movement of people, money and services within the EU requires this and legal opinion appears to support them. Yet France in particular, which allows a massive 60 per cent tax relief on charitable donations internally, overtly refuses to apply the same generosity to charities based outside its borders (Jump, 2009); no EU country appears keen to comply.

The World Giving Index 2010 (CAF, 2011) measures citizen involvement in 153 countries through the giving of money, the volunteering of time and 'helping strangers'. The Index is an average of the percentage of the population that engages in each of these three activities.

The USA, Ireland, Australia, and New Zealand top the table followed by the UK, the Netherlands, Canada and Sri Lanka. At the top of the league the figures differ little from those of the 2010 survey. Seventy-nine per cent of UK residents give money, a figure bettered only by Thailand. Sixty-three per cent of Brits would help a stranger in need but the disappointing figure is the one for those who volunteer time, at only 28 per cent, putting us outside the top 30 on that measure. The 2010 report acknowledged that calculations for domestic purposes may generate a different impression from that given for the purpose of international comparison. A figure often quoted for the UK is that about 70 per cent of people carry out some sort of voluntary work during the course of each year. The rank orders are perhaps more interesting than the numbers themselves.

People tend to engage in ways which are appropriate: in Liberia only 11 per cent give money but 81 per cent would help a stranger. Turkmenistan topped the volunteering poll at 61 per cent compared to under 7 per cent in more than a dozen countries. Most Western European countries made the top 50 for volunteering although Italy, Sweden, Portugal and Greece (at 3 per cent) failed to make the top 100. Happiness proves to be a more reliable indicator of propensity to engage than is wealth.

Private – Third Sector Hybrids

If the three sectors are the three points of a triangle, as in Figure 1.2, then its three lines are the paths along which we find hybrids which share characteristics of both parents. Hybrids between the private and third sectors

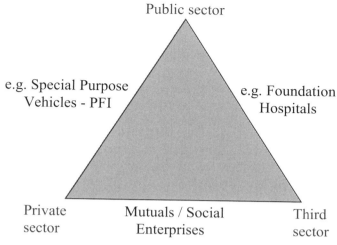

Figure 1.2   The triangle map of hybrids

employ the practices of the profit-driven private sector to pursue the value-driven purposes of the not-for-profit or third (or voluntary) sector. Hybrids are not new: well established examples include the mutuals which employed the ways of high finance to make home ownership available to the many through the early building societies.

In 1844, 28 weavers and others calling themselves the Rochdale Society of Equitable Pioneers established the first successful co-operative enterprise to sell food that they could not otherwise afford. The 'Rochdale Principles' guided the formation of a thousand co-ops over the next ten years in building what is today a world-wide movement.

By 1995, the fourth revision of the principles[5] included:

1.   voluntary and open membership;

2.   democratic member control;

3.   member economic participation;

4.   autonomy and independence;

---

5   See www.ica.coop/coop/principles.html

5.   education, training and information;

6.   cooperation among cooperatives;

7.   concern for community.

Today the line between private and third sectors is a busy road with thousands of social enterprises vying for position as they trade in a not-for-profit manner using models which may be little different from those of their profit-motivated cousins. It is their purpose which gives them their character, which determines where along this line between third and private sectors they settle.

Most of the income of the Glossopdale Furniture Project comes from trade. Over 15 years of existence they have sold furniture cheaply and trained those in need of skills in the arts of furniture-making and the retail trade. They collect, store, repair, recycle, create and re-sell furniture with their modest profits being returned to the business. As a charity providing low-cost home comforts and essentials to needy families they receive tax concessions and cheap or free premises (now stable after a few nomadic years). They directly employ eight people, mostly part time, but in the course of the year thousands of hours are given to volunteering there and receiving skills training. They are managed by a group of volunteers who might be amateur in status but are driven by commitment to the various causes embodied in their work.

When, from 2004, the opportunity arose to register as a Community Interest Company (CIC) they did so. A CIC is a form of limited company designed for those who want to conduct a business or other activity for community benefit, not private advantage. This is achieved by a 'community interest test' and an 'asset lock' which ensure that the CIC's assets and profits remain dedicated to its community purposes.Such social enterprises are the archetypal private sector–third sector hybrid.

Eight thousand social enterprises are members of Social Enterprise UK (SEUK) which exists to represent them and lobby on their behalf. Led by the dynamic Peter Holbrook, whose views on almost everything appear to be of interest to the Coalition Government, SEUK is going from strength to strength. No fewer than four cabinet ministers plus the Minister for Civil Society, Nick Hurd, attended their 2011 annual conference.

Holbrook's excitement at the dawn of a new age of social enterprise is tempered by the reality. Opportunities exist on paper for the movement to create or take over the running of services in communities on a grander scale than ever before and yet … various trends are heading in the other direction or not moving positively fast enough. For social enterprise to make the quantum leap as service providers they need:

1. access to capital (investors who demand equity in a business in return for investment do not find social enterprise attractive);

2. capacity, skills and investment to grow to scale (90 per cent are SMEs);

3. a level playing field in a market place where they cannot compete by using loss leaders;

4. clarity on EU procurement rules;

5. assurances that government will not lump services together in larger and larger contracts that are out of their reach.

All of these are being addressed except perhaps the last: the Ministry of Justice, for example, has explicitly committed to using larger contracts to generate larger savings. Yet the major windows of opportunity for the mutualisation of public services or outsourcing to the third sector, potentially involving a million of UK's six million public employees, will come sooner rather than later. It is difficult to see how all of these issues can be resolved in half a year, let alone the three to five years which Holbrook believes is needed to change the thinking of service commissioners and grow capacity amongst social enterprises. In that time he hopes to see the establishment of a Social Stock Exchange, the development of social enterprise franchising and a more positive engagement with trade unions. The traditional opposition of unions to public sector outsourcing is tempered by the view that something has to happen and much could be worse than a social enterprise – but the representative views of workers need to be more positive than this.

Public – Private Sector Hybrids

In the beginning was privatisation.

During the 1980s and 1990s many state industries – the 'family silver' in Harold Macmillan's words – were sold off by the Conservative Government. The first share issue was of British Telecom (BT) in 2004. On 1 December that year 2.1 million members of the public were allocated almost two-fifths of the shares to ensure wider share ownership (if briefly) whilst British financial institutions bought most of the rest.

Over the years that followed candidates for privatisation were either floated as private bodies on the stock exchange (like BT) or transferred to existing private sector companies (such as the merger which produced UK Coal). In the water and energy industries share purchases led to wholesale acquisition of former state assets by private companies, often owned from outside the UK.

By the late 1990s it was difficult to say that any genuine public–private hybrids existed as a result of this process; even prior to the privatisation era, the demands of profit and subsidy in the state-owned industries had waxed and waned according to Government policy. The appetite for transferring assets away from the state and into private hands had largely disappeared. However, the desire both to offload risk and to access capital from the open market without increasing the Public Sector Borrowing Requirement – the 'up side' of privatisation – certainly did not abate.

By 2001 the Government judged that the previously privatised railway network under Railtrack, a private sector company created for that purpose, had not been a success. The messy creation of Network Rail was a sincere if politically motivated attempt to create a public–private hybrid. Today, Network Rail is technically a private company limited by guarantee. Its principal asset is Network Rail Infrastructure Limited, a private company limited by shares.

However, Network Rail pays no dividend, its debts are underwritten by the Government and it is partially funded by the state ('not for profit' doesn't come into it). The Government may not be keen for Network Rail to be part of the public sector because its debts of over £20 billion would then count as Government liabilities. Network Rail is not a partnership but a single legal entity; a clear public and private sector hybrid.

Over the years the private and public sectors grew ever closer and more inter-dependent without actually merging. In 2009–10 the public sector procured just short of £200 billion of services from the private sector in the form of school dinners, emptying dustbins, managing TV licences and criminal records and running prisons, to name but a few (King, 2011).

If privatisation was the dirty word of the 1980s and 1990s the Private Finance Initiative (PFI) and its successor, Public Private Partnerships (PPP), were the new century's white steeds. Such partnerships typically involved long-term funding deals in which private sector construction and finance companies, with other partners, built new public facilities and then leased them back to the state for a defined period such as 30 years before they reverted to state ownership. Hospitals, schools and roads were built in this way under New Labour; high-quality new public facilities emerged tainted only by the suspicion that if conventional state funding of capital projects had been available it would have worked out cheaper to the taxpayer in the long run. It was a big 'if'.

A PPP itself is not a hybrid; it is a partnership in which no one sacrifices either identity or autonomy. A sophistication is the use of Special Purpose Vehicles or SPVs. The SPV is tied into the contract with the Government and then manages the constructor/manager/landlord role. SPVs are legal entities created with the single purpose of acquiring a specific asset and managing it on behalf of the Government in a cautious way which minimises the risk of bankruptcy. Where that new entity is created between the construction companies and the financiers and the Government holds an equity stake then a public–private hybrid exists.

Public – Third Sector Hybrids

Foundation hospitals were one of the Blair Government's more controversial initiatives. They had a degree of financial autonomy in their borrowing ability and their power to vary employment agreements distinguished them from the rest of the National Health Service (NHS). Their boards had a directly elected element usually appointed quietly, on a tiny turnout of those qualified to vote. In short, they enjoyed a large degree of independence within the public sector and were able to organise themselves in ways that the Rochdale pioneers would have recognised.

Thus they were loved by some in the Co-operative movement and hated by Labour proponents of the beneficent and indivisible state. In 2004 the NHS described Foundation trusts and hospitals as:

> *... the cutting edge of the Government's commitment to the decentralisation of public services and the creation of a patient-led NHS ... They have been created to devolve decision-making from central government control to local organisations and communities, so they are more responsive to the needs and wishes of their local people. The introduction of NHS foundation trusts represents a profound change in the history of the NHS and the way in which hospital services are managed and provided.[6]*

The Co-operative Party is that part of the wider labour movement that grew from the principles of Robert Owen in the nineteenth century. Whilst welcoming both Foundation hospitals and moves to transfer public housing stock and leisure services into the hands of mutuals – years before the phrase 'Big Society' came into being – the Co-operative Party criticised the then Labour Government for not going far enough:

> *The establishment of foundation hospitals was strongly supported by the Co-operative Party as an example of mutualism. But [Co-operative Party General Secretary, Peter] Hunt said that initial government funding to help hospitals become membership organisations had now dried up. (Little, 2007)*

The Hinchingbrooke Hospital in Cambridge is not a Foundation hospital but is run by an NHS Trust. Or rather, it was. In November 2010 the East of England Strategic Health Authority announced the first franchising of an NHS service in which this hospital would be run by a social enterprise. Circle is an employee-owned health company often described as run on the 'John Lewis model'. Over 2,000 clinicians and other employees each have a share in 49 per cent of an enterprise which has produced spectacular results – both financially and in terms of patient care – in the first few hospitals and clinics it has established or taken over.[7] The remaining 51 per cent is owned by finance institutions which makes borrowing easier and capital investment more attractive.

The much delayed transfer of Hinchingbrooke to Circle was finally achieved late in 2011, arguably the first franchising of a major hospital to a third sector organisation.[8]

---

6   See http://webarchive.nationalarchives.gov.uk/+/www.dh.gov.uk/en/Healthcare/Secondarycare/NHSfoundationtrust/index.htm
7   See www.bbc.co.uk/news/health-13446084
8   See www.huntspost.co.uk/news/business-news/prime_minister_urged_to_unblock_hinchingbrooke_franchising_1_926986

The first public–third sector partnership was also health inspired: the Treasury contributed to Captain Thomas Coram's Foundling Hospital charity in the 1750s. Coram was a philanthropist who, after a career establishing colonies in the new world, cared for street children in the hospital he founded in Bloomsbury in 1737. William Hogarth was a governor there and George Frederic Handel dedicated performances to help fund it, even selling the original manuscript of the Hallelujah chorus to raise funds. Such was the support of artists that the hospital was a milestone in the formation of the Royal Academy.

The Fourth Sector

In our triangle model we have seen three points and three lines as distinct sectors and groups of hybrids existing between them.

Some argue that social enterprise should be regarded as the 'fourth sector' (such as Ellis, 2010) whilst others say that the community sector, often qualitatively different from its voluntary sector cousins, deserves that title. But in our triangle model neither definition is sufficiently distinct from that of the third sector. The triangle has three points, three lines and a space in between. For me, the fourth sector is that space – as shown in Figure 1.3 – where bodies

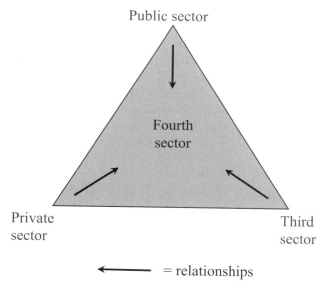

Figure 1.3   Defining the fourth sector

from the other three sectors interact and relationships are formed; an idea which has traction in the United States and to which we will return.[9]

Ethical Business: The Door to Charity Partnerships

My first memory of ethical demands on business was in the 1960s when my parents refused to eat anything from South Africa; in practice, oranges and a certain sickly mint. I remember too their frustration at not finding anything Rhodesian that they could boycott following the Unilateral Declaration of Independence in 1965. In 1972, on my first day as an undergraduate, 'Boycott Barclays' banners fluttered in the campus square, a campaign which became the effective 'disinvest from apartheid' demand of the 1980s. There are still those who cannot forget the past despite the fact that Barclays has contributed more than most in working for stability across southern Africa in the last 20 years.

Whatever pressure there has been for business to behave in an ethical manner has proved relatively easy to resist until relatively recently. There remains a school of thought that says 'the business of business is business'[10] and devil take the hindmost. Whereas public sector bodies do good because they have to (they are intended to produce a positive and measurable benefit to society) and third sector ones because they want to, private business has traditionally been characterised by the view that doing good must either involve making a profit or be incidental.

In India in 1984 Bhopal saw the antithesis of social responsibility. A subsidiary of Union Carbide negligently allowed poisons to escape into the atmosphere, killing up to 15,000 people over several years. Twenty-six years later seven people were convicted of negligence, each sentenced to two years in prison and a $2,000 fine. No doubt the company was in India in 1984 because it could exploit the workforce through low wages. No doubt planning and other controls were more lax and running costs lower than in other countries. The bottom line was king.

Other scandals perpetrated by multinationals in developing countries came to light over the years involving child labour, exposure to harmful substances and irresponsible marketing.

---

9   Such as can be seen at www.fourthsectorconsulting.com/
10 This quote is widely attributed to the free market economist Milton Friedman (1962), but probably predates him by several decades.

THE EXTRACTIVE INDUSTRIES

Ten years before Bhopal, in 1973, British Prime Minister Edward Heath described 'Tiny' Rowlands of the mining giant Lonrho as 'the unacceptable face of capitalism' when the company put itself above the law in bribing African leaders and smashing the international sanctions imposed on Rhodesia.

How times change.

When Rowlands died in 1998 the eulogies flowed generously: 'He made an enormous contribution, not only to South Africa, but to the whole of Africa', said Nelson Mandela, 'We will remember him as a long-standing friend in the struggle against apartheid'. The former President of Zambia, Kenneth Kaunda, said, 'We worked together to empower Africans … He is a great loss to us'.[11]

Today no one believes that African development can make progress without the heartbeat of business and commerce driving it from both within and outside the continent.

Some of the extractive industries are regarded as amongst the most upstanding of corporate citizens in Africa. The 2003 Extractive Industries Transparency Initiative (EITI) was a British creation. It is an international commitment by countries, companies and CSOs to 'the prudent use of natural resource wealth' in the pursuit of sustainable economic growth and poverty reduction in developing countries, whilst reducing mining's negative economic and social impacts. Fully supported by the third sector's leading anti-corruption campaigner, Transparency International, EITI pre-dates the ratification of the UN Convention on Corruption. Its list of 28 full country members or candidates includes much of central and western Africa. Liberia has gone furthest, insisting on the same openness and transparency in the exploitation of rubber and timber.

One large extraction company, the giant Anglo American Corporation, claims to be the world's largest private purchaser of antiretroviral drugs. It sees a clear commercial benefit in protecting its workforce from having their HIV-positive condition degenerate into AIDS and inevitable death. Such is the toll from AIDS in parts of Africa that the company is reputed to recruit two employees for every vacancy. The extraction industry cannot choose where

---

11   See http://news.bbc.co.uk/1/hi/world/africa/139596.stm

to invest, where to get the best return. In Anglo's case it has to go where the platinum, diamonds, metals and coal take it.

Once committed, the company can either work with the local community that provides their workforce, bringing qualitative benefits to local people as well as income, or not. Anglo American, currently creating economic hubs around its plants, is one of a growing number of companies which has decided that their bread is buttered on the side of being a good neighbour and a supporter of the local community.

COMMON PURPOSES

The UNGC is the world's largest voluntary corporate sustainability initiative, with over 5,000 company members in 135 countries.[12] It seeks to embed ten universal principles in the fields of human rights, labour, environment and anti-corruption in business activities around the world and to promote broader UN goals.

Doing good in business these days is not entirely voluntary. The International Labor Organisation (ILO) is responsible for drawing up and overseeing international standards.[13] Created in 1919 and incorporated into the UN in 1946, its partners are 183 governments plus employers and workers' representatives, though Britain ceased contributing to its funds in the 2011 public spending cuts. Laws exist in every country to reflect commitments made under ILO conventions although in some they are more comprehensive and better enforced than others. Those commitments include job creation, rights at work, dialogue and social protection of workers.

Aware that minimum ILO standards were not being universally enforced a group of UK companies, trade unions and charities came together in the early 1990s to go a stage further and create the Ethical Trading Initiative (ETI).[14] The companies are few (just over 50) but they include major procurers of goods from the developing world: the founding fathers were ASDA, Premier Brands, Body Shop, Littlewood's and Sainsbury's. The ETI now guarantees decency at work in 38,000 suppliers employing over eight million people in these companies' supply chains.

---

12   See www.unglobalcompact.org
13   See www.ilo.org/global/about-the-ilo/decent-work-agenda/lang--en/index.htm
14   See www.ethicaltrade.org/about-eti/why-we-exist

In 2001 a group of UK retailers and major suppliers set up the Supplier Ethical Data Exchange, a not-for-profit organisation known better as Sedex. Sedex exists to drive improvements in global labour standards and ease the regulatory burden on suppliers who were being audited many times over in respect of ILO and other legally binding standards. Today it is genuinely international with around 30,000 members. Marks & Spencer, an original Sedex member, explains why they use it:

> ... to collect and manage data on the ethical risk of suppliers. As the ethical issues of interest to M&S and our customers are continually evolving and our business commitments are increasing, we need a tool that is sustainable and also flexible enough to accommodate changing requirements. Sedex provides that tool for our business.[15]

Sedex focuses on four pillars: Labour Standards, Health & Safety, Environment and Business Integrity. As we shall see in Chapter 3, these reflect the seven pillars of the first international standard on social responsibility, ISO26000.

Sedex collects, manages and processes data and reports its findings to clients. This prompts them to address any problems of non-compliance in the supply chain hopefully through amelioration or by sourcing from elsewhere. If inadequate company policy caused the breach this is addressed and codes of conduct are amended.

Despite the existence of international standards compliance is not universal and Sedex reports frequent violations. In 2009 its audit revealed 1,294 'non-conformances' from 165 site visits to members of supply chains for the Co-operative Group, of which two-thirds were for lack of a Healthy and Hygienic Working Environment. Three-quarters of all breaches were resolved within the year.

FAIR TRADE

The Fairtrade Foundation[16] was born from the NGO movement in 1992, specifically by CAFOD, Christian Aid, Oxfam, Traidcraft and the World Development Movement. They were later joined by Britain's largest women's organisation, the Women's Institute; the movement is now worldwide. The Fair Trade label was launched in the Netherlands four years earlier.

---

15 See www.sedex.org.uk
16 See www.fairtrade.org.uk

The growth in the fair trade economy in the last decade has been phenomenal. From chocolate, coffee and tea it now includes wine, cotton, biscuits, sweets, honey and flowers.[17] Mainstream large-scale manufacturers like Cadbury and Nestlé now champion fair trade chocolate in some of their most popular brands.

The biggest vendor of Fair Trade products in Britain is the Co-operative Group which aims for a 20 per cent year on year increase in fair trade sales. It was the first to sell many fair trade products: Café Direct in 1992, own-brand chocolate in 2000, wine in 2001, mangoes and pineapples in 2002, cotton carrier bags in 2007 and charcoal and Palestinian olive oil in 2009. All the Co-op's tea and coffee range is now fair trade.

The UK turnover of fair trade goods has gone from nothing to £1.17 billion per year in 20 years, aided by the UK Government and recently the EU, and it is now mainstream. UK fair trade imports grew by 40 per cent in 2010 alone, despite the recession. It is difficult to buy a banana these days that is not fair trade, despite fears that prices are too low for the market to be sustainable.

Whilst there is still a premium on the price of some fair trade products it is not as heavy as it was; products of all kinds are now much more competitive than they were for the conscientious consumer.

Actively promoted by Government, fair trade certification of a supply chain which starts in a developing country and ends in a UK home is much sought after; supermarkets and Marks & Spencer now carry the baton that in the 1990s was held by Traidcraft, charity shops and churches. A third sector-led initiative is dictating, in the nicest possible way, how private sector institutions behave.

THE GREEN AGENDA

The environmental agenda has been led by scientists and some politicians but most would accept that high levels of popular understanding and concern result from third sector activity. Greenpeace, Friends of the Earth and others have delivered convincing and effective warnings that if we (consumers, businesses and governments) go on as we are then global warming will ensure that we won't go on much longer. There is no country in the world that currently

---

17 The transport by air of Kenyan roses to Britain is controversial but has a lower carbon footprint than locally grown flowers as in Kenya growers require little energy other than the sun.

enjoys decent living standards whilst at the same time producing sustainably low carbon emissions.

Business has realised that environmental sustainability has to be in their bottom line calculations and that being 'green' in their use of energy and other resources can save money. 'Greenwashing' is readily exposed; good environmental stewardship, often with the assistance of a third sector partner, can help boost sales.

Sustainability is not just a green concept. When the word initially surfaced in the Bruntland Report of 1987 it had a broader meaning; it is only with the urgency of the debate on climate in recent years that sustainability has been skewed to mean 'reducing our carbon footprint to a sustainable level'. Thus a large company's 'Head of Sustainability' will often be an environmentalist.

That original meaning continued to be championed by John Elkington, best known for his million-selling *Green Consumer Guide*. In his book *Cannibals with Forks* (Elkington, 1997) he coined another meaningful term.

The 'triple bottom line' acknowledges that the economic, environmental and social outputs of a business, sometimes referred to as 'people, planet and profit', are all important enough to deserve 'bottom line' status. This holistic approach to sustainability is advocated by this book and we will return to it in our discussion of Corporate Social Responsibility (CSR) in Chapter 3.

In Chapter 4 we will look at practical ways in which co-working happens across sectoral borders, in the fourth sector.

Philanthropy and Foundations

For those who are incredibly wealthy there are tax effective ways of managing wealth and there are philanthropic ones. Whether you are an individual or a corporate entity these can, fortunately, overlap; philanthropy is now a major industry at the interface of cross-sector partnerships.

Britain's 50 largest family foundations held assets of over £24 billion in 2008–09. Whilst this is not surprisingly down from the pre-crisis peak of almost £28 billion in 2005–06, the amount paid out to good causes actually increased over the same period by 40 per cent to £1.4 billion in 2008–09 (5.6 per cent of assets or 9 per cent of all charitable giving) (Pharaoh and Keidan, 2010).

If you are a company, creating a foundation can allow you to discharge duties both of conscience and fiduciary responsibility at the same time. As the foundation achieves charitable status and joins the third sector it gains operational independence from the host company. The originators will, of course, have established the fund's field of work in its charitable objects. The Wellcome Trust, for example, Britain's largest charity, spends £600 million each year on medical research, over half of the total sum paid out by all family foundations together.

Sir Henry Wellcome was born to a poor family in the American mid-west in 1853. His philanthropic instincts were inspired by his shame at the murderous treatment of Sioux Indians in Wisconsin. In his early twenties whilst visiting the Andes in search of natural sources of quinine to fight malaria he expressed concern about the destruction of the forests – an idea well ahead of its time. A trained pharmacist, he came to England in 1880 at the invitation of a college classmate to sell 'compressed medicines' or pills.

Pill-making by compression had been patented by an artist who had wanted the graphite in his pencils to be less friable. It led to the first accurate and consistent measurement of drugs and (fortunately for Wellcome) great commercial success. He set up the Wellcome Foundation in 1930, initially to house his personal collection of museum pieces.

Most foundations of business origin have charitable purposes related to the host organisation's field of business. It is understandable that the corporate passion that brought success should at least influence the foundation's work, though operational independence is essential.

The Innocent Foundation was set up soon after the eponymous soft drinks company launched in 1999 and for several years the agreement that it would receive 10 per cent of company profits was upheld. In 2008, half a million pounds of the charity's money was held back in the company's bank account, since when trading pressures have caused profits to be minimal. The Foundation's spending in 2010, at £127,000, was half that of 2008 (Ball, 2011).

Innocent and the foundation that bears its name share the same three directors, which is not good practice. Even though debt interest is now being added at 2 per cent per annum this does not detract from the suspicion that the Foundation exists as much to benefit the benefactors as the recipients of its benevolence.

Many major British companies – banks, supermarkets, insurers, manufacturers – now have associated foundations. BHP Billiton, a South African company, was able to enter the chart of UK corporate giving at number one in 2010 courtesy of a one-off donation to its own newly established foundation (Lillya, 2011).

What the UK's 12,000 foundations have in common is that they give money away, often the interest earned on an endowment. Some come together as the Association of Charitable Foundations (ACF). Although its 160 members are just the tip of the foundation iceberg they distribute the vast majority of the funds that follow this route. The Wellcome Trust, the Big Lottery Fund (not technically a foundation) and the Diana, Princess of Wales Memorial Fund are amongst its largest members.

ACF cannot be said to be the voice of foundations; as a population foundations maintain their independence, even from each other, ferociously.

There is a debate about the size of reserves or endowment that a body should hold. Even amongst the largest charities there are different views: some, like Oxfam, hold just a few weeks running costs in reserve, whereas the RNLI, whose lifeboats cost £2 million to replace, hold considerably more in order to plan their replacement strategy of boats and buildings over a 50-year horizon. There is no 'right' amount for a foundation to hold and recent low interest rates may have prompted some to hold on to capital to maximise investment income; others play the market, with a diverse portfolio to help control risk. Others like the Diana Fund take the brave and rare decision to 'spend out' their endowment, effectively closing down their operation within five years.

Difficult choices of reducing reserves or the endowment are all guided by perceptions and predictions of risk; there is pressure from some quarters to reduce reserves under the guise of efficiency and increase spending power at a time when cash flow from other sources is being restricted (Smouha, 2011). Is this not the rainy day they were saving for?

Philanthropists can be large or small; the word describes an attitude of mind, not a wallet size. Small philanthropists in Britain might join The Funding Network where the emphasis is on giving to create social change: charities which support animals, the environment or the arts are not encouraged to apply.

Meeting several times a year in London to socialise and network, up to 100 Funding Network members hear five shortlisted charities each give a six minute pitch on 'How we would spend £5,000'. These are charities to whom £5,000 means a lot, often those which arise from an individual's passion, such as helping local children with learning difficulties through the medium of music, promoting embroidery amongst prisoners to reduce re-offending or fighting child cancer in an African country.

All gifts are made semi-anonymously and only honour commits the giver to pay up. It is rare for a shortlisted charity to fail to reach its £5,000 target and common for £40,000 to be raised in an evening.

The issue of anonymity divides the philanthropic world. Much is donated to good causes in silence; too much giving, some say, is designed to promote the name of the giver rather than the cause itself. The need to be recognised as a philanthropist, perhaps where a family charity based on aristocratic 'old money' is doing good nearby their historical home, can stand in the way of a good cause. In one village I heard of, the county council was struggling to fund a computer literacy course in the local library when a local philanthropist decided to fund a rival one 400 yards away in the village hall that bore the family name.

Ultimately no one can tell a philanthropist, individual or corporate foundation what to do. They are not obliged to give away their money at all or cooperate with anybody and they can cease to fund a project whenever they like. Philanthropic input cannot be relied upon when public or third sector initiatives seek partners to further the public good. If someone wants to spend their money providing hypnosis for three-legged cats rather than tackling cancer in children then that is their right.

There are notable exceptions: no discussion of philanthropy would be complete without mention of Bill Gates and Warren Buffett. Currently the third richest man on the planet, super-investor Buffett has pledged to give away 99 per cent of his wealth during his lifetime. Much of it has already gone to the Bill and Melinda Gates Foundation, established from Gates' own wealth acquired through his former company, Microsoft. Because of the sheer size of their multibillion dollar investments, notably in health in Africa, the Gates Foundation is a formidable player on the world charitable stage, more important than many donor countries, though the same rules apply: no one can oblige Gates to do anything.

Gates is the archetypal philanthrocapitalist, a concept explored by Matthew Bishop and Michael Green in their excellent book, *Philanthrocapitalism* (2008). Concentrating mostly on America, where more billionaires live than anywhere else, Bishop and Green show how the most successful entrepreneurs are, through their foundations, increasingly using the skills that made them rich to engage in strategic funding in the economic, social and moral fabric of the world and the neighbourhoods that make it up.

In the UK, one of the largest foundation grant makers is the Esmée Fairbairn Trust. With a reputation for funding innovation and taking risks in the field of social change, it funds other charities to the tune of £30 million each year. Its brief is wider than most, covering the arts, education and learning, the environment and disadvantaged people generally. Esmée Fairbairn was a pioneer of the Citizens Advice Bureau and Women's Royal Voluntary Service (WRVS). She died in a Second World War air raid and her family, who made their money from unit trusts, created the Foundation in 1961.

Partnership in Action

Back in Paul Kennedy's office in Glossop, Derbyshire, CEL continues with its everyday work. CEL was established in 1987 by Ken Spencer and Ian McCrae who had shown entrepreneurial flair even back in their left-wing student days in the 1970s. One of CEL's first customers was the National Union of Students, establishing a 25-year history of a private company serving the needs of the not-for-profit third sector. CEL's philosophy is that bulk purchasing and clever procurement can support the cause of not-for-profits by making significant savings for them. The same applies to back office and business services more generally. Organisations as large as Best Western, the not-for-profit co-operative chain of independent hotels, use CEL's central procurement services.

In recent years, starting shortly before Spencer and McCrae took early retirement and sold the business to Paul Kennedy and his business partner, Mohammed Ramzan, the model was diversified by two significant initiatives.

The first was a new organisation called Foundations.[18] In 2000, CEL won the contract from the Department for Communities and Local Government to run a national body for Home Improvement Agencies (HIAs). There are 230 HIAs in England, third sector organisations often using the name 'Care and Repair'.

---

18   See www.foundations.uk.com

HIAs help vulnerable people maintain their independence and live in comfort and security in their own homes. Although the service is available to elderly, disabled or housebound homeowners much of their work is with tenants. Each year they deal with over 220,000 enquiries and deliver work with a value of over £110 million, a situation tailor-made for the centralised organisation of procurement, training and events. With a fine reputation, Parliamentary receptions and national awards all now established, Foundations has made its name as a privately owned body, commissioned by the public sector to co-ordinate a sub-sector of the third sector.

No less innovative is Digital Outreach.[19] Tasked by Government to support elderly, disabled, confused and housebound people, including those on the 'official' BBC help scheme, Digital Outreach Limited (DOL) gives practical advice and assistance to people with the conversion of their televisions as digital switchover rolls out across the country a region at a time.

That was the idea: but digital switchover is a one-off event. It would have been wasteful of resources and energy to have stopped there. Since it was set up as a unique special purpose vehicle (SPV) between a private company (CEL) and two third sector bodies (Age UK and Community Service Volunteers) – DOL has shown itself to have the CEL hallmark traits of ambition, innovation and diversification.

Under its director, Ian Agnew, DOL now uses the same model of home visits from trained, knowledgeable and sympathetic volunteers that it developed for digital television to promote internet access for older users, the 'silver surfers', on behalf of Ofcom. Other services are being developed for regional and national clients which build on this impressive network of trained volunteers under the name 'Convey'. Ian is confident that this is the beginning of a new era of personalised third sector service provision.

In Chapter 7 we will ask how all this fits in with the flavour of the political moment, the Big Society.

---

19 See www.digitaloutreach.org.uk

2

A Word About History

There are records of voluntary associations in Britain a thousand years ago. Acts of philanthropy and mutual aid in centuries gone by tended to be associated with religious institutions, with some 500 voluntary hospitals being set up in the twelfth and thirteenth centuries alone.

Charitable trusts were established in the sixteenth century, when the dissolution of the monasteries removed a hitherto reliable source of charity from the needy. In 1552, Parliament appointed alms collectors to redistribute voluntarily donated cash to the poor – and a 1563 Act distinguished between those poor who were 'deserving' and the rest. The 1601 Act is still the basis of charity law today. It prevented fraud within charities, which could by then be found within secular movements, laid down basic definitions of charitable purposes and established the need for commissioners to regulate them.

In the seventeenth century education and employment joined hospitals and poverty relief as major causes for philanthropic and charitable activity.

Most schools at that time were religious, though the secularisation of good deeds bloomed with the industrial revolution and the growth of wealth within the business classes: new money rather than old. During the eighteenth century urban facilities like parks and libraries were endowed by philanthropists and, by the turn of the nineteenth century, the breadth of good causes had grown to include maternity provision, child welfare and support for the colonies.

Campaigners and Providers

Campaigning organisations blossomed in the age of enlightenment. The Society for Effecting the Abolition of the Slave Trade (1787) was established in Britain 100 years after Dutch and German Quakers had made the first anti-slavery statement in Pennsylvania. The Society was non-denominational, led by nine Quakers and three Anglicans whose presence gave them credibility in Parliament. By 1823 the Anti-Slavery Society's gradualist approach was in conflict with that of the Female Societies of Sheffield and Birmingham who demanded immediate abolition, although as women had no vote their voice was seldom acknowledged in high places.

Women not only wore their hearts on their sleeves but also on their collars, hair slides and bracelets. Business joined force with campaigners when Josiah Wedgwood manufactured a pottery medallion in support of the anti-slavery movement. Amongst the most famous works of eighteenth century art depicting a black person, a man in chains is asking 'Am I not a man and a brother?' It was an effective awareness-raising tool.

As early as the 1830s, following the repeal of the Combination Act that was designed to prevent insurgency in Britain following the French revolution, workers started to organise themselves. In the second half of the nineteenth century a particular type of friendly society developed with echoes of the medieval guilds. Such bodies came together as the Trade Union Congress (TUC) in 1868.[1] Trade unions evolved from mutual benefit societies at a time when the state did not provide for the poor or the workless. They are not normally regarded as being in the third sector although they are bona fide members of civil society, not least in developing countries. Their principal purpose is the benefit of their members rather than the public as a whole, hence they cannot be charities, though they certainly embody the principles of volunteering, campaigning and organising that the third sector has made its hallmark. Membership of trade unions in Britain has been stable for some years, though it has fallen by a third since 1970 (to eight million in 2008).

It is no accident that as the economy grew in the nineteenth and twentieth centuries so the size of the voluntary sector grew also. Business was providing personal wealth for both the rich, whose passion for philanthropic deeds of various kinds it fed, and the ordinary, whose new access to wealth led to larger numbers of more modest acts of both volunteering and giving and the development of overt charitable fundraising.

As we shall see, some of the very businesses whose names are found on every larder shelf today were involved in good deeds from the outset, with their founders committed to helping those most in need. First let us look at a nineteenth century philanthropist and a charity which dominates its field today.

---

1   For a potted history of trade unions see www.unionhistory.info/index.php

ROYAL NATIONAL INSTITUTE OF BLIND PEOPLE (RNIB)

Thomas Rhodes Armitage was the sixth of seven children in a wealthy family. Born in Sussex in 1824, he grew up abroad before becoming a medical student at Kings College, London, where his sight began to fail. By 1860 he could no longer continue his doctor's practice.

'I cannot conceive', he wrote, 'any occupation so congenial to a blind man of education and leisure as the attempt to advance the education and improve the condition of his fellow sufferers'.

Too many blind people spent their time begging, he reasoned, only a minority was educated and too few were employed. A blind patient introduced him to Lord Shaftesbury's Indigent Blind Visiting Society, through whom he realised that education for blind people of all ages required a common system of embossed script. Several existed so he convened a committee with three blind colleagues to decide which to promote.

This British and Foreign Blind Association for Promoting the Education of the Blind was the precursor of the Royal National Institute of the Blind (RNIB). After two years they decided upon a system created by a Frenchman, Louis Braille.

The use of braille as a teaching medium grew slowly across Britain, Europe and America; Armitage's organisation became a braille publishing house. Today the RNIB is the world's largest publisher of braille in the form of books, magazines, exam papers, knitting patterns, bills and bank statements. Since 1927 over six million copies of braille radio and television listings and 14,000 titles of sheet music have been produced.

Queen Victoria became the organisation's first royal patron in 1875 and both the Queen Mother and the current Queen have served in that role. There have been several mergers and name changes along the way so it was the National Institute for the Bind which received a royal charter in 1948 and became 'Royal' in 1953.

Armitage also established the first dedicated school for blind children, then took on training, employment and rehabilitation and the development and sale of equipment to meet blind people's needs. This included the Talking Book Service in 1935 which now has 40,000 regular users. In the 1990s a telephone helpline was established and then a fully accessible web site; over recent years RNIB has emerged as a formidable campaigning organisation winning many new rights and opportunities for people with visual impairments.

Today RNIB is a professional and aspirational organisation aimed at helping people 'find their life again' yet only a fraction of Britain's two million people with a visual impairment access its services to the full. RNIB's network of volunteers supports those who need help: from Talking Newspapers to reading out correspondence and driving to appointments, charity box shakers to more ambitious fundraisers. Much of this work is franchised to local associations.

Armitage had been well off when he started his pioneering work, but not as wealthy as his contemporaries who became captains of industry. Some of them used their profitable and growing companies as agents of social change.

CADBURY'S

In the same year as Thomas Armitage was born, 1824, John Cadbury opened a grocer's shop in the centre of Birmingham. Cadbury believed that drinking chocolate, a recent and exciting import from the New World, was a healthy alternative to the evil of alcohol for the working man. He ground the powder himself with a mortar and in 1847 he and his brother opened a factory to produce it on an industrial scale.[2]

Fame and fortune in the early nineteenth century were either inherited or earned through the professions or military rank. Quakers like Cadbury were not allowed to attend universities, which were controlled by the church against whom they had rebelled 100 years earlier, so neither law nor medicine were accessible to them; as pacifists, neither was military service.

However, they clearly had an eye for business: Cadbury's chocolate rivals included other Quakers, Fry (which was taken over by Cadbury in 1919) and Rowntree. Quakers also pioneered the iron and steel industry and established bodies like Lloyds and Barclays Banks, Carr's biscuits and Clarks shoes.

John Cadbury retired in 1861 when his sons Richard and George took over, allowing him to concentrate on his philanthropy and his favourite good causes. These included the abolition of child labour (epitomised by boys sweeping chimneys) and his Animal Friends Society, a forerunner of today's RSPCA.

---

2   See www.cadbury.co.uk/cadburyandchocolate/ourstory

George Cadbury had worked in the Adult School Movement providing education for working class adults so he was well aware of the conditions in which working people, including his own employees, lived. A Royal Commission in 1840 had described the streets of central Birmingham, home to over 50,000, as 'quagmires' due to the lack of drains, sanitation and clean water. The death rate there was double that of nearby affluent Edgbaston.

By the 1870s the cocoa and chocolate business required a new and bigger factory. 'No man ought to be condemned to live where a rose cannot grow', said George, so in 1878 he and his brother established not only a new factory but also accommodation for its workers on a greenfield site at Bournville. Here was fresh water, good transport links (the milk came in by canal, the chocolate by rail) and an absence of pollution. They built parks, lakes and sports facilities and for 50 years began each working day with a bible reading. True to the family credo, Bournville had no licensed premises, a tradition which maintains to this day – apart from the sports pavilion which has had a private bar since 1940.

Workers were treated with respect and dignity: they were amongst the first to benefit from subsidised travel to work, a works committee, works pensions and a company health scheme. By 1915 death and infant mortality rates at Bournville were significantly lower than for Birmingham as a whole. Evening classes were provided for the workforce. A conservation area, Bournville village is still run in accordance with Cadbury values by a residents' committee established in 1900.

In 1935, the Cadbury Foundation was formed, the explicitly charitable arm of the organisation, funded by 1 per cent of the company's pre-tax annual profits.

In the Second World War 'Mercy Vans' delivered chocolate drinks to victims of air raids and the company issued advice to people on getting the best from their ration books. In the 1950s they produced their first educational materials for schools and throughout the 1990s their community investment ran at £1.8 million per year.

In 2007, to celebrate the centenary of the importation of cocoa from Ghana, the Cadbury Foundation together with the charity Water Aid built a well each day for a year in the country's main cocoa growing area. An immediate reduction in water-borne disease and social stress followed. It was followed in 2008 by the launch of the Cocoa Partnership, in which Cadbury pledged to invest £45 million over several years in cocoa-producing communities in key developing countries. This investment would lead to improved yield for small farmers, new rural businesses, an improved quality of life for cocoa workers and their families and better partnership working between Cadbury and governments, development agencies and NGOs both international and local.

The Cocoa Partnership was 'highly commended' in the Responsible Supply Chain category of Business in the Community's (BITC) 2010 Excellence Awards.

Back in the UK, as a committed member of BITC, Cadbury has long recognised the value of employee volunteering to workforce and community alike. Supporters of the UK Paralympic team, they also sponsor Games Makers, the volunteers that will service the 2012 Olympics.

The British public believes that homelessness is the second largest social problem that business can help solve; business itself ranks it eighth.[3] Since 2002 Cadbury has found work placements for 62 homeless people in Birmingham alone, of whom over 50 have moved into permanent work with the company. The Head of Manufacturing at Bournville, Mark Jones, chairs the Birmingham branch of Business Action on Homelessness (BAH) through which employee volunteering opportunities to work with rough sleepers have been created. BAH is part of the BITC portfolio of services.[4]

Employee volunteering, say Cadbury, has led to enhanced team working, higher staff morale and retention and a more open-minded approach to homelessness.

Despite concerns, the takeover of Cadbury by the American food giant Kraft in 2010 has not damaged its reputation as a leader in ethical business. Kraft too, in a tradition more widely found in USA than in the UK, has a reputation of caring for its domestic workforce and acknowledging its wider responsibilities in society. According to Cadbury's own web site:

> *Cadbury recognises that it doesn't operate in isolation but has responsibilities to its employees and society in general. As Cadbury*

---

3   1998 research by Bain et al., quoted on the Business in the Community web site www.bitc.org. uk/resources/case_studies/cadburybaoh.html

4   See www.bitc.org.uk/community/employability/homelessness/

has grown as a business, the expectations of consumers, customers, colleagues and communities have also increased.

At the 2007 launch of Purple Meets Green, Cadbury's sustainability programme, CEO Todd Stitzer said:

> *We recognise that if we are serious about tackling climate change, we need to be absolutely committed. This means re-thinking the way we do business, embedding sustainability into every decision we take. Not only will this have a strong social and environmental impact but also a positive economic impact too in the long term.*

These two statements – on the recognition of relationships and the broadest definition of sustainability – go to the heart of the issue of corporate responsibility (CR) in Britain today. 'Sustainability', the 'triple bottom line', 'Social Return on Investment' (SROI) and the implications for partnership working with the voluntary sector and others are all explored further in Chapter 3.

A History of National Council for Voluntary Organisations

There is no better way of showing how the voluntary sector bloomed in the twentieth century than by looking at its principal national co-ordinating and umbrella body with 8,000 members, the National Council for Voluntary Organisations or NCVO.

Before the First World War, Edward Vivian Birchall helped found the National Association of Guilds of Help, the first umbrella body for volunteering. But he was ambitious: he wanted to see better co-ordination of 'voluntary social work' in all parts of the country and support for those who volunteered. Unfortunately, Birchall died in the Great War and never saw his dreams bear fruit. However, he did leave a £1,000 legacy to his friend, SP Grundy, to 'do some of the things we talked about'.

So Grundy became the first Honorary Secretary to the National Council for Social Services (NCSS), the ancestor of NCVO.

Fully established by 1924 and achieving charitable status in 1928, the main thrust of NCSS's work appears to have been to stimulate the creation of other charities, with an early bias towards those which would provide services such as village halls in rural areas.

Over its early years NCSS spawned the Youth Hostels Association (YHA) (1930), the movement of Young Farmers' Clubs (1931), Citizens Advice Bureaux (1939) and the National Association of Parish (later Local) Councils (1946). Its activities generated Councils of Social Service in each local authority area, the Charities Aid Foundation (CAF) and even the Charity Commission itself in the 1960s. Again in the 1960s it prompted a major debate on promoting volunteering within the statutory services, the impact of which within hospitals is very evident today.

Over the years the organisation shifted its focus several times, raising the profile of older people's issues (Age Concern was one of its offspring), international development (establishing Bond, the umbrella group for such charities), women, young people and communities. Its lobbying influence on legislation over the past 50 years has been significant.

In the 1970s NCSS received a Government grant to establish 141 volunteer bureaux around the country, now independent and considerably more numerous, and in 1980 it changed its name to the National Council for Voluntary Organisations.

From 1989 NCVO's doors were opened to corporate membership of supportive companies, pre-dating the idea of cross-sector partnerships. Through such membership companies can demonstrate social responsibility and gain access to services, markets and information.

In 1991 the organisation spawned the National Association of Councils for Voluntary Service (NACVS) which changed its name to National Association for Voluntary and Community Action (NAVCA) in 2006. Each local Council for Voluntary Service (CVS) in England supports local charities, voluntary organisations and community groups in various ways.

In its first year NCSS's turnover was £2,000. In the 1960s it started to receive direct Government funding. By 2009–10 the Government's strategic grant to NCVO was £1 million per year, on a turnover of ten million, but the grant was cut by half in March 2011. This was part of a programme to reduce the Government's 'strategic partners' in the sector from 42 to 15 and the placing of two caps on partners' funding at £500,000 or 50 per cent of their turnover. The total bill for strategic partners was reduced from £12.1 million to £7.5 million.

Table 2.1   **The Office of Civil Society's strategic partners receiving more than £500,000 in 2008–09, the year before the 50 per cent and £500,000 caps were introduced**

v (see note)	£54,594,000	Promotion of youth volunteering
Volunteering England	£1,575,900	Promotion of and research into volunteering
Mentoring and Befriending Foundation*	£1,050,600	Support to those involved in mentoring and befriending
Community Service Volunteers*	£1,050,600	General support for volunteering and training
NCVO	£1,040,000	Umbrella body for 8,000 voluntary organisations
Youthnet UK*	£994,933	Online charity supporting young people in life choices
Citizenship Foundation*	£841,100	Promotion of civil engagement
Timebank*	£525,300	Volunteering brokerage
Social Enterprise Coaltion (now SEUK)	£534,000	Umbrella body for social enterprises

Note: v was exceptional as it was a Government creation receiving over 95 per cent of its funding from government and thus fell into both categories of the 'cap'.

In 2011, those organisations marked * in Table 2.1 had all of their Government funding withdrawn. NCVO lost 55 per cent and a quarter of its staff; Volunteering England lost 70 per cent and half of its staff and the SEUK lost 22 per cent.

NCVO has been led since 1994 by one of the sector's statesmen, the indomitable Sir Stuart Etherington. It continues to operate on many fronts including helping the sector deliver high-quality services in the most efficient manner on limited resources. Its 8,000 member organisations have over seven million volunteers and 240,000 staff, constituting half of the third sector workforce even though they are only 5 per cent of all registered charities.

Who Volunteers Wins

'There has never been a better time for a volunteer to work for free', says Sheila Moore in her *Essential Handbook of Voluntary Work: Working for Free*. She goes on, on page 24:

> *There are two more reasons why people should get involved now. First, the current expenditure cuts are seriously affecting the social services*

and this could bring genuine suffering to many people. Time and again in this country volunteers have sprung up – often in astonishing numbers – to rescue the victims of disaster. If volunteers do not arise today to fill the widening holes in the statutory social services, the cost in human misery is going to be brutal.

Second, volunteer organisations themselves are drowning in the sea of financial troubles flooding the country. If they go down in great numbers I think our society will lose the following irreplaceable and precious things: genuine freedom of opportunity to contribute to the community in the way each person thinks best; important counterweights to counterbalance the monolithic power of the State; and the variety, spontaneity and volatility that are both the identifying marks and the foundations of a democracy.

How history repeats itself! Both supporters and critics of the 'Big Society' in the second decade of the twenty-first century will recognise the sentiments in this passage, though it was written 35 years ago (Moore, 1977).

The late Sheila Moore's husband John, now Lord Moore of Lower Marsh, was a 40-year-old Conservative MP when she wrote the book. He went from student politics to an active role in the Democrat Party in Sheila's native Illinois in the 1960s. From 1987 to 1989 he had cabinet responsibility for the 'widening holes in the statutory social services' his wife had identified.

Volunteering is the practice of people working on behalf of others outside their family without being motivated by financial or material gain. It is altruistic, intended to promote good causes or improve the quality of life.

Volunteers work long hours or short hours, regularly, irregularly, frequently, infrequently or as needed. They are highly trained (First Responders are a breed of paramedic), not trained at all (parents keeping a children's sports team going) or selectively trained to a relevant level (sorting clothes in the back of a charity shop). They work in dedicated teams with a common purpose (such as mountain rescue) or they are jacks of all trades (the staff of a volunteer centre). They may use existing skills (as a treasurer) in a voluntary context or gain new ones (as in furniture recycling). They may be on the front line (in a playgroup) or in the back office (trustee). They may volunteer in a developing country (through Voluntary Service Overseas (VSO)), in an institution (listening to children reading at school or prison visitors), in their communities (special constables, magistrates, scout and guide leaders, Neighbourhood Watch), from home (writing postcards for Amnesty International or taking part in a telephone befriending scheme), in the fresh air (British Trust for Conservation Volunteers) or over the internet (mentoring via Skype).

Volunteering offers three types of benefit: economic, community and personal. Where an activity is undertaken by volunteers that might otherwise be carried out by the state there is often a clear saving of public expense (such as the Royal National Lifeboat Institute (RNLI) or hospital 'Friends'). However, outsourcing of services to volunteers should not be regarded as the cheap option: lower costs mean that more staff, or a better quality of service, or an additional complementary service can be provided without incurring additional cost.

Volunteering brings communities together in common purpose, aiding community cohesion and capacity-building (such as in tenants' associations) which will help create the right circumstances for economic regeneration and the localism agenda.

Again, Sheila Moore reports from 1977:

> There is even a timid trend in industry to release some of their people for community service while keeping them on salary.

This is still the case. Employee volunteering still needs to step up a gear to play its part in any strategy to engage employees in active corporate citizenship. This is discussed in detail in Chapter 3.

The personal benefits from volunteering can be very significant: developing new skills and talents, accredited training and other experiences can help with career development. Using existing skills in a new environment can make a worker more productive and effective. People for whom teamwork is a new experience can gain very significantly whilst others gain in confidence, expression and other character-building traits.

Volunteering England is the charity which promotes the quality and quantity of volunteering, as summarised in Table 2.2. Their 2011 mission was to promote both Investing in Volunteers accreditation for public and third sector bodies, of whom 440 had qualified by summer 2010, and the new Investing in Volunteers for Employers standard of which Barclays Bank, the BBC and Microsoft were amongst the first to qualify.

Table 2.2   The impact of volunteering – in numbers[5]

- £18 billion: the value of volunteer time to the UK economy in 2010
- 22 million people volunteer each year
- In 2008–09, 71 per cent of adults in England volunteered at some point with 47 per cent doing so more than once a month
- 96 per cent of volunteers say they 'really enjoy it'
- 62 per cent of volunteers started volunteering because they wanted to improve things/help people
- 73 per cent of volunteering organisations would engage more volunteers if they could secure more resources
- 86 per cent of Volunteer Centres saw an increase in the number of enquiries in 2009–10
- 63 per cent of Volunteer Centres are now carrying out work specifically focused around volunteering and employability
- 87 per cent of employers think that volunteering can help career progression

The 2012 Olympic Games will have its own cohort of volunteers[6] but Volunteering England is working with others, including the Cabinet Office and various sports bodies, to make sure that volunteering in sport will thrive after the Olympic torch has moved on. Most Volunteer Centres are now delivering volunteering opportunities designed to increase the employability of those out of work, often in association with Jobcentre Plus. This will prove valuable at a time of high unemployment.

Training for volunteer managers is a key element of Volunteering England's programme and it receives direct Government funding. However, this was only possible because of the work of the Commission on the Future of Volunteering.

THE COMMISSION ON THE FUTURE OF VOLUNTEERING

The Commission sat from 2006 to 2008 under the chairmanship of Baroness Rabbi Julia Neuberger. Its 18 members, of whom I was one, were drawn from a variety of faiths, professions, regions, ages, ethnic backgrounds and political outlooks. It is worth summarising our unanimous recommendations, published in January 2008 (Neuberger et al.):

1.   To raise the profile of volunteering.

---

5   From Volunteering England Impact Report, 2010.
6   In July 2011 it was announced that Olympic volunteering would be extended to 16–18 year olds. Sportsbeat web site reported that I had called for this when an MP.

2.   To create an Access to Volunteering fund (akin to Access to Work) to help disabled people better participate in civil society.

3.   To remove administrative obstacles to volunteering.

4.   To create more and better employer-supported volunteering, with Government leading by example.

5.   To modernise volunteering's infrastructure and organisations.

6.   To recognise volunteering in career development, training and accreditation for volunteers and volunteer managers.

7.   To allow full cost recovery where proposals to use volunteers are put forward.

8.   To have a Cabinet minister responsible for volunteering policy across departments, with a select committee to oversee the same.

9.   To accept promotion of volunteering as a criterion by which public services are assessed.

10.   All Government departments to adhere to the Compact and the Volunteering Code of Practice.

Within a year many of these ideas had been implemented by the Labour Government with cross-party support. Some were approved then but implemented by the Conservative-led coalition, such as the establishment of a de-regulation task force for the voluntary sector. This was led by Lord Robin Hodgson, the President of NCVO and a former Conservative MP, who reported in May 2011 (Hodgson et al., 2011). Far from being a litany of 'bureaucracy gone mad' the report was constructive and wide ranging. It called for clarity on trustee and volunteer liabilities, the elimination of duplication in regulation, taking a stiff broom to licensing and incentives to volunteer – especially from Jobcentre Plus which had a reputation of being ambiguous on these matters.

Appendix 2 of the Hodgson report deserves to be reprinted and displayed in every civil servant's office, town hall, volunteer centre and school: it is a joyful list of 20 practices that are allowed, contrary to popular opinion and urban myth, such as playing conkers without wearing goggles. On the role of the private sector the report was almost silent, noting only that it had its profits to protect.

A £2 million Access to Volunteering Fund two year pilot to support disabled people as volunteers was set up by the Government in 2009 in three regions. After the pilot ended it disappeared without trace: see Chapter 7 (Fresh Minds, 2011).

No one can say that the profile of volunteering has been hidden under a bushel as the Big Society, with its ethos of volunteering and community engagement, has been on the lips of every politician since before the 2010 election.

The Cabinet Office announced in 2011 that its staff could volunteer a day a year of work time, 30,000 days between them, and that other departments should follow suit. It is not clear whether this is to be an average or whether the previous Government's allowance of up to five days each still applies; certainly senior managers in Government now have 'encouraging volunteering' as an element of their annual appraisals. The Government announced in early 2011 that charities will be able to request help from civil servants when they need it, perhaps creating a demand for that volunteering time to be made available.

By 2006 Government policy for the third sector had already been centralised in the new Office of the Third Sector (OTS) within the Cabinet Office. OTS inherited much of the activity, policy and even workforce from the Home Office's Active Community Unit but for the first time the minister in charge was called the Minister for the Third Sector. Previous incumbents in the Home Office had tended to be minister for something else, with volunteering and third sector issues tacked on.

The first three Ministers for the Third Sector were Parliamentary Under-Secretaries of junior rank: Ed Miliband in his first ministerial role, Kevin Brennan and Phil Hope. The fourth, Angela Smith, was a Minister of State which was taken to be a sign of Gordon Brown's elevated regard for the sector. Whether this was the case, or whether this experienced minister was being rewarded for her years as his Parliamentary Private Secretary, we shall never know.

When the name of the unit was changed to the Office for Civil Society the first incumbent of the coalition era, Nick Hurd, reverted to the more junior rank.

The Commission on the Future of Volunteering's idea of a select committee to oversee all third sector matters was never going to happen. The cost and Parliamentary manpower needed to set up and run it would have been difficult to justify; and the reason why there is no select committee specifically to oversee the Cabinet Office is political. No Prime Minister would tolerate a select committee free to walk down its metaphorical corridors, peering into allegorical filing cabinets and waste bins in a department which included both his own office and that of the newly empowered Deputy Prime Minister, would they?

Instead, the Public Administration Select Committee stepped up to the mark under its forensic Chair, Dr Tony Wright. They somewhat trumped the Commission by holding their first ever inquiry into such matters, on Commissioning from the Third Sector, whilst the Commission was still sitting.[7] Their recommendations relating to full cost recovery and to the Compact were dealt with when the Compact was refreshed, as we will discuss in Chapter 5.

The Committee also looked into 'Public Benefit'. In examining 'The Work of the Charity Commission in 2008–09' a Conservative member of the Committee grilled the Commission's Chair, Suzi Leather, in a manner so hostile that it would have broken lesser witnesses, parroting the *Daily Mail*'s description of her as a 'quango queen'. The Chairman and other members of the Committee publicly apologised to Dame Suzi.[8]

In his time at the helm following the 2010 election, Public Administration Select Committee's new chair Bernard Jenkin has made up for lost time with several inquiries focusing on the third sector.

BRINGING THE UNIONS ON BOARD

In the early days of public and voluntary sector co-working it had not been lack of imagination of managers alone that had held back constructive engagement. There had been real shop floor concern amongst employees that unpaid volunteers would undercut their labour costs – by up to 100 per cent – and force them out of work. This did happen in some poorly managed environments. So in December 2009 Volunteering England reached a historic agreement with the

---

7   See http://www.publications.parliament.uk/pa/cm200708/cmselect/cmpubadm/112/112.pdf
8   See www.publications.parliament.uk/pa/cm200910/cmselect/cmpubadm/109/09121002.htm#n9

TUC[9] that spelled out a professional approach to maximise common interest and minimise conflict between volunteer and paid staff in any workplace.

The Charter principles were that:

1. all volunteering is undertaken by choice and all individuals should have the right to volunteer or not to volunteer;

2. while volunteers should not normally receive or expect rewards for their activities, they should receive reasonable out of pocket expenses;

3. the involvement of volunteers should complement and supplement the work of paid staff and should not be used to displace paid staff or undercut their pay and conditions of service; and

4. all paid workers and volunteers should have access to training and development.

The Charter applies to employee volunteers as much as to others. It recognises the value that 22 million volunteers make to the UK economy and wider society, estimated (by various sources) to be worth between £18 billion and £23 billion each year.

Voluntary Organisations Delivering Services

In trying to understand how private sector businesses might best work with third sector agents for mutual benefit, we must look at how the relationship between public and voluntary sectors has matured.

For much of the second half of the twentieth century a significant part of the voluntary or third sector delivered services complementary to those of the state. That complementarity was not planned and there was no strategy to fill the holes left in the informal network between the weft and the warp of public and voluntary services. An example of complementarity might be found with Shelter, one of the UK's leading charities, now led by Campbell Robb who had previously moved from NCVO to be the first director of the OTS.

---

9   See www.volunteering.org.uk/magazine/Issues/2009+issues/December+2009/news/TUC+and+
    VE+launch+charter.

Since 1966 Shelter has campaigned for decent housing and against homelessness. It is today the principal source of independent advice for people in housing need and by 2007 a quarter of Shelter's £50 million income came from Government grants – a level that would have been unheard of in its early days. Where a government acknowledges a social need for good housing advice it is better to fund an expert to provide an enhanced service than to set up a rival one.

We will return to housing in a moment.

CHARITABLE STATUS AND PUBLIC BENEFIT

Back in 1966 the only direct assistance available to charities from Government was the variety of tax reliefs that came with charitable status. 'Charitable status' is defined by HMRC under the 2006 Charities Act[10] and it relies on the delivery of public benefit.

In consulting on 'public benefit' following the Act the Charity Commission opened a can of worms. A charity must deliver through its activities a benefit, tangible or otherwise, consistent with its charitable aims; the benefit had also to be available to the public. In most cases both the 'benefit' and the 'public' criteria were readily met. The Commission's web site gives examples of how the test might be failed: a cancer research charity could bring benefit even if its research duplicated that carried out elsewhere, but if its research was useless it would bring no benefit. If its findings were never published then any benefit would not be public.

The elephant in the room was the fee-paying and essentially private public schools which receive the tax benefits of charitable status. Everyone could see they brought benefit to those who used them – the fast track to an elite university, leading roles in the professions, a disproportionate chance of becoming a cabinet minister of any hue – but how public was it when families had to pay thousands of pounds a year to avail themselves of the service?

Politically, the elephant became the dog that never barked. Backbench Labour MPs were expected to take up arms to persuade their own Government to at least remove charitable status from Eton and Harrow, thereby smashing the means by which thick rich kids purportedly did better out of life than bright

---

10 See www.hmrc.gov.uk/charities/guidance-notes/chapter2/chapter_2.htm [and] www.hmrc.gov.uk/charities/tax/basics.htm

poor ones. Although this was a policy the Party had almost condoned several times during the previous half century there was no such rebellion – apart from a few die-hards in the House of Lords (and one on the Public Affairs Select Committee).

I sat on the committee stage of the 2006 Charities Bill as it then was. The Bill would not ban anything: it merely asked the Charity Commission to rule on public benefit in each individual case. As such it attracted almost no attention in the Commons outside the committee room.

To be on the safe side public schools made important but not earth-shattering gestures, increasing the number of scholarships available to children from poor backgrounds and offering to share their often superior sports and drama facilities with neighbouring state schools.

The change in government in 2010 prompted the Independent Schools Council to seek legal clarification on 'public benefit'. The referral was supported not only by the Attorney General (an alumnus of Westminster School) but also by a confident Charity Commission as a way of clarifying its own position. The outcome, supporting the Commission's general principles but requiring them to rewrite significant parts of their guidance, was a 'score draw'.

HOUSING

1966 was also the year of one of television's most memorable dramas, 'Cathy Come Home'. This story of unemployment, homelessness, squatting and family break-up was watched by a quarter of Britain's adult population at its first showing and raised the political profile of housing significantly. The Reverend Bruce Kendrick had already set up a housing association in Notting Hill to serve the more disadvantaged members of his flock but taking advantage of the popular mood following the play he established Shelter. The charity's early work drew attention to the crisis of both quality and quantity of housing available to poorer people in inner cities.

Shelter does not build houses. During the first 100 years of local authorities the mass building of homes for rent was led by the public sector. Prior to that, anything that would today be described as social housing had been the responsibility of the church (the first recorded alms house being in the tenth century) or philanthropists such as the Cadbury family in Birmingham, as we have seen, or George Peabody's Trust in London which owns 19,000 homes.

The building of council houses peaked in the post-war years and by the 1970s housing associations, themselves charities, were making the running in the homes for rent market. As we have seen, government borrowing can be a touchy subject. Council borrowing shows up on the public sector balance sheet but that of housing associations need not. The vast majority of social housing receives public subsidy and is subject to local authority nomination rights; it is a public service comparable to council housing although it is in the third sector.

Councils opposed to the Government's policy of selling council houses from the 1980s also realised that 'public' housing stock belonging to a housing association was not covered by Right to Buy legislation; so stock transfers and tenant involvement in management were introduced to put the brake on such sales.

PRESCHOOL CARE

The world of preschool playgroups is dominated by the voluntary sector which, over the years, has seen its functions gradually nationalised. Although the first preschools were created in Lanark in 1816 by Robert Owen, the founder of the Co-operative movement, the first large-scale provision was the German kindergartens from 1837.

There is no legal obligation for local authorities to provide education for the under-fives although many chose to do so in more deprived wards. In 1982 Princess Diana became the patron of the Preschool Playgroup Movement of voluntary providers, founded in 1961 and later renamed the Preschool Learning Alliance (PLA). The PLA believe that parents should play a role in their work, not only to meet the demand for volunteers but to demonstrate partnership in their children's social upbringing.

Until recently there was only basic regulation of preschool education outside the small public sector. This changed as the Government decided to fund places for four- and then three-year-olds from 2000, initially for 12.5 hours a week and then for 15. Such funding was initially seen as a threat to preschool playgroups and membership of the PLA fell from around 15,000 to 13,000 as state schools looked to expand in a toddler turf war.

The 2003 white paper, Every Child Matters, brought stability and a more level playing field to the preschool sector and was welcomed by the PLA. It was followed by more regulation the outcome of which was to define the independence of the sector by its means of governance rather than its activity.

PLA members include private companies but the majority are still voluntary organisations including charities, social enterprises and latterly Community Interest Companies (CIC). Some of its members are engaged in formal partnerships, often with Sure Starts or local authorities, to provide services in deprived areas or for hard to reach families. There is understandable sensitivity amongst some parents that some private sponsors might be offering reduced rates on their products and services to PLA members as a marketing ploy in return for publicity with little benefit to the service, so such partnerships are not common.

FROM GOOD DEEDS TO SERVICE PROVISION

In areas like social housing, preschool education and care for the elderly, the boundaries between public and voluntary sectors have become increasingly blurred. The private sector, active in all three fields, has largely retained its operational independence. The growing dependence of the voluntary sector on government funding has arguably produced a more cohesive, comprehensive and reliable service than the voluntary sector could have generated alone. It has also avoided competition on price for the basic service. Political responsibility for each service has remained with government, local and national.

In 2008, the voluntary and community sector provided over a quarter of the social care workforce in the UK. In England, 87 per cent of voluntary sector adult care homes and agencies in England met national minimum standards compared to 84 per cent in the public sector and 82 per cent in the private sector.[11]

Have these trends been at the expense of originality, variety and true localism? It is more likely that services provided through the regulation and funding of voluntary sector providers has enabled the Government to ensure that the services exist at all, and that the real choice was between encouraging them in this way or not having them. With the best will in the world, because of its dependence on volunteers, initiatives and circumstances, one quality the voluntary sector could not guarantee in the past was universality of service. Coalitions of the willing, on which smaller voluntary organisations are based, are dependent on the right people being in the right place at the right time, being not just willing but ready and able to step up to the mark.

Part of the Big Society ethos is a trust in the capacity of local communities to generate local services. Communities lacking the expertise, 'elbow power'

---

11   Source: Volunteering England, *Guardian* online debate on Public Sector Reform, 12 July 2011.

or resources to do this, or lacking people with the strength of character to sustain it do not have the capacity to set them up. They will not be able to take localism to its logical conclusion, no matter how many community organisers are appointed to coax and goad them into doing so. Such ambitions cannot be fulfilled overnight or whilst local authority services – the natural complement to local action, however small they may eventually become – are being withdrawn.

What is unarguably true is that what capacity there is to enable voluntary organisations to take responsibility for the delivery of services within communities – or within public sector organisations – is already being utilised in Britain where we have one of the largest proportions of people who engage in voluntary work in the world.

Where the will and the competence do exist, does the scale? No. Taking small operations to scale through merger and investment over a period that is feasible in order to contribute to a universally available service is the biggest challenge that Big Society faces. Those with the highest expectations of the Big Society still have to learn these lessons, as we shall see in Chapter 7.

Some people have berated the increasing professionalism of parts of the voluntary sector as 'not playing the game' so it is worth summarising the story up to the early 1990s.

We went from:

> The voluntary sector delivering services independently of the state, relying on fundraising or philanthropy. Some services inadvertently complement or copy those provided by the public sector

To:

> A culture of grants from the public sector to sustain the voluntary sector. Arbitrary by nature, largely one-off or short term, not totally strategic and, whilst influenced by outcomes, not wholly dependent on results

To:

> An acknowledgement that some third sector services complement those of the state and should receive state funding accordingly, with little strategic planning and still largely not related to results.

THE CONTRACT CULTURE

In the 1990s all this was to change. With the advent of the contract culture, where the assumption was that 'traditional' public services need no longer be provided from within public bodies, the same mood that brought privatisation in the 1980s caught up with the voluntary sector. It was not originally conceived that voluntary bodies would play a major part in delivering mainstream services as authorities embarked on direct privatisation, outsourcing and compulsory competitive tendering. On the other hand, why not? With £30 million being cut from local authority grants to voluntary bodies in 1991–92[12] there was considerable uncertainty, scepticism and fear within the sector.

At the same time, some charities were heavily reliant on direct funding from the Government. The Citizens Advice Bureau (CAB), which received money for providing financial and benefits advice to the public, was being warned that such grants could be withdrawn if they did not cease criticising aspects of the Government policy on benefits through their campaigns.

Such a threat went to the heart of the very existence of CAB, which has incomparable data on the impact of the welfare system on people in receipt of benefits. The challenge was resisted, loudly, but the threat only went away with the change in government in 1997.[13]

Would the provision of services based on value for money alone place greater emphasis on low-cost provision than on high-quality services? How would charities cope with competing for funds? Did they have the skills, the capacity, the wherewithal to function in a cross-sector competitive market place?

The answer to the third question was the clearest: in most cases it was a resounding 'no'. Whilst NCVO provided what help and advice it could, even many large charities could not thrive in an environment of raw competition. Whilst there was big money to be won they had no experience of bidding, tendering or dancing to someone else's tune. Smaller, local charities had the same problem – in spades.

---

12 A lot of money in those days. Source: NCVO.
13 After the Iraq war in 2003, Save the Children was highly critical of US and UK policies on reconstruction, whilst delivering aid programmes there on behalf of both governments. In responding to their concerns the US withdrew its funding but Britain did not.

It is little wonder that in the 1990s the private sector did not, by and large, regard voluntary sector organisations as credible and reliable business partners. However, the introduction of the Compact in 1998, a memorandum of understanding on co-working between the Government and the third sector, was to help the sector move in this direction as we will see in Chapter 5.

Modern Times

Government funding on the third sector boomed between 2004 and 2010 as more and more services were commissioned from the sector; the proportion of spending that came as grants fell considerably. Those funding streams will crash between 2011 and 2014. The Association of Chief Executives of Voluntary Organisations (ACEVO) and others have estimated that some £3 billion to £5 billion will be lost from the third sector over this period when direct cuts and the knock-on effect of reduced local government spending are taken into account.

The Government set up a transition fund of £100 million to help charities forced into hardship by 'the cuts', at best a 3 per cent plaster to cover a 100 per cent hole. To add insult to that injury, in April 2011 the three year protection of Gift Aid, a tax relief that charities can claim from donations given to them by UK taxpayers, ran out. Gift Aid is related to the level of basic rate income tax, which is currently at 20 per cent. This means that on a £100 donation from a basic rate taxpayer a charity can claim back £25 from HMRC because an income of £125 less 20 per cent tax would have produced a sum of £100. Prior to 2008 the basic rate was 21 per cent, so the £100 donation would have generated £28.21 for the charity. That protection, which kept Gift Aid payable at 2008 rates, was only intended to last for three years.

It has been estimated that the loss to charities from 2011 caused by the tax change in 2008 is around £100 million a year; a cut about the same size as the money made available to protect the charitable sector from all the other cuts.

Direct funding of the sector's umbrella bodies – NCVO, NAVCA – was cut in 2011 and others receiving direct funding such as the young people's volunteering body, v – lost half their staff. Even the Charity Commission, frustrated at never having had enough funding to deliver some of its new obligations under the 2006 Charities Act, lost a quarter of its budget and a third of its staff in the 2011 spending round (Wiggins and Cook, 2011).

At the same time, expectation of what the third sector might do to compensate through the Big Society is very high. Many argue that it is unrealistically high, especially as the timescale for the cuts, front loaded at the beginning of this Parliament for obvious political reasons, is so short. What the Big Society is, what it might become and how the third sector and business will or could relate to it, is discussed in Chapter 7.

The Diversification of Funding

Every two years *Third Sector* magazine and the research group nfpSynergy carry out a 'State of the Sector' survey which identifies the key issues and priorities for the third sector. The 2012 survey confirms many of the trends identified in post-recessionary 2010 when the last one was carried out, with 'Creating a stable funding base' emerging as the number one priority (69 per cent) and only one charity in five holding out any hope of improved funding from Government. Just one respondent in 12 thought the Government's approach to their sector was 'coherent and promising'.[14]

Fundraising was identified by more than two in five as the skill in shortest supply, well ahead of digital media, which had overtaken strategic planning for second place. Many of the skill shortage areas identified are those where trading skills with businesses could be advantageous for both parties.

In December 2010 a report published by an ad hoc grouping of NCVO, Unity Trust Bank, Capacitybuilders and the Joseph Rowntree Foundation called for a 'ten year framework for civil society' to bring certainty and stability to the funding environment (Funding Commission, 2010). It took into account the financial environment of the Spending Review of a few weeks earlier, the Big Society and localism but also future demands on the sector's services: an ageing and more diverse population, climate change, new technology and ethical consumerism.

Doing nothing would lead to a decline in third sector services based on the 'unrealistic assumption' that voluntary effort and income could fill the gap created by the state's withdrawal, they said. The alternative, growth in funding, clearly could not be guaranteed by Government but could be financed from:

---

14 See http://www.thirdsector.co.uk/Finance/article/1110963/low-scores-government-state-sector-survey/

- a doubling of 'giving' (from £10 billion to £20 billion);

- £10 billion from social investment;

- more effective spending all round.

This would be complemented by increased research into social impact, improved financial capability, better investment of charity assets and grant making, investment in social enterprise, partnerships with business, better commissioning practices, help with restructuring and mergers and proper funding of Big Society initiatives and outcomes by central government.

As we saw in Table 1.2, charities spend over £52 billion each year. A 1 per cent increase in efficiency would generate the equivalent of ten £1 million donations to charity every week.

The economy of 2011 forces voluntary groups and charities to think out of the box to fund their activities. Essentially fundraising falls into four categories: Active fundraising, Philanthropy, Grants and Trading. Active charity fundraising includes many traditional forms: events, lotteries and raffles, collection boxes and sponsorship.

Philanthropy, bequests and legacies tend to be more passive although the market is increasingly competitive. The lifetime legacy is an attractive idea which has never been implemented: the owner gifts an asset to a charity through a legally binding agreement which allows the charity to make use of it by, for example, borrowing against its capital value. The donor continues to use the asset during his lifetime and the agreement would transfer the physical asset to the charity at the donor's death. This process is often advocated for the donation of works of art but there is no reason why it could not apply to property and other major capital assets.

Let us dwell on the other two categories, grants from third parties and trading.

Grants from Third Parties

Grants are essentially gifts to charities and voluntary groups from a grant-making body on a one-off or repetitive basis, tied to some extent to a particular activity. Traditionally grant-making bodies have included central government, local government and foundations. Foundations exhibit different patterns of giving: most operate in specific policy or geographical fields and few are comprehensive in their scope. Some are proactive rather than reactive, discouraging funding requests.

Council grants respond to local needs as represented by applications from voluntary and community groups. Typically they will set aside a budget each year for this purpose and treat applications on merit. In many top tier councils a small 'no strings' budget for micro-grants is devolved to each councillor to help address their ward's needs. Even today, grants as low as £50 can make a difference to a small community group.

London Councils is the umbrella body for the Borough Councils of London. In 2010 they announced that the £26.4 million collective 'pot' from which they made grants for London-wide organisations would be cut by £10 million. A group of charities took London Councils to court as they had failed to make a proper assessment of the impact of the cut under the 2010 Equalities Act. In essence, they argued that charities working with disadvantaged groups like refugees, who could have expected to receive a share, would be disproportionately disadvantaged by the cut: a legal advice centre in North London, promised £83,000 per year from 2009 to 2012 from the fund, could have lost it all. The court agreed with the claimants and forced London Councils to think again by making the proper assessments. The court had no power, however, to stop the cuts from happening; the subsequent review brought about a halving of the cut.

THE BIG LOTTERY FUND

In 1994 the biggest single source of grant funding for the third sector appeared: the National Lottery. With 28p of every pound spent by punters going to good causes it is the most generous national lottery in the world. The Big Lottery Fund currently distributes almost half of that 28p to organisations and projects in communities across the UK and a small programme in developing countries. BIG (as it is sometimes called) came into existence in 2004 when the Community Fund and the New Opportunities Fund merged, since when it has distributed almost £4 billion to communities and humanitarian causes. Thirteen other distributors divide the balance between the arts, heritage and sport. About £1.5 billion will have supported the Olympics by 2012; this revenue stream will be available to other good causes, together with one-off funds from the sale of assets such as the Olympic village, after the games are over.

Several programmes running on different time scales work in different ways within BIG. As well as grants, large and small, it has diversified into loans and endowments. Although it is not strictly a foundation, having no endowment of its own and being tightly regulated, BIG is one of the largest members of the Association of Charitable Foundations.

BIG's annual report for 2009–10 gives an idea of the balance between supply and demand for their funding:

> ... *14,000 commitments were made to groups the length and breadth of the UK, totalling £440 million. These ranged from £300 for small community projects, to more transformative investments of over £1 million ... In 2009/10 we received over 28,000 applications requesting [a total of] more than £1 billion.*

Awards for All is a small programme for grants up to £10,000 although many applicants request much less than this. At the other end of the scale, BIG has given £11.25 million to Social Finance, of which £6.25 million is to help establish the first Social Impact Bond (SIB) (more in Chapter 7) with the rest dedicated to creating a market for such bonds in the future.

BIG calls this intelligent and creative grant-making: making grants to aid projects which are most likely to succeed and valuing projects according to outcomes rather than inputs: 'real improvements to communities'.

BIG has not been without controversy. Whilst some of their programmes, like 'The People's Millions', overtly seek public engagement in the grant-making process the tabloid newspapers are always looking out for BIG 'gaffes'. Grants to groups of lesbians, asylum seekers and AIDS sufferers have been derided and mocked in the press but it remains important that disadvantaged groups have access to funds to meet their unmet needs.

Additionality is a concept with which supporters of the Lottery and of BIG in particular have struggled in the past and will do so again in the new environment of cuts to statutory services. In the 1998 Act ministers went out of their way to lay down in law that BIG was independent of government in its funding streams and that all grants must be additional to and not substituted for cash that came – or should be expected to come – from government.

There were accusations that distributors were sailing close to the wind, being used by the Government to pump money into projects favouring disadvantaged groups of potential Labour voters. BIG defends its legal framework and independence stoutly. Although they might fund work in the same communities as other agencies they argue that this reflects local need, not Party-political motive. The Reaching Communities programme has pulled together different elements within deprived areas, going to the heart of what makes them tick, helping them achieve more than the statutory agencies can because they are not mired in the silo thinking too often inherent in the statutory system.

On the other hand, they would not be as effective as they are without leaning on existing frameworks. Funding such programmes irrespective of what public sector service providers were doing would risk duplicating rather than complementing them and would be irresponsible.

BIG funding puts spending power into the hands of local people in those communities. It is committed to giving 80 per cent of its spending to voluntary and community sector (VCS) groups in the period 2009 to 2015. It got off to a good start, with 92 per cent going to the VCS in 2009–10.

The additionality clause in the BIG constitution is safe. Those who questioned it in Parliament in the past are now in Government, where they appear to be content with its current interpretation which is very 'Big Society'. Even though the Government is reducing BIG's share of lottery funding from 46 to 40 per cent, it will be a smaller share of a larger pot once the diversion to the Olympic funding stream has ended, assuming lottery ticket sales remain constant.

Whilst BIG funding appears safe, this is not certain. It is politically safe because the Government wants BIG as a friend, not an adversary. As services are withdrawn from communities by cuts, especially by local authorities, the additionality question becomes more fraught, not less: does the rule that says 'thou shalt not fund a service which would reasonably be expected to be provided by government' still apply when the service is no longer provided by government?

Everyone in the worlds of politics, charity and volunteerism would prefer that this question was not even asked for a few years yet.

Trading

Charities and other groups have become more professional over the years, more 'businesslike'. The growth in social enterprise, businesses designed for social benefit rather than profit is testament to that new philosophical environment. As organisations became larger, businesslike behaviour became essential not only to manage larger finances, payrolls and premises but also to hold one's own in what has increasingly become a market place – both for services and for the giving of time and money on which the third sector depends.

Charity shops have had their share of controversy in their time. They may not be big business (though collectively their value is massive) but they are lucrative; the growth in thefts of charity clothes bags and door to door scams is testimony to the fact that money can be made here. Perhaps charity shops nowadays deserve to be classed as a 'traditional active forms of fundraising' listed at the start of this section. Scope alone raised £150,000 from clothes donated via clothes recycling banks in just two counties, Hertfordshire and Northumberland, in 2010 (Boffey, 2011).

The trading of new goods by charities is a relatively new phenomenon. You can buy almost anything as long as it carries an organisation's logo. Your credit card may give 25p to your favourite charity for every £100 you spend and charities get similar deals from insurance companies, holiday companies and energy companies. Charity shops are only allowed to sell a token amount of new goods, such as Christmas cards, for fear of losing the privileged status that the local council, responsible for collecting business rates, may have afforded them – a privilege often resented by their private sector High Street neighbours.

Today through the internet you can buy a tree with your name on in a fine oak wood or a porpoise somewhere in the Atlantic; you can become the proud owner of a flock of goats in the Sahara, a feast of pencils in New Guinea or a box of vaccines in India, all by proxy.

But the business of selling services is what the commissioning revolution is all about. The Coalition Government wants to take this process to another level.

CASE STUDY: ROYAL NATIONAL INSTITUTE FOR DEAF PEOPLE (RNID) (NOW ACTION ON HEARING LOSS)

One of the first services to be commissioned by the Government from a charity was the choice of the RNID to oversee and manage the introduction of digital hearing aids into the National Health Service (NHS).

The National Institute for the Deaf was founded in 1924 although its roots date back a dozen more years to Leo Bonn, a deaf merchant banker. The Duke of Edinburgh became its patron in 1958, adding the prefix 'Royal' in 1961. In 1992 'the Deaf' became 'Deaf People'. To mark its centenary it changed its name to 'Action on Hearing Loss' in June 2011. Chief Executive Jackie Ballard says that now 'it does what it says on the tin'.

Today RNID is a clearing house for every imaginable service for hearing aid users, sufferers of tinnitus, lipreaders, sign language users and anyone else with impaired hearing – potentially nine million people in Britain. Their vision is of a world where deafness or hearing loss do not limit or determine opportunity and where people value their hearing.

It is an effective lobbying organisation: in 1948 Aneurin Bevan chose the organisation's conference to announce that the new NHS would provide hearing aids free of charge.

But 50 years on NHS hearing aids no longer enjoyed the best of reputations. They were unsophisticated analogue devices the size of a hazelnut, worn behind the ear. They had tubes which could get blocked and were unreliable when wet, their battery power faded over time and to cap it all their sensors faced backwards. About half of all patients prescribed hearing aids did not use them on a regular basis. Users looked with envy at their neighbours whose privately sourced digital aids were small enough to be hidden within the ear, compatible with hearing loop systems and capable of producing great clarity of sound. Then they saw their price tag: £2,000.

RNID did not relax. Why should two million NHS patients accept second rate, one-size-fits-all models when private patients could enjoy the state of the art? In 1997 they began a lobbying campaign which was both effective and admired. By 1999 their profoundly deaf Chief Executive, James Strachan, had persuaded manufacturers to offer the RNID digital hearing aids in bulk containing technology only slightly behind the times, at just £150 each.

This was not good enough for the former banker, who was later to become Chair of the Audit Commission. In 2000 the Government agreed in principle to digitise audiology services and invited RNID to manage an NHS pilot project. In September 2001 MPs were deluged with one of the largest postcard lobbying campaigns ever and Alan Milburn, Health Secretary, agreed to the national roll-out of digital aids. He asked Strachan to lead the negotiations with the providers and he managed to halve the price again: hearing aids that would have cost £1,000 just a year previously were now available for £75 to the NHS and through them to patients for free. From 2003, by then with John Low at the helm, RNID took on and rolled out the £95 million, two year programme of delivering NHS digital aids to those who needed them.

Between 1998 and 2003 I was a trustee of RNID. It was an exciting time though not without moments of doubt and hesitation. This was a unique role for a charity provider to play on this scale.

> *The key to success, observers believe, is that the RNID offered the NHS both time-honoured voluntary-sector expertise in delivering services and understanding particular user-groups, as well as private-sector expertise in risk management, project management and negotiation. This new partnership, then, is another take on the public-private debate in the NHS, but less controversial because the voluntary sector is the conduit to bring in that private-sector knowledge. 'It is', as Strachan puts it, 'a somehow more publicly and politically acceptable channel'. (Stanford, 2002)*

Why was it more acceptable for a charity to deliver a programme independently of but within the NHS than for a company to do it? RNID made no profit from the deal, but was that the only reason?

> *The history of third-sector involvement in the health service has rarely seen charities prepared to take such a risk. Strachan acknowledges the danger but believes that it had to be overcome in order to move beyond traditional constraints on voluntary-sector involvement. 'I would say that what we are achieving proves that you can be very close – working in partnership as project managers – but, at the same time, preserve your independence and still be an extremely aggressive campaigner with the Government when the need arises'. (Stanford, 2002)*

No one would disagree that RNID had the energy, knowledge, passion and common touch to see its goal won in the best interests of hearing impaired people – and everyone in the country knew one.

Labour's Alan Milburn was clearly comfortable with this ground-breaking deal. It allowed him to argue that dogmatic insistence on state provision for state provision's sake may not be in the interests of either patients or public, whose interests both his Government and the NHS were committed to serve. Even after leaving Parliament he maintained this position, criticising the Cameron Government for lack of commitment to its own 2011 NHS reforms.

The gate had been opened and the precedent for asking the best person for the job to deliver an NHS service was established, whilst retaining the basic principle of being free to all at the point of use.

From that moment onwards, the door was open to a new form of privatisation, not selling off but buying in elements of health provision from alternative providers. Ten years later a Coalition Government is in power which is not proposing to sell off parts of the NHS but instead intends to ask its own staff to run vast parts of it as independent, not-for-profit mutuals.

But that's another story.

3

Social Responsibility and the Corporate Sector

If stories of business-based philanthropists like Buffett or Gates suggest that the private sector is enjoying a Golden Age of Social Responsibility, think again. Dozens of astonishing stories of good practice exist but they represent the shining tip of a grey corporate iceberg. Recent research in Sweden suggests that most companies believe they make a positive contribution to society but less than half of the public agree; and even their positive view is skewed by a few prominent corporate saints. There are a million registered companies in Britain for most of whom 'responsibility' has three principal elements: to the shareholders, the bank manager and the law.

Too many acts of intended corporate kindness do not engage with communities and have little strategic value, Corporate Social Responsibility (CSR) policies which tick boxes but do not arouse passions. Too many corporate values are stuck in the Friedman era, when the business of business was business and business alone. Here the response to external challenges like recession and climate change, which should spark new ways of thinking and doing, are as likely to prompt entrenchment and an 'as you were' attitude.

The evolutionary path goes something like this:

1.   *What I do with my company is my business. I don't see why the Government has to tell me how to run it, all this health and safety and equality nonsense. It's not right. What do you think we are, a charity? The reason we can't employ disabled people is because – well, they wouldn't like it. I know my staff have the right to join a trade union, but that's not the way we do things around here. Green? What's that? Do you mean inexperienced or bilious?*

2.   *Oh yes, I'd say we're a socially responsible company. Family values, that's us. The staff like a get-together on Red Nose Day each year, after work, and they pass a collection box round. It's good for morale, I'm sure. Each time a light bulb fails, we replace it with a low energy one, you know, but they're not as bright, are they? Payroll giving ... I think I know what you mean, but no one's ever asked for it.*

3.   *Sustainability is very important. We've cut water consumption, packaging, staff travel, saved a bit of money. After we put extra insulation in the buildings we turned down the thermostats but staff objected so we turned them up again. Oh yes, we're sorted on the environment front. Next time we change the Chairman's limousine we'll get one of those hybrids. Community engagement? No, we're not that sort of company. We give prizes to the school raffle, of course.*

4.   *We follow all the Energy Trust guidelines. It cost a bit, but it will be worth it. We pay London Living Wage and the canteen uses fair trade stuff. We've got a partnership with a children's charity – the staff CSR committee suggested them. We give them surplus stock occasionally and we top up whatever staff raise at events. Some staff have a rota for helping out at the children's home, they get a day off for every eight hours they spend volunteering there, maximum three days a year. One of our managers is in Kenya volunteering, actually, working with a social enterprise for three months. That experience of problem solving will mean he comes back a more aware and skilled manager, I bet!*

There is a business case for being actively 'responsible': ethical, efficient, considerate, balanced, fair. As far back as 2004 Elliot Morley MP, a respected Minister for the Environment long before his fall from grace, wrote:

> *Stakeholders and customers are increasingly concerned about the environmental and social impacts of the products they buy. It follows that businesses can maximise their long term returns by minimising their negative impacts. Through responsible action business can become more competitive, not less. (DTI, 2004)*

There is always a good excuse for not acting. According to research carried out in Holland (Brandsma, Moratis and Cochius, 2009) the main reasons companies gave for not having a policy of social responsibility were:

1.   no clear action plan – 57 per cent;

2.   too little time – 48 per cent;

3.   too little knowledge of CSR implementation – 43 per cent;

4.   too little knowledge of CSR itself – 39 per cent;

5.   obtaining buy-in from board of directors – 32 per cent.

Financial reasons and buy-in from other stakeholders were also significant.

In 2010 the Doughty Centre for Corporate Responsibility, part of Cranfield University School of Management under the enthusiastic Professor David Grayson, reviewed seven years and 167 documents of academic research and company reports.[1] They concluded that the field had matured rapidly since an earlier report (BITC and Little, 2003); some general trends could be identified.

The top seven types of benefit to business from specific and overtly responsible behaviour were, in rank order:

1.   brand value and reputation (each supporting the other);

2.   employees and future workforce (attracting, developing, retaining);

3.   operational effectiveness (through stakeholder engagement);

4.   risk reduction and management (including improved compliance);

5.   direct financial impact (cost savings);

6.   organisational growth (access to new markets);

7.   business opportunity (rethinking role leading to new products).

Two new trends cited in recent years were:

–   responsible leadership (redefined according to CSR values);

1   See www.doughtycentre.info

—   macro-level sustainable development (supply chains and
      Millennium Development Goals (MDGs)).

A number of fascinating trends occurred over the years. Brand value and
reputation (1) was more important for smaller companies than larger ones,
with those pursuing an active social responsibility policy more likely to give
priority to operational effectiveness (3). Employee issues (2) were also favoured
by Small and Medium-sized Enterprises (SMEs) but there was a marked change
from 'employee satisfaction' in 2003 to 'employee innovation and learning'
which was ranked higher than 'satisfaction' more recently.

Business in the Community (BITC) started its benchmarking Environment
Index in 1996 and extended it to a broader Corporate Responsibility Index (CRI)
in 2002. At that time three-quarters of business leaders agreed that companies
would become more competitive if responsible business principles were
evident throughout an organisation. This integrated approach to managing
environmental, social and economic issues was the beginning of the 'triple
bottom line' in Britain. We revisit BITC in Chapter 7.

The Triple Bottom Line

The triple bottom line, or 'people, planet and profit', was ratified as an approach
to urban and community reporting by the United Nations (UN) in 2007 as a
standard for public sector full cost accounting, though it has not yet been formally
adopted by great numbers in the private sector. It encapsulates the philosophy
that organisations are responsible to their stakeholders, including shareholders,
rather than to shareholders alone. Stakeholders are defined by the international
standard ISO26000, which we shall discuss, as anyone who might reasonably be
affected by the organisation's activity. The idea is represented in Figure 3.1.

It was perhaps inevitable, as climate science pervaded the public domain in
the last ten years, that 'going green' became synonymous with good corporate
citizenship. Even so, companies were hardly enthusiastic about innovation and
insulation at first and the best do stand out from the pack. Carbon fuels were
running out and oil prices were going up: these factors alone proved enough to
make even the most reluctantly green business people take notice. A future in
which supply chains were disrupted by extreme weather in the tropics and the
vague threat that half of London would be flooded by melting ice caps added
to the imperatives; was it not rapid climate change that killed off the original
dinosaurs, after all?

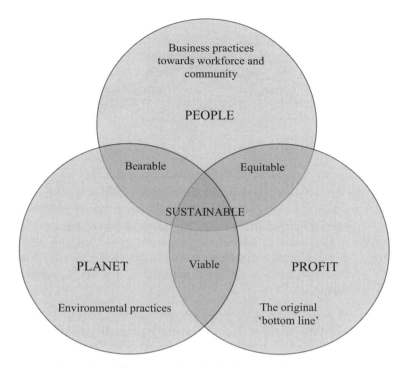

Figure 3.1   Sustainability and the triple bottom line

Management Today's Green Business Awards have become the hallmark of good environmental practice and in 2010 Marks & Spencer was a worthy winner. During the year its impressive 100 green commitments in its 2007 'Plan A' ('Because there is no Plan B') was increased to 180, including the over-riding ones of being carbon neutral by 2012 and the world's most sustainable major retailer by 2015. The competition in this field is limited, however. The judges found the holistic and inter-related measures of the plan particularly impressive, including the company's commitment to fair trade and sustainable timber and fish products. Its 88 per cent reduction in waste and 18 per cent increase in energy efficiency had produced £50 million in savings for the company.

In June 2010, Ipsos-MORI carried out research for BITC and Legal & General. They compared the total shareholder return (TSR) of 28 companies that had taken part in all eight of BITC's annual CRI assessments to TSR values more generally. TSR is the net change in share value plus the total dividend per share as a percentage change year by year.

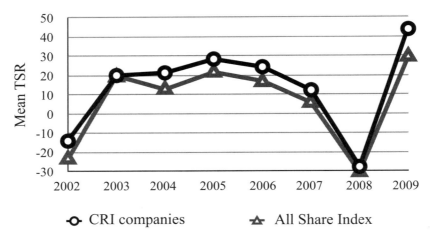

Figure 3.2   **Total Shareholder Return: CR Index vs FTSE All Share Index (Extrapolated from data published by BITC and Legal & General)**

Whether we compare CRI companies to the All Share Index or FTSE 350 makes no difference; over the period 2002 to 2009 socially responsible companies that allowed BITC to assess them annually had an average TSR significantly higher than those who did not, over a whole economic cycle. Indeed, the figures suggest that socially responsible companies were hit by recession later and recovered faster than their more traditional colleagues (Figure 3.2).[2]

Back in 2000, another piece of research by MORI for the Corporate Citizenship Company showed that employees who were aware of or involved in CSR would speak more highly of their employer and be less likely to be critical.[3]

Table 3.1   **Employee attitudes and Corporate Social Responsibility**

	I would speak highly of my employer	I would be critical of my employer
Not aware of CSR programmes	50%	23%
Aware, not involved	65%	19%
Involved	82%	13%

2   See http://www.bitc.org.uk/resources/publications/ft_2011.html
3   Quoted by Volunteering England, see www.volunteering.org.uk/WhatWeDo/Projects+and +initiatives/Employer+Supported+Volunteering/Resources/Research/CSR+Research

This research (Table 3.1) supports the widely reported impression that good CSR policy helps to both retain and attract the best and most highly motivated staff.

In 2002 the European Commission outlined a strategy for promoting the business case for CSR, especially to SMEs; promote external evaluation and benchmarking; and make sure that European Union (EU) policy and practice was CSR-friendly.[4]

SMEs employ over half of the EU workforce, yet CSR has been slow in taking off in this sector where margins are small, competition and overheads are high and communication and awareness are less sophisticated than in their larger cousins. Authorities recognise that being small is a constraint: the speed and manner with which ISO26000 could be implemented would be different in smaller companies compared to larger ones.

All is not lost. Following a survey the Federation of Small Business (FSB, 2007) disputed that their larger cousins had all the best policies. 92 per cent of the self-selected 1,700 online respondents believed that they were already acting in an environmentally and socially responsible way and that good practice was simply common sense. FSB has 210,000 members. The low participation rate combined with the fact that the survey showed members to be largely unfamiliar with CSR terminology raises the question of how effective 'common sense' might actually be.

For example, whilst four out of five were engaged in waste minimisation and recycling (aided, no doubt, by their local councils) only two in five had taken action on energy efficiency and other green measures scored even lower. Cost, lack of time and being 'too small' were the main reasons for not being more environmentally friendly.

Three-quarters of respondents considered their business to be focused on local communities and over half were actively engaged with local charities or schools. The survey was silent on what these answers meant in practice.

Back in 1996 the British Chamber of Commerce reported that eight out of ten small companies gave funds to 'good causes' and one in three donated time and services (quoted in Quirke, 1998).

---

4   See europa.eu/rapid/pressReleasesAction.do?reference=IP/02/985&format=HTML&aged=0&l
    g=sl&guiLanguage=en

The FSB supports the European Commission's definition of CSR as 'a concept whereby companies integrate social and environmental concerns in their business operations and in their interaction with their stakeholders on a voluntary basis'. This is borne out by the fact that three-quarters of respondents to the survey would welcome financial incentives from Government to promote CSR (why wouldn't they?) whilst only a minority thought other forms of encouragement would work. They strongly opposed introducing legislation.

Anecdotal evidence suggests that smaller SMEs are more community aware than larger (medium-sized) ones, probably because they are literally closer to the communities in which they operate; and that workers in smaller businesses are generally happier than those in larger ones. The average SME has four employees, the average FSB member six. Once the workforce reaches somewhere between ten and 50 it is thought that external pressures and bureaucratic demands on time cause a change in behaviour of leaders which tends to lower the priority given to community matters.

Little objective research has been done on SMEs' approach to CSR, let alone how 'S' and 'M' Es do it differently from each other. The FSB exists to reflect its members' views rather than lead them, though they acknowledge that more information on CSR and SMEs would be helpful.

The Guardian's Sustainable Business web site accepts that sustainability is not simply a 'green' concept. In December 2010 they reported some astonishingly optimistic figures from a survey by Echo of 50 members of the International Business Leaders' Forum (IBLF) (Macleod, 2010) which showed that:

- the number of CEOs who believed CSR was integral to improving commercial success had risen from 10 to 91 per cent in ten years;

- 96 per cent said that sustainability efforts needed to be integrated into their strategies and operations;

- 88 per cent believe that businesses should demand similar commitments from suppliers.

Neither sets of data can represent a true picture of business generally. IBLF is an excellent organisation which embraces the most forward looking members of the international business community. Most have experience of working in developing countries where pressures on business to act in a socially responsible way are more acute, as we discuss in Chapter 6. But multinationals working in challenging environments may not be typical of UK companies and the statistical rigour of both samples of businesses calls the figures into question.

One problem of studying CSR is that wherever you look – to BITC, Business Fights Poverty (BFP), Business Action on Homelessness (BAH), the IBLF, the Business Charity Awards and the Green Business Awards – the same corporate names keep cropping up. One can only conclude that the best practitioners in the field are excellent but that they are as yet a select group.

Nevertheless, the *Guardian* article's conclusion is intuitively sound:

> ... *those companies that best integrate CSR into overall business practices will reap the rewards born of increased consumer confidence.*

The same statistical problem arises with an annual survey carried out by the CSR agency C&E Advisory, which started in 2010. But this time the results are of more qualitative interest. In 2011 they again asked businesses and their charity partners why they had entered into business-charity partnerships (Figure 3.3).

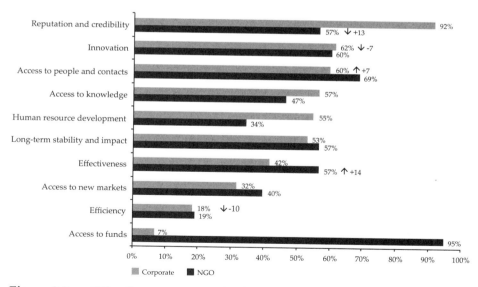

Figure 3.3   **Why does your organisation engage in corporate-NGO partnerships? (C&E Advisory, 2011)**

Although the figures represent bodies already in a healthy partnership abroad there is a remarkable degree of common understanding of the purpose and value of partnerships between charity and business.

There is no reason to believe that the relative importance of these qualities to successful partnerships is not universal and most values have changed little between the first year and the second. The value where the two partners' views significantly differ most significantly is the understandable one of access to funds.

For business it is all about reputation, innovation and Human Resources (HR) development; for charities it is access to funds – with reputation, access to contacts and innovation some way behind.

Diversification of funding is essential to many charities in an economic climate with fewer grants and riskier government contracts, even with the promise of a golden dawn. Larger charities are at greater risk as they tend to have the service delivery contracts in the first place but they are also more capable of making the most of both existing and novel sources of revenue.

Nudge, Nudge

The provision of financial incentives to move along the CSR route, willed by FSB members, is not going to happen except in relation to green behaviour. Even here, I guess that FSB were asking for carrot-shaped tax allowances rather than being beaten with sticks such as rising landfill prices and fuel tax. Even where direct incentives exist, like feed-in tariffs for creating your own zero carbon energy, the lure of market rewards is often self-evident.

FSB members, so I hear, don't mind being encouraged to behave in more responsible ways but resent being told – as they have recently – that salt should no longer be provided on the tables in works' canteens. That is not a nudge.

Business Link, the Government's web-based business advice service, lists a number of reasons for adopting a CSR approach to business, each of which is a nudge:[5]

---

5   See www.businesslink.gov.uk/bdotg/action/detail?itemId=1075408491&r.i=1075408480&r.l1= 1074404796&r.l2=1074446322&r.l3=1075408468&r.s=sc&r.t=RESOURCES&type =RESOURCES

1.   a good reputation makes it easier to recruit employees;

2.   employees may stay longer, reducing the costs and disruption of recruitment and retraining;

3.   employees are better motivated and more productive;

4.   CSR helps ensure you comply with regulatory requirements;

5.   activities such as involvement with the local community are ideal opportunities to generate positive press coverage;

6.   good relationships with local authorities make doing business easier;

7.   understanding the wider impact of your business can help you develop new products and services;

8.   CSR can make you more competitive and reduces the risk of sudden damage to your reputation (and sales). Investors recognise this and are more willing to finance you.

UK legislation reinforces a lot of socially responsible corporate behaviour. Human and labour rights, anti-discrimination practices, consumer rights and health and safety at work have changed significantly over 50 years as the law has led public opinion and vice versa at different times.

The church, too, is playing its part in nudging. Professions Group Wales is a forum which brings together five professions in the principality under the banner of 'working in the public interest': the Association of Chartered Certified Accountants, the Chartered Institute of Marketing, The Law Society, the Institute of Chartered Accountants and the Royal Institute of Chartered Surveyors. In a fascinating speech to their conference in January 2011,[6] which was welcomed by the Welsh Confederation of British Industries (CBI), the Archbishop of Wales, Barry Morgan, said:

In the end, all companies are social organisms – they have a social purpose and have corporate social responsibilities ... Wealth cannot

---

6   As reported on the BBC News Wales web site, 12 January 2011. I am grateful to the Archbishop for providing the full text of his speech. He also wrote an article based on it for the *Financial Times*.

be pursued regardless of the consequences. Economic decision-making raises questions about the common good, but also about human character and integrity.

He went on to call for all graduates of the Master of Business Administration degree (MBA) to take an oath of ethical and responsible behaviour in business, akin to the Hippocratic Oath which doctors are required to take when entering the medical profession. As the Archbishop pointed out, such an Oath already exists.

The MBA Oath[7] was drawn up by Harvard Business School's 2009 graduates and is affirmed voluntarily by MBA graduates and students. Inspired by the global financial crisis and Harvard's centenary, it calls on graduates to 'create value responsibly and ethically'. In its first year it attracted 4,500 signatories from over 300 business schools around the world including four in the UK: Cass, London, Oxford and Strathclyde. The Oath's content speaks for itself (Table 3.2).

Table 3.2   The MBA Oath

As a business leader I recognise my role in society.
- My purpose is to lead people and manage resources to create value that no single individual can create alone.
- My decisions affect the well-being of individuals inside and outside my enterprise, today and tomorrow.

Therefore, I promise that:
- I will manage my enterprise with loyalty and care, and will not advance my personal interests at the expense of my enterprise or society.
- I will understand and uphold, in letter and spirit, the laws and contracts governing my conduct and that of my enterprise.
- I will refrain from corruption, unfair competition, or business practices harmful to society.
- I will protect the human rights and dignity of all people affected by my enterprise, and I will oppose discrimination and exploitation.
- I will protect the right of future generations to advance their standard of living and enjoy a healthy planet.
- I will report the performance and risks of my enterprise accurately and honestly.
- I will invest in developing myself and others, helping the management profession continue to advance and create sustainable and inclusive prosperity.
- In exercising my professional duties according to these principles, I recognise that my behaviour must set an example of integrity, eliciting trust and esteem from those I serve. I will remain accountable to my peers and to society for my actions and for upholding these standards.

---

7   See http://mbaoath.org/ and *The MBA Oath: Setting a Higher Standard for Business Leaders* (Anderson and Escher, 2010). The Oath echoes to some extent the Sullivan Principles of 1999: www.thesullivanfoundation.org/about/global_sullivan_principles

Taking the Oath changes nothing. But it is a signal for the future, a change of emphasis and purpose, a promise that somehow business will do things better than before. As we shall see, partnerships with charities may be one way to help this along.

Those who produced ISO26000, the international standard on Social Responsibility, tell us that its principles apply equally to business, the public sector and the not-for-profit sector; but the body corporate at whom the thrust of corporate citizenship is aimed is the private sector.

In the same way as aid to a developing country is only a fraction of the money that circulates even in the poorest lands, and taxation represents a tiny fraction of Britain's wealth (expressed in hundreds of trillions of pounds on the stock exchange), so the expectation is growing that if only some of the riches held by private companies can be at least voluntarily recirculated to address social and environmental problems then we will all be better off.

And if on the way there is money to be saved or made, so much the better. This is capitalism, after all.

The lessons of taxation are that, above a certain level, the biggest players will always try to minimise their obligations by, amongst other ways, using the global nature of their business to legally relocate tax liabilities to their best advantage.

Early in 2011 Barclays surprised the media and the public with the disclosure that it had paid a very low level of Corporation Tax on its profits, which were bouncing back after the 2008 crisis. Although Barclays went on to infuriate many still further by paying its leadership stellar levels of bonuses, it remains one of the most generous and strategic of social investors and voluntary funders of international development activity. In 2010 it was the ninth largest UK company in terms of market capitalisation, the fifth largest donor of cash and the third largest donor of services in kind or 'community contributions'.

The United States has the highest level of personal giving in the world (in terms of GDP) which many claim is linked to low levels of personal taxation. However, the US figures have been distorted in recent years by massive levels of giving by a handful of extremely rich donors: Gates, Buffett, Turner et al.

Death and taxes, we are told, are certainties. Voluntary ethical corporate behaviour, as advocated by ISO26000, is not.

The International Standard Blueprint: ISO26000

Like any other international standard ISO26000 took several years to compile. Business, workforce and the third sector were all involved in drawing it up; they have produced a common sense, comprehensive and convincing programme for action.

At its London launch in December 2010, the Trade Union Congress's (TUC) Ben Moxham put aside an innate scepticism of companies' approach to CSR – 'Being socially responsible is about impacts, not sponsoring fun runs' – and warned that the social responsibility standard should not replace collective bargaining. He gave it a guarded welcome, stressing that the co-operation of trade unions was the best way to pursue it. In an email to me he explained that unions could help take the process forward in four successive stages:

1. 'Companies need to understand that unions in their supply chains can drive sustainable improvements in labour standards and that freedom of association is something that needs to be promoted rather than tolerated. To start with, this needs training and guidance across companies' buying and key decision-making teams, not just CSR departments'.

2. 'Companies need to build longer term and stronger relationships with their suppliers to be able encourage them to reach out to local unions – usually through [such as] in-country roundtable discussions, access agreements, joint training, etc'.

3. 'There must be a local union willing and able to engage – this involves careful mapping with the right international union partner and resources to help with capacity building where necessary'.

4. 'There often needs to be collective pressure on (or support for) governments to enforce labour laws, and on local suppliers and their associations to adopt an open and positive attitude to local unions'.

Cynics have suggested that ISO26000 will inform campaign groups what standards are deemed acceptable and thus turn up the pressure – through the media, boycotts and demonstrations – on allegedly recalcitrant corporates. This would be a messy and unintentional consequence but it does have precedents: campaigns like Baby Milk Action in the 1970s and high-profile stunts by Greenpeace supporters on Rainbow Warrior, up factory chimneys and in Monsanto's genetically manipulated crop fields spring to mind.

The standard commences with these words:

> *An organisation's performance in relation to the society in which it operates and to its impact on the environment has become a critical part of measuring its own performance and its ability to continue operating effectively.*

It reminds readers that it does not replace existing laws, international agreements or conventions but it brings them together in a holistic manner. And there are plenty of them, ranging from the International Labor Organisation (ILO) codes, through responsibilities under Health and Safety legislation, the National Minimum Wage and CITES – the convention that prohibits the import, export and sale of protected animals and plants and products thereof. The latest, the UK Bribery Act 2010, came into force on 1 July 2011.[8] Under that Act it became illegal for a UK citizen to give or receive a bribe, or attempt to do so, anywhere in the world even if the practice were tolerated in the host country.

I spoke about the need for such an Act when representing the UK Parliament at the inaugural conference of the Global Organisation of Parliamentarians Against Corruption in Ottawa in 2002. The UN Convention followed, Britain ratified it in 2006 and legislated for it at leisure thereafter.

The standard goes on:

> *The essential characteristic ... is the willingness of an organisation to incorporate social and environmental considerations into its decision making and be accountable for the impacts of its decisions and activities on society and the environment.*

But what if they don't? There is no mechanism for enforcement other than customers and other stakeholders looking down their noses in admonition or taking their custom or talents elsewhere. Unlike most British Standards, ISO26000 is not the subject of accreditation. If a company tells you that they are certified to BS or ISO26000 standard don't believe them. As things stand, they cannot be.

---

8   *The Daily Telegraph* helpfully listed '10 DIY tips to avoid breaking the Bribery Act' on that day (Cowie, 2011).

This is causing problems. It is an international standard so, were it to be accredited, the accreditation should be recognised globally. Consultants in Hong Kong, Switzerland and elsewhere offering 'ISO26000 accreditation' (in some cases based on draft versions) are unauthorised and flouting the deregulatory spirit of advisory guidance.[9] National standards bodies can however choose to require certification. In Denmark DS 26001 has been approved and is certifiable under Danish law; it is ISO26000 under a different name and it applies to their biggest 1,100 companies.

ISO26000 is more than a nudge, it is also a wink. 'You are already standing in the shallow end of a swimming pool', it says, 'because you are already working inside the same legal framework as the rest of us. We are nice people in here, good customers, good suppliers, so come on in and join us, the water's lovely!'

The document identifies seven principles which are paraphrased in Table 3.3. I have slightly rephrased and reordered them to create a memorable mnemonic: Rochdale. By a delicious coincidence Rochdale – as we saw in the first chapter – was the historic home of the pioneers of the Co-operative movement.

Table 3.3   Seven principles of social responsibility (based on ISO26000)

Accountability	Responsible
Transparency	Open
Respect for stakeholder interests	Considerate
Ethical behaviour	Honest
Respect for human rights	Dignified
Respect for norms of behaviour	Aware
Respect for the law	Legal
	in Everything!

The list is not unlike the Seven Principles of Public Life[10] drawn up by Lord Nolan's Committee on Standards in Public Life in 1994. Designed as a standard of political integrity 'Nolan' covered the fields of Selflessness, Integrity, Objectivity, Accountability, Openness, Honesty and Leadership.

---

9   See http://www.british-assessment.co.uk/news-story.asp?newsTitle=ISO-warns-of-rogue-
     certification
10 See http://www.public-standards.gov.uk/

ISO26000 then applies its principles to six core areas of social responsibility:

1.   human rights;

2.   labour practices;

3.   fair operating practices;

4.   consumer issues;

5.   environment;

6.   community involvement and development.

And one over-arching theme:

7.   organisational governance.

The first four themes are covered by UK legislation as, to some extent, are Environment and Organisational governance.

REASONABLE ADJUSTMENTS

Whilst companies must behave in a manner that is legally compliant, best practice can often be achieved through consulting or acting with charities. For example, under the heading of Human Rights, the Disability Discrimination Act rules that reasonable adjustments must be made in workplaces and public areas to meet the access needs of people with disabilities. Employers have discretion in deciding what adjustments they will actually make; but if they don't exercise the responsibility of acting reasonably then a court might.

The list of potential 'reasonable adjustments' is huge: if a wheelchair ramp is provided it must meet building regulations, some colours of paper are easier for some people to read from than others, some induction loops are more appropriate for hearing aid users than others. Some organisations produce simple illustrated guides to their services aimed at people with learning difficulties. Who better to advise the responsible body how their property and services can be made compliant than a local charity's disabled access group?

Employers should not be worried that an inexhaustible list of unreasonable and disproportionate demands would be generated in this way: many such groups have 20 years of experience. If their suggestions went significantly beyond what the law would regard as 'reasonable' their access teams would get no work and the charity would lose income. If in doubt, the Equalities and Human Rights Commission provides independent advice.[11]

The Commission's web site also provides comprehensive and comprehensible advice to employers about the 2010 Equality Act.

It could be argued that a business cannot know what is 'reasonable' until a case has arisen and been tested. That is not the path of the conscientious corporate citizen. Reasonableness should be considered whenever the builders are called in, a publication is produced, an event organised or a room decorated. A reasonable employer not only anticipates, going beyond a strict interpretation of the law, but also discovers that adjustments made at the planning stage are cheaper to implement than retrospective ones and can bring unforeseen benefits.

Since 2005, Professor John Ruggie has served as the UN Secretary-General's special representative on business and human rights. In 2008, as the UN renewed his three-year term, they welcomed the three complementary but independent pillars of his proposed framework:

- the state duty to protect against human rights abuses by third parties, including business;

- the corporate responsibility (CR) to respect human rights;

- greater access for victims to effective remedy, both judicial and non-judicial.

In 2011 he published the guiding principles on the 'Protect, Respect and Remedy' framework to facilitate their implementation.[12] The key to making this work is not to regard human rights as a compliance issue, which would tend to encourage the minimum acceptable standard to become the goal, but to make the most of what a good record on human rights can do for a company.

---

11 See www.equalityhumanrights.com/
12 See www.business-humanrights.org/SpecialRepPortal/Home

Even though legal compliance is a minimum level of engagement it does not apply to all strands of ISO26000 (see Table 3.4).

Table 3.4   Legal compliance as a minimum level of engagement

Strand	Minimum	Socially Responsible Approach
Human rights	Legal compliance (e.g. Human Rights Act 1998)	See opportunities rather than constraints, e.g. positive anti-discrimination practices
Labour practices	Legal compliance (e.g. ILO conventions)	Minimum legal compliance not acceptable. Employees and unions regarded as partners
Fair operating practices	Legal compliance (e.g. OHSAS18001 on health & safety)	Stakeholder engagement, reputational advantage
Consumer issues	Legal compliance (e.g. ISO27001 on information security)	Customer engagement, reputational advantage
Environment	Legal compliance (e.g. ISO14001 on environmental management)	Stakeholder engagement, market advantage, cost and energy savings, waste minimisation, environmental sustainability
Community involvement and development	Very few standards exist (e.g. SA8000 on supply chain working conditions)	Employee/community engagement, social investment, supply chain standards, win–win partnerships, skills exchange, market advantage
Organisational governance	Legal compliance (e.g. Companies Act 2006)	Engaged corporate leadership, fully integrated social and environmental reporting to agreed sector standards

BEYOND COMPLIANCE: THE MINIMUM WAGE

'Labour practices' in Britain includes observing the National Minimum Wage. Introduced in 1999 against protests that unskilled workers would be priced out of jobs, it is generally accepted to be a success. New Zealand had the first minimum wage in 1894 and today nine out of ten countries have one. As of October 2011 the National Minimum Wage in the United Kingdom was £6.08 an hour for someone 21 years old or over.

In 2000, London Citizens held a conference on work/life balance in the East End. They discovered that family life was disrupted by the long hours people were working, holding down perhaps two or three jobs at once to make ends meet. A thousand people came together in 2001 to launch the London Living Wage (LLW) campaign, arguing that housing and other costs in London were so significantly above those elsewhere that any Londoner working on the Minimum Wage was condemned to poverty.

In 2003, urged on by the trade union Unison, four London hospitals introduced the first LLW. The Mayor of London, Ken Livingstone, established a department within the Greater London Authority in 2004 to calculate what LLW should be. His successor, Boris Johnson, showed himself to be an equally vocal supporter and introduced an annual award for participating employers. The team working on the London Olympic Bid accepted LLW at an early stage and thereafter the idea caught on in the banking community around Canary Wharf.

Over 100 employers across the public, private and third sectors have now adopted LLW, which in 2011 was £7.85 per hour. LLW has already benefited 10,000 families and put £75 million into the London economy.[13]

LLW puts no legal obligation on any employer to join. It is a voluntary act of corporate citizenship undertaken by those who have calculated that the cost to their company of not introducing it is by some definition greater than the cost of raising living standards for the poorest employees.

Community Involvement and Development

Legislation proliferates in most of the core areas of ISO26000. Community Involvement and Development, however, is almost a blank sheet offering a wealth of collaborative opportunities.

ISO26000 strongly suggests that socially aware bodies should not only advocate social responsibility amongst their stakeholders but actively promote it through their supply chains. This raises the possibility of contract compliance by consent being used to further the CSR cause.

Stakeholders exist on four levels:

Local: close to the business' base(s), especially where it draws its workforce from a discrete geographical community.

Market area: this may be the nation but will often be too vaguely defined to be helpful other than for marketing purposes.

Distant: that which is impacted by a company's supply chain.

---

13 See www.citizensuk.org/campaigns/living-wage-campaign/impact/

Virtual: those who relate to a business through web sites and the blogosphere.

How businesses impact upon local communities is discussed below. The distant community will be considered as part of the 'Humanitarian Approach' to community development in this chapter and, insofar as it affects developing countries, in Chapter 6. Let us put the virtual community to one side, perhaps redefining it as a media stakeholder group.

Essentially there are four avenues by which companies can engage their operating practices with the Community Involvement and Development strand of ISO26000. They are:

1.   Legal compliance (yes/no) (obligatory, no other partners required).

2.   Financial or other giving (quantitative: 'Cash and Kind') (corporate, payroll or employee-generated fundraising, or goods or services in lieu of cash).

3.   Volunteering of time and skills (quantitative: 'Time and Talent') (with a charity, community group or social enterprise, actively or passively promoted by the company, involving groups or individuals, low skill time donation, pro bono skills donation or skills exchange).

4.   The 'humanitarian' approach (qualitative: 'Head and Heart') (strategic or holistic engagement with communities).

Partnership working between a business and a charity can assist the implementation of socially responsible policies in all four ways. As we have seen, most of the strands of ISO26000 can be implemented through legal compliance as a minimum; in all likelihood, this is already happening. But there is no legislation relating to Community Involvement and Development so legal compliance is not relevant: at least one of the other three methods has to be deployed. Here partnership working is essential, even unavoidable.

The delivery of the Community Involvement and Development strand tends to evolve within an organisation. Table 3.5 suggests that three levels of engagement within the corporate body develop for each means: ad hoc, organised and strategic. The arrow that runs across the table, from the bottom

Table 3.5   The evolution of corporate community involvement through charity partnerships

PHASE	Financial: Cash and Kind	Volunteering: Time and Talent	'Humanitarian': Head and Heart	Benefit to Company	Benefit to Charity Partner
3 Strategic	Long-term relationship with partner charity or social enterprise where partner mission complements business goals or values Strategic donations in kind in lieu of cash – goods or services Ongoing (even if time-limited) commitments Payroll giving promoted	HR programme of enhancing employee skills through volunteering Pro bono volunteering of professional services Promotion of wider volunteering ethos e.g. three days paid leave per year for voluntary work Sabbatical volunteering e.g. VSO	Collaboration with charities (and unions) to create economically viable, desirable, sustainable outcomes in line with common goals (Shared Value approach, in the UK and/or developing country) Ethical management of supply chain Social Return on investment (SROI)	Skills acquisition – greater employee capacity, fulfilment and effectiveness Boost to global reputation Access to new market sectors; improved bottom line justifies even greater social investment Reciprocal access to charity services	Increased profile and piggy-backing of message globally Volunteer time and skills available Sustainable funding enabling longer term planning and mission enhancement Improved potential of future partnerships
2 Organised	'Charity of the Year' approach One-off fundraising events Donating surplus goods Payroll giving available Matched funding of employee initiatives	Organised employee volunteering opportunities (little emphasis on skills exchange or development) Sharing opportunities with other local employers	Address local needs with agreed and defined outcomes Liaison committee Wider fair trade procurement policy Affinity marketing	Informal acquisition of employee skills Enhanced employee engagement Enhanced reputation amongst community and stakeholders 'Ticking CSR boxes'	Increased profile and messaging opportunities Volunteer time available Short term funding gain
1 Ad Hoc	Allowing employee-led initiatives No payroll giving (No employer engagement)	Business supports 'responsible' employee volunteering: school governors, magistrates, TA, emergency services Local volunteering organised by staff	Limited community action, local awareness-raising around national initiatives such as Red Nose Day Some fair trade items	Team building, improved motivation of employees and their view of their workplace	Limited but immediate

Note: Arrow indicates trend of 'evolution' or 'maturity'.

left to the top right, shows a sort of evolution: as often as not employee generated fundraising for a particular cause will be the first act of engagement, in which the body corporate may not even be involved.

The second stage will either be a slightly more organised fund-raising regime or the first steps on the road to employee volunteering (or both). The pinnacle is the box at the top right: a fully integrated partnership between a corporate body and one or more charities showing a qualitative and sustainable commitment to a community.

Although the bottom left box can be delivered by employee 'push' the top right cannot be achieved without employer 'pull' from the highest level.

At the ad hoc or basic level charities are the major beneficiaries of the relationship though employees gain from team building and other 'soft' activities. Employee contentment brings intangible benefits to the corporate.

At the organised level there is positive employer response to CSR initiatives, with reputational benefit to the organisation.

At the strategic level of engagement CSR is mainstreamed into the organisation's core operations and the missions of the charity and the business partners are to some extent aligned. Positive outcomes for the employer, charity partner and other stakeholders are maximised on several fronts, not least long-term profit.

Giving: 'Cash and Kind'

In its simplest form, fundraising for a charity within a company is employee-led and intermittent, possibly inspired by Red Nose Day for Comic Relief, BBC Children in Need or a major disaster appeal. It involves simple fundraising ideas – collection boxes, cake stalls, dress down days – and is focused either out of work time or without impinging on it too much. Corporate engagement would move from blindness to tolerance and then engagement, with the next step being making payroll giving available.

PAYROLL GIVING

Payroll giving is a simple way of making a donation from wages to support a cause. The value of charity donations made in this way in 2009–10 went up by

2 per cent to £106 million due to greater numbers participating – though some argue that this is not a great return for 25 years work. Today 4 per cent of UK employees use payroll giving compared to 35 per cent in USA.

The Payroll Giving Centre, part of the Institute of Fundraising, sponsors national awards and a certification scheme which recognises employers with 1, 5 and 10 per cent employee participation. Over 3,000 employers hold Gold (10 per cent) certificates. The overall winner of the Payroll Giving Awards in 2010 was the Police Service of Northern Ireland where more than half of all new recruits signed up.[14]

All modern payroll software supports payroll giving. There is little cost or administrative time involved in setting up monthly payments to an HMRC-approved agency with charitable status which top-slices around 4 per cent from donations to pay its running costs. The law requires that employees choose freely which charity to support so the employer does not need to know which charity an employee has nominated. Some employers promote their chosen charity; some like RBS Group use the system to top up employee donations from their own resources.

Since direct debits have become easier to control online through personal banking some have questioned the value of payroll giving (Saxton, 2011). Payroll giving can allow for different tax rates, direct debit cannot; it allows the company to top up donations; and it is more popular amongst men than amongst women who are more likely to give in other ways. It is an easy, popular and stress-free way of engaging employees. The email promotion of payroll giving is a positive, cost effective and inclusive tool for corporate communications teams to have. Claims that it allows employers to bully employees into using it in a particular way lack evidence. The employer need not know who the employee is favouring – and the rarity of a 10 per cent take up rate suggests that any such persuasion is ineffective! In common with direct debit, payroll givers tend to keep paying over the long term.

CHARITY OF THE YEAR

There is evidence that partnerships between businesses and charities are growing more sophisticated as the old model of a 'Charity of the Year' falls

---

14 For more information see www.payrollgiving.co.uk, www.hmrc.gov.uk/businesses/giving/
    payroll-giving.htm and www.payrollgivingcentre.org.uk/

out of favour. Why should this be happening – and why do charities see it as a positive development?

At its most basic, a company chooses a charity to support for 12 months either to appease a vocal workforce (or the Chairman's wife) or to tick a CSR box. 'Support' can mean tolerating employee fundraising for a popular cause through to the company matching the funds its workforce raises, promoting payroll giving and time off to volunteer, a grand ball and the ubiquitous 'three peaks challenge'.

Having a 'Charity of the Year' can engage and motivate employees and bring a five- or six-figure cash boost for charities. So what is the down side?

First, the competition. Capturing the imagination of a market leading company involves increasingly professional marketing and competing with other charities. Success is not guaranteed, even if that investment wins a place on the shortlist before an employee vote. Winning a 'pitch' worth having might cost several thousand pounds, money that could have been spent on the charitable cause itself. Usually only one pitch can win.

Secondly, the practice of an employee vote – defended by companies that welcome the vote as an HR exercise rather than fuelling the engine of social change – can produce irrational results: children and animals are more likely to elicit a positive vote than are young men at risk of reoffending.

The ephemeral nature of the 'Charity of the Year' means that no sooner have you won one year's support, if not before, you are thinking about the next. You take your eye off the ball. Things that don't gel this year can't be corrected the next if the relationship is over. For companies too, the bureaucracy is never ending.

Whilst 'Charity of the Year' may be fading, business–charity partnerships are thriving. How have they evolved beyond this annual commitment?

Companies and charities are increasingly looking for a 'strategic fit', like Boots has with Macmillan cancer care; a responsible chemist benefits from having advice for cancer patients in-store whilst the charity broadens its 'reach'. A partnership which maximises employee engagement to benefit both company and charity will need to involve them; increasingly this is done through inviting nominations to staff CSR advisory panels rather than raw votes.

Some partnerships nowadays last three years or even five; longer ones bring certainty and better working relations than the previous in-out and innovation prevents donor fatigue. National Grid, one of the most comprehensive charity engagers of all, eschews the 'Charity of the Year' in favour of promoting payroll giving, matching each employee's charitable fundraising up to £400 per year and making local donations to staff-nominated charities. It has made a six-year commitment to funding for the Special Olympics for people with learning disabilities.

Although some charities find matchmaking frustrating others are in the enviable position of having suitors knocking at their door. Some have such a strong, clean and positive brand that companies vie for their attention. Turning Point Chief Executive Lord Victor Adebowale takes an interesting view: if the applicant for his charity's favours is from the CSR or communications team then he won't even meet them. He wants to engage with mainstream core business departments or nothing. The lesson from this is that if you want to impress a charity, make sure your CSR operations are themselves a core function of your organisation; don't give the impression that CSR is an add-on.

The rationale for a company choosing a charity partner might include:

1.   a geographical link, perhaps to a local community;

2.   a health issue which might stimulate the workforce to live more healthily, reduce absenteeism and thereby increase productivity;

3.   a link arising from an employee's personal experience such as cot death;

4.   an issue with wide family identification such as hearing loss or dementia;

5.   an international cause related to the company's supply chain;

6.   a product link, such as a construction company with a housing charity.

A good match between the company's market and the charity's cause is a good place to start: Mothercare has a global partnership with Save the Children.

We have seen that fundraising for a charity in the workplace includes both employee and corporate giving. Corporate giving without a rationale – a random act of kindness – is understandably rare and becoming rarer.

The choice of a truly strategic fundraising partner will present options for the volunteering and humanitarian elements of the engagement strategy. As a select few experts know, this can be achieved within the constraints of a 'Charity of the Year'. In 1974 Anthony Nolan was born with a rare condition called Wiskott Aldrich. The only known cure was a blood stem cell (or bone marrow) transplant, but there was no process or system to find a matching donor. Shirley Nolan, Anthony's mother, started the Anthony Nolan register to connect potential donors to people like her son. By 2010 the charity had fought its way into the major league – if turnover (over £26 million a year), the size of the potential donor register (over 420,000), its transplant provision (937 in 2010) or staffing (over 170) are any measure.

Helped in the early days by personal contacts linking it to the NatWest Bank, Anthony Nolan was an official race charity for the 2006 Flora London Marathon and has enjoyed recent corporate support from Easyjet and Betfair. However, they capped it all with a million pound deal with Wilkinson, the home and garden retailer with 351 stores across the UK, which started in May 2010. If you're going to do 'Charity of the Year' properly you need to invest heavily in it and plan it long in advance.

The task of raising money from customers, employees, supply chain members and other sources is not something the company is left to do alone: Anthony Nolan produces a whole brochure of fundraising runs, cycle rides, abseiling opportunities, balls and dragon boat races – you name it – in which employees can take part. Anthony Nolan also provides Wilkinson with all the sales and marketing material they need to promote their own in-store events.

And the employees do not just fundraise: within months of the start of the relationship 250 of them had registered as potential stem cell donors. Some are ambassadors acting to promote the register, others talk to schools about the charity's work and others put their skills to use mentoring young people with blood cancer.

'This is a partnership of equals', says the charity's Senior Corporate Partnerships Manager Lila Dowie, 'with clear and constant communication at its heart'.

That communication, starting with the two organisations' shared values, commenced 18 months before the Charity Year began. It engaged all departments of the Wilkinson company at all levels from the board to the shop floor, not just CSR or media professionals. Suppliers were recruited at an early stage and the need for an employee vote was avoided by management consulting on the general field of charity that the workforce would support. The company then went to some lengths to explain to employees why this particular partner had been chosen, an exercise which was successful as staff have clearly taken Anthony Nolan to their heart.

COMMUNITY FUNDS

In 2010 NatWest Bank, part of the RBS Group, launched a community fund of just over £1 million per year to distribute to good causes local to each group of six to ten branches in England and Wales (RBS did similar in Scotland). Local nominations were invited and knowledgeable people joined the local team to draw up a shortlist to be a winner and two runners up, who would receive £3,000, £1,000 and £1,000 respectively. Customers were then invited to vote for who gets the £3,000 in each locality and both NatWest and the local charity winners received good local publicity.

The vote was via the bank's web site and open to abuse. There was no guarantee that the voter (who only had to submit a postcode as means of identification) lived locally, was a NatWest customer or was voting only once. Some local charities stretched the rules to claim dubious celebrity endorsement for their bid and the web site of a local branch of a certain political party appeared to suggest that the fund was its own idea. In summer 2010 the Meningitis Trust, a national charity, published on its web site a list of postcodes of the eight areas where it had been shortlisted for NatWest funding. It invited its supporters to follow a web link and vote in those local areas – whether they actually lived there or not – and even suggested they consider multiple voting.

This subterfuge did not actually work: every shortlisted organisation was already guaranteed a minimum of £1,000 per area and that is what the Meningitis Trust got, rather than eight victories generating £3,000 each, which is what they desired.

All this fuss, simply to decide whether a local group would receive £3,000 or £1,000 from a fund worth only around £20 per branch, per week, seems highly disproportionate. As well-organised, larger charities could potentially exploit it better than smaller local ones it was poorly focused.

The same bank raised eyebrows in the CSR world in 2010 when its billboard advertising both featured its Community Fund and boasted that its employees would donate 15,000 days of volunteering time to local communities that year. The aspiration was modest compared to BT's 48,000 days and Boots' 84,000.

Early in 2011, true to its word, NatWest published Deloitte's independent assessment of its Customer Charter commitment performance: it had delivered 18 out of 23 pledges. The most significant failure was employee volunteering where just 7,547 days had been given (Deloitte reported the target as having been 22,000 rather than 15,000).[15] The NatWest web site at that time claimed both that the target was both 7,000 (which had been achieved) and the original 15,000 depending on which page the claim was viewed.

In 2011, I pointed out to NatWest some of the weaknesses of their approach and they made some sensible changes. The voting process became more local, funding was linked to community engagement by the staff, local charities got a higher media profile and the process was renamed Community Force rather than Community Fund.

The approach of Waitrose, the supermarket within the employee-owned John Lewis group, is less sophisticated but possibly more effective. Every customer takes a plastic token as they leave the checkout which they place in one of three perspex voting 'bins' at the store exit. Each bin is labelled with the name of a local charity and each month a thousand pounds is allocated to the three charities in proportion to the tokens they receive, typically £250 to £400 each. Thus 36 local charities benefit from the company's largesse in each store's area each year. Even though the voters are likely to be local and both charities and company get a positive profile from the attendant promotion, there are concerns within the company that more attention should be given to how effectively these gifts are spent.

DIRECT DONATION: CORPORATE PHILANTHROPY

There are league tables for everything these days; the one which covers corporate giving is assembled each year by the Directory for School Change (Lillya, 2011). The guide is intended as a reference work for those seeking funding, with advice on which companies and their associated foundations use what criteria for doling out how much money to which causes. The research is longitudinal and tells us a lot about developing attitudes. Unfortunately a lack

---

15 Reported in a free booklet distributed through NatWest branches.

of consistency in the way companies report their donations or evaluate non-cash contributions makes direct detailed comparisons difficult.

With the weak economy the figures for 2010 show an annual fall in the community support given by the corporate sector of 5.9 per cent to £762 million. Somewhat counter-intuitively the cash element of this actually appeared to rise by 2.3 per cent to £512 million. The difference between cash and the total is accounted for by the value of goods in kind, services and employee volunteering (where its value has been calculated), which showed a significant fall. The Guide speculates that in future the tangible non-cash element will rise as a proportion because it represents an efficient use of resources in challenging times, not least against a background of big rises in the tax on landfill sites, where much surplus material would otherwise be bound. Work by the London Benchmarking Group (LBG) appears to confirm this hypothesis.

The value of employee-generated cash is unlikely to be included in this list. It will be a relatively small part of the total contributed and the way it is directed is outside companies' control. Matched funding by the company certainly will be included: RBS Group, the parent group for NatWest, doubles an employee's charity fundraising efforts up to £500 per year and matches their payroll giving by up to £100 per month (a generous act of community support that NatWest failed to mention in its advertised commitments described above).

In 2010 the list of significant donors, compiled from annual reports, questionnaires and data from Companies House increased from 500 to 600, which possibly explains the apparent increase in cash donated. The top 25 companies account for 62 per cent of the total (compared to 50 per cent last year) which also suggests that smaller companies are feeling the pinch.

At the top is BHP Billiton plc which donated £39 million. It is a holding company for a suite of minerals-based industries which has never before been in the top 25, its previous 'best' being three-quarters of a million. This year's figures reflect their new policy of putting 1 per cent of profits into a new charity, BHP Billiton Sustainable Communities. On that basis the figure should rise again before the next guide comes out.

Despite their well-known difficulties four financial institutions are in the top ten corporate donors: RBS Group (second), Lloyds TSB Group (third), Barclays (fifth) and Northern Rock (seventh).

Previous lists have been ranked on the basis of UK spending only. As it is often difficult to distinguish UK from other spending the two are combined this year. This has allowed Tesco (which does not distinguish) into the list in fourth place at £28.3 million. Shell, Execution Ltd, Diageo and British Nuclear Fuels, all donating over £10 million, complete the top ten.

Three of those ten are not amongst BITC's 850 members whilst both the Co-operative Group and Marks & Spencer, featured elsewhere in this book, are in the top 20.

Esparto Santo Investment Bank (formerly Execution Noble but Execution Ltd at the time of the Directory of Social Change (DSC) research) is an interesting case. Their stockbroking arm is based in Brick Lane, one of London's poorer areas. One of the largest fundraising events by any company is their Charity Trading Day, when all commission earned on a designated day is donated to its Trust: £1.3 million in 2009–10, £9 million in their first seven years. The Trust takes the advice of the think tank New Philanthropy Capital, which processes applications for funding for them, on the potential effectiveness of any donation before it is given. A particularly remarkable element of good practice is that all of the beneficiaries from deprived areas of the country are invited to an annual one-day workshop to discuss lessons learned from the Trust's investment. This shows a commendable interest in meaningful outcomes and social impact in the areas that it targets rather than using the usual short-term, qualitative, easily measured tick box outputs.

It is important to keep these figures in perspective: corporate giving accounts for less than 6 per cent of charitable income. However, it is important because it usually represents a source of unrestricted funds for charities and it can often leverage other sources of funding. It is also a very tax-efficient tool for companies to manage their pre-tax profits.

COST FREE GIVING

Corporate Britain gave half a billion pounds in cash to charity in 2010 and half as much again was donated in goods, labour, premises, facilities, time and skills. This is likely to be an underestimate as not all companies go to the trouble of costing the assets that they donate either directly or through an intermediary.

In Kind Direct, a charity founded by Prince Charles in 1996, has redistributed over £100 million-worth of goods from 850 member companies to over 8,000 charities. Almost half of the gifts support international disaster relief, the rest going to a variety of UK causes – with a predisposition towards disabled people, children and community projects.

In Kind Direct matches the right gift to the right cause. No longer does a budding philanthropist who thinks they know best need to arrive unannounced on a charity's doorstep with a van-load of well-meant furniture which will never get used, yet companies can offset even these donations against tax.

Following China's 2001 floods there was an American donation of large quantities of expensive ($120) sports shoes, size 12. They were far too big for Chinese feet even though they were manufactured there; they went to waste. More common in disaster relief is the gift of medicines which are past their expiry dates and useful machinery, like X-ray machines, lacking either manuals or spare parts (Osman, 2011).

Gifting 'stuff' rather than skills or time brings benefits to the donor: offloading surplus office furniture to the local CVS will save on Landfill Tax and Computers for Africa will even collect old IT equipment for free. The third sector can find homes for clothing, household goods, office supplies, toys and games and more. Most such gifts will be perfectly good products, perhaps last season's range, shop soiled or wrongly packaged or even brand new products with an insignificant fault. And gifts create a better photo opportunity than the boring giant cheque.

FareShare provides free food to homeless people using products which would otherwise have gone to landfill. Typically this is food close to or past its 'display by' date but not yet at its 'use by' date. Sainsbury, Nestlé, Marks & Spencer and Kraft are amongst its larger regular food-giving donors and other employers have volunteering relationships with the charity. FareShare was 'Britain's Most Admired Charity' in 2010 and its operations are now franchised across the UK.

Foodcycle does something similar on a small scale, providing community meals in 13 centres around the country at least once a week. It is different from FareShare in that all the food donated is fresh and vegetarian, sourced within a bicycle ride of the community kitchen and providing one meal a week for up to 100 homeless people or housebound pensioners. Training young people to design and cook the meals is an essential part of what Foodcycle does.

READ International is a student organisation which takes surplus books from UK secondary schools and embeds them in schools in Tanzania. I am one of its patrons. In summer 2011, year five of operation, they delivered their millionth book, knowing that it will support the local curriculum and that this is the only source of books for many of the schools they serve.

A third of READ's £160,000 per year income comes from gifts in kind by companies. In an award-winning partnership, Big Yellow Storage provides free book storage in 20 university towns whilst marketing its facilities back to the student body. Veolia, the waste disposal company, collects books from the public and recycles those that the charity can neither use nor sell. DHL carries the books to Dar Es Salaam using surplus shipping capacity and British Airways subsidises over 60 student volunteers to go to East Africa each August to distribute the books. KPMG, British Library, Staples and others also support READ through gifts in kind.

Under the inspirational leadership of founder–director Rob Wilson READ won the Best New Charity award in 2007 and International Charity of the Year in 2010.

Everyone who has ever dropped a paperback into a charity shop or donated a raffle prize has taken part in in-kind giving but corporate in-kind giving is clearly in a different league. General Motors, for example, gave £100,000 in cash to good causes in the UK in 2009 but nine times as much in kind, including 21 vehicles to educational institutions to assist the study of motor mechanics. The value of the Co-operative Group's gifts in kind to charity in 2009 was over half a million pounds.

Share Gift[16] allows donors to give to charity the value of assets they cannot sell in their own right: orphan shares. Some people own tiny numbers of shares acquired from inheritance or privatisation. Others have shares which have suffered a devastating loss in value. Either way, some portfolios are so small that the cost of selling the shares is more than their face value. You can donate such shares to Share Gift and specify the charitable area you want your donation to go to. The shares are aggregated, sold through a pro bono stockbroker and the charitable gift made.

Share Gift started in 1996 and now operates in the UK, Australia and USA. In 2002, when BT split to become two different companies it wrote to its 1.8

___

16 See www.sharegift.org

million shareholders – many of whom were in the Share Gift target group – to invite them to donate via the charity. Around £700,000 was raised and BT won an Institute of Fundraising award.

Pressure on cash budgets will be tight for the foreseeable future so corporate giving in kind may rise both in real terms and as a proportion of the total as cash donations fall. Corporate giving of goods is a significant source of income for a hard pressed third sector and much appreciated. Like all corporate giving its guiding force is not so much philanthropy as enlightened self-interest.

PRO BONO WORK

London's East End contains some of the most deprived communities and marginalised people in the country. Hogan Lovell, a leading international law firm based in the area, was nominated for the 2011 Business Charity Awards for their partnership with the charities Body & Soul and Community Links, alongside ITV and a legal aid centre. They provided free legal advice initially to people with HIV/AIDS and then to refugees, asylum seekers and others in the locality.

A third of Britain's 83,000 people with HIV have suffered discrimination. Through Hogan Lovell's legal clinic, training sessions and a commitment to take serious cases further, 300 now have an increased awareness of their legal rights and responsibilities. This is a significant step in enhancing safety, dignity and justice thanks to a thousand hours of work per year by 50 Hogan Lovell volunteers.

The Bar Pro Bono Unit supports people who need a barrister but can neither afford one nor qualify for legal aid. £450 million-worth of pro bono work by solicitors was performed in 2010, 19 per cent more than the previous year, worth 2 per cent of UK solicitors' gross revenue. Half of all solicitors had done some pro bono work during the year (Baksi, 2011). The work is co-ordinated through a handful of groups including ProbonoUK.net where a portal allows public access to free work of guaranteed professional standard. The charity was established at the behest of the Attorney General in 2003.

Architects, planners, economists, the medical profession and others provide pro bono services. The British Trust for Conservation Volunteers (BTCV) claimed in 2010 that it had saved £850,000 on the lease of a single property in London thanks to the services of a pro bono chartered surveyor arranged through Geoffrey Barber's Return Foundation (Jones, 2010).[17]

Barber's is a text book story. Following a near-fatal car crash in 2001 the property company owner decided to 'put something back' in the form of advice to charities. His philosophy was that whilst charities were good at doing what they did, property sales, lease management and purchase were not usually in their skill set. In the early days he told one charity they were paying three times as much as they needed to purchase a new office: 'But we've budgeted for it', they cried and went ahead. Since then Barber has saved charities literally millions.

The value to Beatbullying of huge donations of professional skills from a variety of advertising companies has been immense. For a charity whose key role is awareness raising this is the result of canny targeting of donors. Their inclusion as a Royal Wedding Charity in 2011 was a boost for them both for messaging and fundraising reasons; the boost came just weeks before the demise of one of their high-profile supporters, the *News of the World*.

Such corporate generosity need not be a one-way street.

Employee Volunteering: 'Time and Talent'

The border between pro bono skills donation and high-level skills volunteering is necessarily vague: suffice to say that the recipient may not notice the difference. Pro bono skills donation is the one-way giving of an intangible product which might otherwise be bought; high-level skills volunteering is the donation of time given by a professional person in a novel context from which the recipient gains benefit but so does the volunteer and his/her organisation.

Pilotlight delivers genuine exchanges of high-level skills through volunteering. They recruit high ranking business people in London, Scotland and Wales as volunteer mentors for charities and social enterprises in need of help. A team of three business people from different companies, Pilotlighters, is allocated to a not-for-profit organisation; skills and experience required and on offer are matched up. Pilotlight, working with both teams, helps draw up the desired outcomes, methodology and timetable required to turn the organisation around and facilitate the process.

---

17   Return Foundation's web site had lapsed as of March 2011.

Up to 90 charities and social enterprises benefit from this process each year and there are over 300 Pilotlighters. Unlike other high-skill employee volunteering partnerships the support from Pilotlight lasts a year and the benefit to the volunteer is assessed and reported back to the host company. Although relatively small numbers of volunteers per company are involved the impact is profound. The outcomes for companies include better team working and problem-solving, motivation, happiness, awareness of community issues and specific skills acquired through mentoring and facilitating the charity's work.

Pilotlight works. Two years after working with Pilotlight, the charities they support say that the number of people they reach has doubled and their financial turnover has gone up by half. In 2009, 84 per cent of Pilotlighters from business said that their experience had helped them to become happier and more fulfilled in their day jobs and 90 per cent said the experience had refreshed or improved their skills. One in six Pilotlighters had become charity trustees and a further one in six intended to; the time they spent in general volunteering following the Pilotlight experience was 50 per cent more than it was before.

Pilotlight is the pinnacle of high-skill exchange employee volunteering; it defies the image of employee volunteers doing all the giving and charities doing all the taking which might otherwise be assumed to happen.

Gone are the days when the only volunteering that was tolerated in work time were Territorial Army officers or the prestigious white collar roles of magistrate, councillor or school governor. Today volunteering is more diverse: people pop out of work for an hour to listen to children read in the local school or they keep in touch with a housebound person by a 15-minute phone call from their desk, agreed with their managers in advance.

More than a million over 75-year olds in Britain report feeling lonely 'often' or 'always'. An acclaimed befriending scheme, A Call in Time, started life as an in-house telephone volunteering service at Zurich Insurance. In 2005 the Zurich Community Trust (ZCT, Zurich's charitable arm) and Help the Aged relaunched it together and today it includes several other employers under the merged Age UK umbrella. Academic research has shown that this 15-minute per week volunteering experience is highly valued by the vulnerable people it supports as well as being fulfilling for the volunteers themselves. Zurich is still a major sponsor of A Call in Time.

Back home in Swindon, ZCT is engaged in other volunteering initiatives. Involve Swindon is a consortium of 20 local employers and 60 local charities which share a pool of employee volunteering opportunities, initiated by ZCT and co-ordinated by the town's independent Volunteer Centre. Although 30 or more other such city consortia exist, under the 'Cares' banner of BITC, Swindon appears to be the biggest.

Clearly there are advantages to organising volunteering in this way for one-off team days, regular small episodes or mentoring, not least economies of scale and the benefits of having a dedicated co-ordinator. As with Pilotlight, the employers providing the volunteers make a financial contribution but when compared to the HR budget it is likely to be modest.

Some employers including Government allow or promote time off for volunteering, typically one to three but as much as five days per year. A few corporate HR departments use opportunities like those provided by VSO (the organisation formerly known as Voluntary Service Overseas) for sabbatical volunteering (aka personal capacity building) opportunities.

VSO was inspired by a letter to the *Sunday Times* from the Bishop of Portsmouth in March 1958. He wrote:

> *A number of headmasters in this country are very much aware that many of their senior boys including the most gifted are having to wait a year (in some cases even longer) before vacancies become available in universities and in technical training. So many of these young people have something very worthwhile to give; but where and how?*

He went on to recommend that 'the underdeveloped territories of the Commonwealth' presented opportunities for service and for doing good. Over 1,400 young people spent a year doing a VSO project in its first decade and it was soon expanded to include volunteers from several countries and projects in many. Although the initial target was school leavers and students – it became known as the 'gap year' charity – the organisation soon realised that the giving of enthusiasm alone was not as productive to the cause of development as the giving of skills and experience. Since then the average age of its participants has doubled, to around 40.

Today VSO sends volunteers to over 40 countries and works with qualified professionals with at least two years working experience. Most volunteering is for a year or two, though shorter terms are available for those who bring greater experience to the table and a youth programme has recently been reinstated.

VSO's development goals include Disability, Secure livelihoods, HIV/ AIDS, Health, Education and Participation and governance.

For over ten years VSO has encouraged strategic partnership with companies and others; they currently exist with Accenture, the Royal College of Midwives and Randstad.

ISO26000 does not discriminate in its advice to business, public or third sector bodies; all are equally urged to behave in a socially responsible manner. Public and third sector bodies may feel that community engagement is their day job, but there is no reason why the HR and good community relations arguments that encourage businesses to engage with their localities should not apply to them, too. The Youth Hostels Association is a major charity which allows its staff five days paid time off each year for volunteering – for charities other than itself.

In our discussion of fundraising we started with the more basic levels and in considering employee volunteering we will end with the same.

VOLUNTEER CENTRES

Many employers allow, tolerate or promote employee volunteering within local communities. At its most basic this involves identifying tasks which are useful to local charities and communities such as decorating a building or organising a day out for disabled children. Ongoing one-to-one activities might include the donation of time and patience to listening to a child learning to read or mentoring an unemployed teenager with low academic achievement.

Many of Britain's 310 Volunteer Centres now cater for employee volunteering in one form or another and they vary in size and nature across the country. They are the High Street expression of the work of Volunteering England, focusing on the act of individual volunteering rather than on the collective work of voluntary organisations.

The Institute of Volunteering Research reports that one in three centres are stand-alone, independent organisations with most of the rest linked to the local Council for Voluntary Service, a support and capacity-building body. The average number of employed staff in a Volunteer Centre is three, whilst many employ none.

Volunteer Centres are highly reliant on local authorities: 84 per cent get some funding from them amounting to half of their total funding nationwide. One in eight is wholly reliant on this source of revenue. Such dependence makes them vulnerable at a time of public spending cuts and increased demand on their services. Unsurprisingly, city-based Centres tend to be larger than rural ones but the level of local activity depends as much on the personalities involved as on turnover or locality.

If any Volunteer Centres receive private sector funding it is so small as to be off the radar – less than 1 per cent of the total – or it is hidden in that element of income described as 'fees', which doubled in importance from 3 per cent of their collective national income to 6 per cent in 2009. Southwark Volunteer Centre works with local employers on 'community day' activities involving up to 20 one-off volunteers at a time, whilst Community Action Dacorum (the volunteer centre in Hemel Hempstead) has a highly sophisticated and multi-faceted employer engagement operation.

Connect Dacorum describes itself as 'CSR for Dacorum Businesses' or:

> ... a partnership between the business, public and voluntary sectors that actively participates in creating a better quality of life for all in the Dacorum and surrounding area.[18]

Most of Connect Dacorum's 100+ corporate members are local SMEs but a spattering of local and national charities, international companies (such as HSBC) and public sector bodies like the Prison Service also take part. A typical quarterly networking lunch can have 80 attendees. They will hear about members' good practice and respond to pleas for help of gifts in kind such as charities requiring office furniture.

Nearby, the Dragon's Apprentice Challenge is the brainchild of Connect St Albans. In September 2010 a dozen teams of sixth form students were given a challenge, a mentor from a local business and a choice of local charities. Both the charity and the mentor company loan £50 to the team and the challenge is to turn £100 into £1,000 for the charity by February. The mentor works with the team and business decisions are made between them. The aim is to raise

---

18 See www.connectdacorum.org.uk/

as much as possible for the charity and prizes are awarded for this as well as innovation, co-operation and presentation. 2010–11 was the second season of Dragon's Apprentice, now an annual event.

Hertfordshire is a wealthy area with a dynamic economy. Just north of London it is home to aspiring and actual entrepreneurs as well as big companies which exploit the area's strategic access to the capital. The most disadvantaged part of the county, working class Stevenage, has not yet managed to emulate the strong and supportive business–charity networks that St Albans and Dacorum enjoy. Is this because the right sort of business is absent or the wrong sort of volunteering opportunity is present? There is a lesson here for the Big Society.

Most volunteer centre opportunities are fairly traditional – decorating, gardening, DIY, escorting, running errands for elderly or housebound people, befriending – but Volunteering England encourages diversity. Innovative work with unemployed young people seeking experience and skills is underway with Government funding.

Meanwhile the centres get on with their work of brokering volunteers with opportunities and helping organisations which use their volunteers to get the best out of them. A quarter of all enquiries translate into acts of volunteering. A quarter of all the volunteers organised in this way are in employment elsewhere – most volunteering in their spare time rather than work time.

Employee volunteering is an area of potential expansion of Volunteer Centres' work, not least as the fees that commercial employers would pay for the service would create an essential diversification of the Centres' funding base at a time when the whole third sector is facing pressures. To the employer such fees are a very cost effective use of HR expenditure.

VOLUNTEERING AS A CORPORATE RESOURCE

Not all employee volunteering is well focused on outcomes. A laughing finance director is wearing his 'I'm a Volunteer!' t-shirt and wielding a paintbrush as the youth centre wall gets re-decorated for the third time this year; behind it the club's treasurer is tearing his hair out. The image is a sobering one.

The motivation for some collective acts of volunteering might therefore go along these lines:

We could use a team-building effort to bring our employees together, build enthusiasm and help convince them that this is a good place to work.

Whereas the path to better community involvement might be:

Our business is a corporate citizen in this community, how best can we discharge our responsibilities through employee volunteering?

Whenever Boots the chemist establishes a new branch they organise a team community volunteering programme not to complement but to replace traditional HR methods of team building.

A conscientious company will not want to be told, 'We only ever see you on your company volunteering day'; ill-focused volunteering, planned without the full co-operation and assent of the target organisation, runs a risk of failure. Failure is something the voluntary sector is both unaccustomed to experiencing (because of their low-risk business model) and finds difficult to cope with. No one volunteers their time in order to fail – though it could be argued that too many do fail to maximise the value of their voluntary work.

A true corporate citizen will help identify needs and priorities and draw up a strategy to address them. It will not restrict its concern to what can be achieved with 200 hours of unskilled casual labour on the annual grand company volunteering day. Above all, it will not – as with some philanthropists – assume that it alone has the insight to decide what needs doing and that its name must be prominent on the project.

In the US employer-supported volunteering is much better established than in the UK and most of the top 500 companies allow their employees to volunteer during work hours. It is accepted as a major part of a company's sustainability efforts and social responsibility activities. Community-based volunteering is less well developed there. Canadian research (quoted in Cohen, 2010) suggests that employees who volunteer are 6 to 7 per cent more productive than those who do not, and in America the skill competency of volunteering employees has been assessed at 14–17 per cent higher than those who do not. It does not matter whether such policies foster high skills or attract them; they are certainly associated with high levels of job satisfaction.

The same research found that employers promoted volunteering in the community because it:

1. complemented core business functions – 82 per cent;

2. supported their corporate mission – 52 per cent;

3. helped develop employee skills – 60 per cent;

4. helped recruitment and retention – 58 per cent.

Members of the '100 best companies to work for' league table, which is closely associated with CSR activity, attracted almost twice as many applications per vacancy as others. Boots reports that since they started pushing CSR more robustly graduate applications have risen four-fold.[19] Aviva reports that although one in six employees take part in workplace volunteering schemes, a high figure, the hours they gave fell during the recent recession and recognition of volunteering achievement attracted insufficient quality control.

The assiduous reader will observe that fewer than 100 per cent of employees volunteer for workplace schemes. 'Lack of time' is the reason almost universally given for not volunteering; half of all volunteers say the reason why they do volunteer is because they were asked (Quirke, 1998). V has found that one in four men and one in six women do not participate because they oppose the idea of employee volunteering (Gammon and Ellison, 2010). These include cynics who claim that by promoting volunteering the company is thinking only of its own image so 'why should I do something for nothing?' How volunteering is promoted is as important as whether it is.

The same IoD/YouGov survey for v reports that women employees were more likely to volunteer then men, younger people more than older and part time more than full time. Those with caring responsibilities were also more likely to volunteer than those without. Companies with an overt CSR policy generated five times the level of volunteering than those without. They also found that a massive 88 per cent of consumers were more likely to buy from a company which was known for generating a positive social impact.

As well as the employee-related outcomes listed above, key drivers for employee volunteering are found to be that it builds brand awareness and

19   Richard Ellis of Boots, speaking to the All Party Parliamentary Group on CSR, July 2011.

affinity, strengthens trust and loyalty among consumers, enhances corporate image and reputation and provides an effective vehicle to reach strategic goals.

You can't say fairer than that.

The Humanitarian Mission: 'Head and Heart'

As the sophistication of corporate citizenship grows and fundraising and volunteering approaches mature, a third dimension emerges, which I call 'humanitarian mission' for convenience. It is a degree of engagement of a company with a community that goes beyond fundraising and volunteering; a qualitative change of gear. It has many means of expression which share a number of characteristics:

1.   it is imaginative, strategic, innovative and sustainable;

2.   it features a genuinely collaborative and co-ordinated partnership;

3.   it is ethical by any definition;

4.   it relates at least in part to the distant communities of the supply chain;

5.   it involves awareness raising and/or education;

6.   at its peak, it provides a social return on investment (SROI).

Examples of this qualitative, community-based approach might include:

A company which identifies needs in the local community through partners including tenants and residents' groups, key third sector players, elected members and council officials and sets about tackling them in an appropriate, strategic, cross-sector manner.

A quarry or construction company which sets up a site liaison committee to give local residents and elected representatives opportunities to raise concerns about site issues, environmental and otherwise, directly with the company and to discuss future plans. The committee meets regularly (at least twice a year) and reports back to the community.

A company which not only funds a charity or social enterprise to do socially valuable work in its community but which takes an SROI approach to assist them to gain the capacity to remain independent and sustainable.

A company which appreciates the legitimacy of trade unions and the value of partnerships with one of the longest established breeds of voluntary organisations within its workforce, fostering an atmosphere of mutual respect and partnership.

A supply chain which is informed by the company's ethical procurement policy so that values of social responsibility are promoted; not just through fair trade but other voluntary compliance schemes such as Forestry Stewardship and Rainforest Alliance certification.

These examples suggest a lot of boxes to tick but the exercise is not about ticking boxes. It is a way for business to recognise that corporate citizens, as any other citizens, have responsibilities as well as rights; and that adopting a 'triple bottom line' approach to social partnership and engagement can pay dividends – literally.

Perfection is not expected and is rarely found: a big High Street name with a fine reputation for CSR is known for not paying its bills promptly (they blame sloppy invoicing by SME suppliers in a complex subcontracting model). Moreover, there is a lack of comprehensive confidence in some certification schemes.

Only one in eight hectares of world forestry is managed in a sound and sustainable way. The good news is that there is a genuine and growing demand for ethically sourced timber. The bad news is that the environmental lobby cannot agree what 'ethically sourced' actually means.

The Forest Stewardship Council (FSC) is based in Bonn, Germany. Since 1993 it has certified ethical timber production as sustainable and not destroying precious human or other habitats unreasonably. FSC dominates the European sustainable timber market. In 2011 over 15,000 companies in over 80 countries possessed FSC certification that their timber is in accord with ten principles of ethical trade and that the timber being sold to the end-user is the same as that so certified at the point of production.

Some environmental groups claim, in effect, that it is possible to buy FSC certification rather than prove that it is warranted. FSC's complaint-handling procedures have been criticised as slow and tending to favour the producer, although independent investigations have led FSC to remove accreditation in some cases. Friends of the Earth UK has withdrawn its endorsement of the FSC brand although in 2011 Greenpeace called FSC 'the only credible certification system' for timber.

All accreditation schemes are probably fallible. Is it not a sign of success that those who would seek to make an unscrupulous buck feel the need to get round them, especially as there is little price differential between certified and uncertified timber these days?

Kraft has long sourced Ghanaian chocolate under the environmentally-focused Rainforest Alliance certification scheme. The chocolate that Cadbury uses for Dairy Milk bars also comes from Ghana but is fair trade accredited. When Kraft took over Cadburys they had a dilemma: which scheme is best? And how can two valid but different ethical routes be combined? The obvious answer is that either route would be ISO26000 compliant if such a concept existed.

TICKING THE FAIR TRADE BOX

ISO26000 is explicit that 'community development' includes the impact of the company's activity on developing countries and the MDGs.[20]

Great progress has been made towards achieving the MDGs in some countries, on some measures. Hundreds of thousands of lives have been saved through the benign actions of governments, charities, individuals – and businesses. There is widespread agreement within the development field that the best way of creating sustainable economies, wealth that can be shared and jobs for the poorest people, is through the growth of the private sector. This includes both that which is local to the developing country and the international business community. Part of that route is fair trade.

As we saw in Chapter 1 the fair trade movement in Britain is 20 years old and has achieved much.[21] Essentially, it is the use of trading partnerships to

---

20 See www.un.org/millenniumgoals/
21 See www.fairtrade.org.uk/

support sustainable development in poorer countries by giving better pay and conditions to marginalised farmers and respecting their human rights.

Although not everyone is convinced of the value of fair trade[22] there is no doubt that it does help the farmers involved; the more widespread it becomes the less it can be accused of distorting the market. Advocates of free trade as the best alternative route out of poverty for poorer countries pose a false dichotomy. In the UK the National Minimum Wage has not only benefited the poorest households but has also helped the economy generally by creating more demand. Ethically it was undoubtedly right to bring it in. The same is true of fair trade, which could and should be part of every company's procurement policy even if it is only relevant to the coffee, tea and sugar it uses.

The question must be raised of how we can best move beyond fair trade to a more holistic approach to ethical supply chain management, closer partnerships with producers and a more effective, cost effective, business contribution to development in poorer countries.

This issue will be discussed further in Chapter 6.

Bringing it All Together

We have already seen a movement amongst academics to imbue future generations of business managers with the highest standards of integrity through the introduction of a MBA Oath parallel to the Hippocratic model sworn by every doctor. Whilst increasingly popular amongst new MBA graduates and business schools it will be generations before it can claim to be universal.

Engagement with charities can be the means through which values are given currency and oaths given meaning. It is possible to be ethical, sound and a good citizen without third sector partners but it is easier when working with those who are already value-driven if you wish such values to permeate your company.

Engagement and the progress towards establishing a coherent strategy of social responsibility and citizenship can emerge from the bottom up in an

---

22 See www.telegraph.co.uk/comment/8353361/Fair-trade-is-neither-fair-nor-good-for-trade. html

organisation or from the top down. Only when both trends are in place can it maximise its potential – for company, charity, employees and community.

CORPORATE SOCIAL HUMAN RESOURCES

There is a growing belief in the corporate sector that volunteering and other forms of third sector engagement are useful and cost effective HR management tools. There is also a view that any approach which prioritises CR can only succeed when the same inclusive values apply to relations between management and workforce.

Picture the scene: an enterprising HR manager in a small town has responsibility for CSR in her company. She decides to call a meeting of her opposite numbers in local companies to see what they might learn from each other. She gets a good response to her email so that today representatives of half the companies she contacted are sitting round the table.

She is a full time HR manager who believes fundamentally that CSR belongs in a mainstream department with influence throughout the organisation; that a company's conscience lies in its people and that the workforce is a link between business and community. She knows too that both her line manager and managing director are on the same wavelength.

As her new colleagues introduce themselves her heart sinks.

Next to her sits a procurement manager who has heard about ethical supply chains but has little experience of other aspects of CSR. Next to him is a communications and media person from a major corporate: 'We need our people to believe that this heart-space is where we are', he says, cryptically.

Opposite sits a secretary: 'I've just been elected to the staff committee for my company's Get Involved community action day', she says. 'Everyone really enjoyed it last year – we all got very messy and a little bit drunk'.

Next to her is a shop steward: 'I only found out about this meeting by accident. My union has a very strong policy on international development and human rights, but can I get management to take it on board? I thought you might have some tips'.

'I don't so much represent our CSR department', says the next person, 'I am the CSR department, a one-woman operation. Well, sort of. I take it very seriously and I get a lot of backing from my boss, but it's a lot of work for two days a week, it's very difficult to make progress'.

Finally, a smartly dressed young woman introduces herself as PA to her managing director. 'He's very interested in this sort of thing and wants me to report back on what our company can do to develop and mainstream CSR'.

No two have the same departmental background and several do not have positions of influence. No one has her level of experience and not all share her aspirations.

'Why couldn't they all have read Elaine Cohen's book?' she thinks to herself.

In *CSR for HR* Cohen (2010), a former HR executive at Unilever, uses an engaging format of following a fictitious HR manager in a medium-sized firm through her growing awareness of CSR and subsequent conviction that the HR department is where CSR responsibility ought to lie. As she says:

> This book is both a wake-up call for the human resources profession and a tool-kit written to help members of that profession to act.

Cohen develops a concept she calls corporate social human resources (CSHR). This directs traditional HR responsibilities such as organisational development, recruitment and training towards CSR practices in a corporate organisation.

Writing about Cohen's work Sian Harrington (2011) says:

> Three years on from [HR Magazine's] campaign to encourage HR to take a leading role in embedding corporate responsibility into organisational culture, there is still, on the whole, a lack of buy-in. Yet HR plays a crucial role in ensuring the right corporate climate and practices that enable businesses to succeed in a responsible way.

I summarise the philosophy as follows: the company that treats its employees with dignity treats its stakeholders and the planet with dignity too. Indeed, unless employees are treated with dignity the company will be unable to fully exercise its external responsibilities in a sustainable way.

Because the HR department is people-centred and pervades the organisation it is well placed to lead, co-ordinate and develop CR, Cohen argues. She advocates a four-tier strategy for CSHR, paraphrased as follows:

Phase 1: Support readiness for CSHR

1. Ethics: assimilate code of ethics into business programme.

2. Stakeholders: survey them about HR satisfaction and expectations.

3. Human rights: examine all business activities for compliance.

4. Culture: identify elements which support or block CSR.

Phase 2: Engagement

1. Community: develop community-based employee volunteering.

2. Environment: establish 'green teams' with cost saving and impact criteria.

Phase 3: Adapting HR processes

1. Recruitment: revise employer brand, ensure diversity and inclusion.

2. Pay: equal opportunity, gender balance, reward for ethical behaviour.

3. Health & Safety: promote and improve health, safety and wellbeing.

Phase 4: Training and communications

1. Training: CSR training for managers, employees and new recruits.

2. Communications: CSR messages in all internal media including social media.

The overlap between this approach and the six strands of ISO26000 is profound. Arguments can be made for other departments taking the CSR lead but any responsible department must have weight and influence. Two which should be avoided, as our HR manager no doubt mused as she looked around the table, were Communications (where commitment would appear superficial if not reflected elsewhere) and a stand-alone add-on with no connections elsewhere.

It is the connections which are essential: internal and external communications should drive the CSR and the engagement agenda and the stand-alone model works well only when the post holder has real authority and responsibility. This is the model used successfully by Boots where the Director of CSR has no department of his own but is responsible directly to the board's CSR committee and has real power to deliver the company's commitments.

As a result of Richard Ellis' influence, Boots was the eighteenth largest donor of community contributions in 2010 according to DSC (Lillya, 2011). That £4.4 million included 84,000 hours of employee volunteering time plus £1.3 million in cash spent mostly in and around Nottinghamshire. One particularly innovative scheme was the deployment of beauty and make-up specialist volunteers to work with women cancer patients in over 50 hospitals nationwide.

The Reputation Index takes a regular snapshot of how companies are regarded by their peers, opinion formers and wider public. In 2010 it ranked Boots as the most highly regarded UK company with an index of 87.2; the average was 64.2. The scale was compared for the first time with ten well-known charities of whom three scored over 90. At 95.1 the Royal National Lifeboat Institute (RNLI) achieved the highest score ever recorded on the Index. Reputations, as we know, are highly influenced by the company you keep (Brindle, 2010).[23]

In 2011 RNLI scored 94.8 with Royal British Legion on 90.1 and Royal National Institute of the Blind (RNIB) on 89.9. Boots had slipped to third place in the corporate list on 83.7 with Rolls Royce Aerospace and Dyson above it. All ten charities surveyed beat all 200+ of the companies on their reputation score.

Research conducted by Reputation Institute since 1999 shows that strong reputations stem from admiration, trust, good feelings and overall esteem.

Corporate Governance

Our chart which showed the three strands of business–charity partnership working at three levels (Table 3.5) has an arrow which leads from the starting point in the bottom left to the most sophisticated top right. The ultimate goal of stakeholders and partners working coherently towards common ethical values is a broad framework of social responsibility. Employee 'push' forces must be complemented by management 'pull'.

---

23 Also the Reputation Index's own UK web site http://reputationinstitute.com/contact/ri-uk

The board of a company consists of non-executive directors and senior executive directors. Their role is to ensure that the company is well run and proceeding in the right direction and to define what that direction should be; management's job is to manage the company.

It would be interesting to ask each board member of a medium-sized company independently what their company was actually for. How many would agree on a common definition? How many would answer 'making money for shareholders' or 'making widgets' compared with those who said 'being a good corporate citizen' or 'making sure our company is still here in 50 years time'? How many could quote the company mission (if it has one)?

The idea of the board having a comprehensive 'stewardship' role is advocated by the think tank, Tomorrow's Company. Whilst there are still business advisors who advise that shareholder value trumps any other consideration, an increasing number of boards are taking the stewardship approach; recognising that whilst management is responsible for day-to-day operational decisions someone has to think of the long term. The 'right direction' in the long term is an economic and environmental concept but advocates of stewardship recognise that it has a community or social element as well. The long-term view sets a framework of values against which short-term and pragmatic decisions are judged and taken.

This framework, which should be tailored to each company's own needs, is spelled out by Tomorrow's Company:[24]

> The starting point ... is for boards to establish their own 'board mandate' – a living statement about what the company stands for and how it wishes to be known to all of its stakeholders. This should capture the 'essence' of the 'character' and distinctiveness of the company, in terms of: its essential purpose; its aspirations; the values by which it intends to operate; its attitude to integrity, risk, safety and the environment; its culture; its value proposition to investors; and plans for development.

The same web site also includes a fascinating tool designed to stimulate board discussion on this issue.[25]

---

24 See www.forceforgood.com/Articles/The-Good-Governance-Forum-566/1.aspx
25 See www.forceforgood.com/userfiles/1724%20TC%20Corp%20Gov_Tool%20Kit%20(4)(1).pdf

A mission statement is slightly different. It defines in a paragraph an entity's reason for existence, its philosophies, goals, ambitions and values. Without a mission statement companies run the risk of wandering through the world without knowing whether they are on course to their intended destination. It is the role of the board to provide the signposts and the Board Mandate is an obvious way to do this. The Board Mandate is a broader prospectus, drawn up to assist the management to progress the company mission.

Neither missions nor mandates are set in stone but nor should they be printed on elastic. Once a mandate is created its ownership should be shared and its stakeholders consulted on proposed changes. A board which inhabits the 'forward space' of the company, the moral leadership, is in control of the mission which is itself guided by the mandate.

As we have seen, ISO26000 lists six fields in which social responsibility can be assessed, promoted, aspired to and achieved – but its authors have added a seventh, a sine qua non: good corporate governance.

The first of many books entitled 'Corporate Governance' was published in 1984 by Gower and written by Bob Tricker, who left school at 16 and served as a Royal Navy officer before finding his academic forte at Harvard and Oxford. Corporate governance refers to how a company is led and managed, how stakeholders are involved, how the leadership is held accountable. Good corporate governance involves well-defined, well co-ordinated and accountable roles, a well-defined mission and an appropriate Board Mandate.

Without good governance the standards and mores of the company will not be delivered, the corporate citizen will not mature and the value the company brings to society will not be shared.

CREATING SHARED VALUE (CSV)

Shared Value has been part of the Nestlé philosophy for some time. In essence, the company believes that:

> *Creating Shared Value is a fundamental part of Nestlé's way of doing business that focuses on specific areas of the Company's core business activities – namely water, nutrition, and rural development – where value can best be created both for society and shareholders.*[26]

---

26 See www.nestle.com/CSV/Pages/CSV.aspx

In 2009, in conjunction with the UN, Nestlé sponsored the first Creating Shared Value Global Forum. They argue that CSV goes beyond CSR because of the way it binds together the interests of shareholder and community:

> Any business that thinks long term and follows sound business principles creates value for society and shareholders through its activities, in terms of jobs for workers, taxes to support public services and economic activity in general.

So argues the Nestlé chairman, Peter Brabeck-Letmathe, in the foreword to their 2009 CSV report. He goes on:

> But Creating Shared Value goes one step further. A company consciously identifies areas of focus, where shareholders' interest and society's interest strongly intersect, and where value creation can be optimised for both. As a result, the Company invests resources, in terms of both talent and capital, in those areas where the potential for joint value creation is the greatest, and seeks collaborative action with relevant stakeholders in society.

In addition to its own efforts, each year the company awards a large cash prize to an individual, Non-Governmental Organisation (NGO) or small business for an outstanding shared value project on water, nutrition or rural development anywhere in the world. Such an incentive makes sense, especially in the developing world, where measures to help people move out of poverty and ill health will make them more reliable consumers over a longer period; CSV may appear philanthropic but it is not a one-way street. A detailed example of Nestlé's approach in Africa can be found in Chapter 6.

In 2011 the philosophy of CSV received a major boost from a well-publicised interview in the Harvard Business Review with Michael Porter, the influential head of the Institute for Strategy and Competitiveness at Harvard Business School.[27] At the World Economic Summit in Davos Nestlé, PepsiCo and the Prudential insurance group were amongst those who rallied to support him.

Sometimes described as the greatest living business guru, Porter believes that sustainability should relate to the triple bottom line but above all he says that there are greater profits to be made by behaving ethically and inclusively than otherwise. News that shares in more ethical businesses on the New York

---

27   See http://hbr.org/2011/01/the-big-idea-creating-shared-value/ar/1

stock exchange performed some 4 per cent better than others over the last five years, and fared better during the financial crisis, would appear to endorse this view. This finding is in line with British research cited in Chapter 2.

Porter has attracted criticism that calls for business to behave more responsibly will invite unwanted and unwarranted 'interference' in markets by government. This is by no means inevitable: advocates of smaller government do not want this and nor do British politicians who support smarter government. Such intervention has always been anathema in the United States.

CELEBRATING BEST PRACTICE

The second decade of the twenty-first century finds business in a different place than where it has been at any other time in its history. It has learnt that size is no guarantee of success and that public tolerance of excess and exploitation has reached its limits. It now recognises that it has a key, urgent and unique role to play in saving the planet through the regulation and mitigation of climate change. And it realises that the power of business to liberate the world's poorest people through sustainable economic development must be exercised if consumers are to continue to consume and markets continue to grow. Bearing all this in mind businesses might feel justified in claiming the moral high ground.

But not all of them. If we look at the membership of the Corporate Responsibility Group, BFP, BAH and the casts of various award ceremonies and other ethical, green and responsible umbrella organisations we see a repetition of star names from the FTSE 100 which is almost depressing; there may be many proponents of corporate citizenship but the top practitioners are relatively few. SMEs are less profoundly engaged and the responsible veneer of the 2007 report by the Federation of Small Businesses (FSB), cited earlier in this chapter, is both thin and fragile. No amount of protesting that 'we are a family firm with family values' can replace the need for strategic and informed thinking and positive engagement that corporate citizenship today demands.

Even though legislation may not be the best way forward from where we are, leadership in this field must include government. The appointment of a minister with CSR in his remit was low profile under Labour, where Stephen Timms ploughed a sometimes lonely furrow, and non-existent in the first few months of the Coalition Government despite Prime Minister Cameron's extolling of business to 'commit'. After a year in ministerial office it became clear that Ed Davey, the junior Liberal Democrat member of the coalition's ministerial team at the Department of Business, Innovation and Skills (BIS), was acquiring both knowledge and enthusiasm about the subject.[28]

Few if any businesses have committed to the 1:1:1 philanthrocapitalist model of contributing 1 per cent of capital, 1 per cent of profit and 1 per cent of employee time to good causes each year as advocated by Bishop and Green (2008).

Nevertheless, the body of good practice that exists in the field of CR, social or otherwise, corporate citizenship, inclusive or sustainable business, shared value and cross-sector partnerships is growing by the day and the value of such approaches is becoming more appreciated.

Such achievements are not, of course, dependent upon having charity partners. The arguments in favour of responsible corporate behaviour are strong enough without; the best charity partnerships arise when the corporate partner has already opened its eyes to the business benefits of taking climate change seriously, going further than legal compliance on ISO26000 themes and acknowledging that sustainability values have a community engagement dimension.

BITC is one of a number of organisations that celebrate excellence in sustainability, taking a triple bottom line approach rather than a green one. In 2010 their Company of the Year was Unilever, whose record suggests that their ambition to double the size of their company whilst actually reducing its environmental impact is credible.[29] Two billion people use Unilever products daily and 70 per cent of the company's environmental impact comes through consumer usage. To achieve their goal they must influence customers more radically than simply through brand promotion and the exercise of choice.

One and a half thousand different Unilever products have had their baseline environmental impact assessed to enable the measurement of their improvement. Their Persil range has halved its use of packaging and lorries; since 1995 Unilever factories have slashed carbon emissions from energy by over 40 per cent. 133 million people in 23 countries have reduced disease transmission through Lifebuoy's Global Handwashing Programme. The

28 Davey was promoted away from this brief in a reshuffle in 2012.
29 See www.unilever.com/mediacentre/pressreleases/2010/Unileveraimstodoublebusinesswhilst reducingenvironmentalfootprint.aspx

judges were clearly impressed by their life cycle impact measurement, the wider social effect of their products, attempts to change consumer behaviour and innovation in all that they do.

Part of Unilever's portfolio of responsible behaviour strategies includes charity partnerships and in 2010 their liaison with the National Childbirth Trust, which included huge quantities of in kind donations of washing, cleaning and baby products, was recognised at the first Business Charity Awards event.

All pioneers of business charity partnerships, such as Wates, BITC's 2011 Company of the Year, deserve to be celebrated; and imitation is the sincerest form of flattery, as we shall see in Chapter 4.

4

The Fourth Sector

The fourth sector is the space between the other three, the place where relationships are formed. Relationships between businesses and charities, like any other, have to start somewhere.

The Dating Game

Charities should not sit around waiting to be asked to dance. Who are their local companies 'seeing' right now? Are they wanting a flirtation, an affair or a relationship? Whose combination of interests, experience and GSOH might make the most fruitful dalliance? How inconvenient might this potential partner prove to be, or how reliable? How much will they spend on the ring?

Neither charities nor businesses should take up with the first potential partner who shows an interest in them. As their mother might say: 'You can do better than that'.

Companies need to take community engagement seriously and decide which department will be responsible for it. If it is the responsibility of a stand-alone unit or the media team, don't be surprised if the good looking charity in the corner turns you down; linking with your Human Resources (HR) department or procurement people is more likely to attract a second glance. Is there an obvious suitor in the form of a defined local community? Have you met the chaperones, the councillors, the residents' association, the local volunteer bureau? Is there a national or local charity or cause that might use your surplus product or pro bono skills to good effect?

There are now people working in that fourth sector space to help build bridges and forge meaningful partnerships. They are a cross between Dateline and Relate, working to help find that missing soulmate (or mates?), providing guidance on planning your future together whilst even daring to think about prenuptial agreements and how to end the relationship, too.

MARKS & SPENCER

We have already seen that Marks & Spencer's Plan A is the most impressive of the high-profile corporate sustainability programmes but green is not the only responsibility that the store tackles head on.

The company invests 1.9 per cent of its pre-tax profits in community programmes; through their electrical goods recycling programme customer-generated income supports six national charities. Much of its surplus but edible display-expired food is diverted to the charity FareShare through local stores. Similarly clothing, samples and business surplus material are given to Shelter for the homeless and New Life for terminally ill babies. Each store has a small budget for use at the manager's discretion to support local good causes and when stores receive their regular 'make over' shelving units and similar are often given to local charity shops.

Cause-related marketing such as that which has supported Breakthrough Breast Cancer and the Prostate Cancer Charity has been very effective and Marks & Start, the company's work experience programme, has supported 2,500 disadvantaged unemployed people since 2004.

Since January 2008 more than 1.5 million customers have given Marks & Spencer clothing to Oxfam in exchange for a voucher worth £5 off the person's next significant Marks & Spencer bill. Oxfam Clothes Exchange has saved over five million items of clothing from landfill and raised over £3 million for the charity, enough to provide safe water for 4.8 million people, 600,000 mosquito nets or three million new school books.

THE CO-OPERATIVE GROUP

The whole structure of the corporate group which includes retail stores, the Co-operative Bank and other businesses remains true to the spirit which drove Robert Owen and the Rochdale pioneers. The group takes its social responsibility seriously: its 2009 Sustainability Report classifies it into Community investment, International development and human rights, Animal welfare, Diet and health, Ethical finance, Social inclusion and Diversity.

The Group's High Street stores have been a driver of fair trade. Its priority since 2009 has been to imbue its values into two major recent acquisitions – the Britannia Building Society and the Somerfield supermarket chain.

Royal National Institute for Deaf People (RNID)[1] was recently the Co-operative Group's Charity of the Year. After setting a £2 million target a magnificent £3.7 million was raised, not only establishing a new record for the company but doing so against a background of recession. In return RNID provided free hearing checks for Co-op customers and staff.

The Co-operative Foundation, the grant-making arm of the business, deploys grants on a two-year strategy cycle. Recently members[2] voted to focus on inspiring young people so a new programme, Truth About Youth, was launched. A Membership Community Fund deploys about £1 million each year to innovative and co-operative community initiatives decided locally by the organisation's 46 local member committees.

The London Benchmarking Group (LBG) comprises over 120 companies mostly from UK which come together to measure, compare and promote a common understanding of corporate community investment. Using LBG criteria the Co-operative Group measured its 2009 community contribution as worth £11.3 million in total, or 3.8 per cent of its pre-tax profits. If other semi-commercial initiatives are included, such as support for the credit union movement and advantageous loans to other co-operatives, the community contribution rises to over 4 per cent compared to an average of 0.8 per cent (2006–09) for Business in the Community (BITC) members.

In that same year over 10,000 Co-op employees took part in community volunteering activity valued at £1.66 million. The Co-op's own volunteering programme included mentoring homeless people into employment, becoming school governors and helping at local credit unions as well as over 100 team challenges. In addition to all this a further £593,000-worth of gifts in kind was made to charities by the group including advertising space on Co-op bags, use of premises and donations of fair trade products. Between 2007 and 2009 Somerfield continued to support Macmillan Cancer Care and raised £2.5 million. Every home insurance policy sold by the insurance wing of the Co-operative Group generates £5 for Shelter, generating well over a million

1   Known since 2011 as Action on Hearing Loss.
2   Tens of thousands of individual members of the Co-operative Group are effectively its shareholders.

pounds to date. Put together, the group's total community investment could be equivalent to 10 per cent of pre-tax profits.

This analysis concentrates on the community investment element of the Co-op's Corporate Social Responsibility strategy but the other strands are equally impressive. It shows that commercial success and the highest standards of ethical and responsible corporate behaviour complement each other when the commitment is both profound and comprehensive.

WATES FAMILY HOLDINGS

Tim Wates is the fourth generation of his family to have run the building company which his great-grandfather Edward founded in 1897. Each generation has vowed to pass on something better in terms of wealth than they inherited and so far, so good. He accepts that being a family business does not guarantee family values in the business arena but again, so far, so good.[3]

Six of the nine members of the board of Wates Family Holdings, which owns the company, are called Wates. The family's stated values of integrity, enterprise, unity, sustainability and leadership are all borne out by the company's conduct; they set the organisation's philosophy and framework and vet capital spending.

In its long history Wates has always been where it needed to be: building speculative housing in the 1920s and 1930s and making a major contribution to post-war reconstruction in the 1940s. In the housing boom that followed they were known for pre-cast or 'system' building which created 60,000 homes, many of the high rise variety. Today their 2,000 employees are more likely to be found working on major public sector or niche projects, interior retail refitting and designing new communities.

Wates argues that, 'business is a force for good', that regeneration 'is about bringing long lasting change to a whole community' so he is not content to simply build affordable homes for ordinary people on well-designed estates.[4]

The family takes a generational, 15–20 year view of their company and its role in society whilst the board is required to observe a three to five year horizon

---

3   See www.wates.co.uk.
4   Tim Wates was speaking at a Tomorrow's Company seminar, March 2011.

in a rebuttal of current short-term business thinking. The firm's activities 'blend wealth creation with social responsibility', says Tim.

And so they do.

In 2008 the Wates Family Enterprise Trust set up a charitable programme to make 'a real difference to the communities in which we live, work and build'. Through Wates Giving, the Trust has given over £2 million to local initiatives including redeveloping community centres, supporting programmes to reduce anti-social behaviour, prisoner rehabilitation and producing classroom resources for 14–16 year olds in vocational education. A distinctive feature of the Wates approach is that community work is carried out in partnership with an existing social enterprise, including secondment of one or more members of staff for a significant time. Part of the service is to ensure the partner's triple bottom line sustainability.

Employees are encouraged to volunteer; they get 16 hours a year paid leave and matched funding of up to £250 per year for their personal giving to charity. In 2009 each project team in the company was given a Wates Giving grant of £500 to donate to a local charity of their choice, totalling over £45,000.

'The local community' to which the business is committed includes localities which are home to Wates's 12 offices and their major construction sites. They work regularly with the Construction Sector Skills Council, The Prince's Trust, Shelter, Working Links and Job Centre Plus. They are active members of BITC and the Confederation of British Industries (CBI) where they promote their values and the good reputation of the construction sector.

Wates creates 40 apprenticeships each year at a cost of a million pounds through the Building Futures scheme whilst the Changing Paths programme does similar for serving prisoners.

If this were not enough, on the annual Wates Community Day in 2010 well over 1,000 employees, customers and supply chain people gave over 13,000 hours to 89 community projects and raised a quarter of a million pounds for good causes.

A formal employee-led partnership with Shelter produced £65,000 in its first year of 2009–10 against a target of £40,000 and over £100,000 in its second and final year. That funding in year one paid for two full time advice workers providing help to over 700 people with housing problems. Wates has developed a charity toolkit to explain to stakeholders exactly why a charity partner has been chosen and what the partnership will achieve. Employee engagement through giving, volunteering and fundraising in Wates is a staggering 73 per cent.

The task of choosing the next Charity of the Year was delegated to Wates's Junior Board, an advisory committee made up of selected younger employees of the company which has a standing input into all policy fronts. Their 2011 shortlist of YMCA, Princes Trust and Barnardo's went to an employee vote.

However, social responsibility does not end there. Wates won the Sustainable Contractor of the Year award in 2008 since when they have directed 92 per cent of all site waste away from landfill and scored 89 per cent on the BITC Environmental Index. Wates was one of the first UK construction companies to introduce a sustainable timber procurement policy, working with Greenpeace to develop it in 2005.

In 2010 BITC gave them a Platinum award for corporate responsibility followed by Platinum Plus and Company of the Year in 2011;[5] the *Sunday Times* listed them as one of the 100 best companies to work for and they won other awards for their employment, training, green and leadership qualities. Wates has received a Royal Society for the Prevention of Accidents (RoSPA) gold medal for preventing accidents six years running.

Given the plethora of responsible silverware on the family mantelpiece let us ask: what is so special about the Wates's commitment?

Wates demonstrates that active community engagement based on cross-sector partnerships, common understandings, common missions and common sense is highly desirable, cost effective and mutually beneficial. Key decisions which have brought this about include:

- the choice of an initial charity partner, Shelter, whose mission is completely at one with a builder of homes and communities;

- working with existing social enterprises rather than re-inventing the wheel shows confidence in local initiatives and capacities;

---

5   See www.bitc.org.uk/cr_index/results_and_ranking/wates_platinum_plus.html

- investing in sustainability by embedding staff in a social enterprise and developing its business avoids the traditional problem of the benefits of the liaison being lost when the project is completed;

- the high level of staff engagement with the company's mission brings business advantages to the company as seen in the accolade of awards won. A high degree of transparency contributed to this;

- this scale of involvement of customers and supply chain alongside employees in community work is rare. It builds a feeling of membership of a wider company family;

- the bold decision to work with fringe disadvantaged groups such as offenders;

- the total commitment to corporate citizenship, at 5 per cent of profits, is very high compared to others;

- the high level of recognition that Wates has achieved from its peers has bolstered its image still further whilst doing good.

It would be remiss not to point out that Wates is also a substantial sponsor of the Royal Opera House in Covent Garden.

PASSION, ANGER AND RATIONALITY

Water covers 70 per cent of the planet's surface yet only one drop in a hundred is potable liquid fresh water. Over a billion people have no adequate access to clean water and habitats are dying through lack of it. At the same time over 350 billion litres of water are used every year by the Coca-Cola company, the world's largest producer and distributor of soft drinks whose product is found in every town on the globe.

Having been stung by concerns that a global drinks company shouldn't be locating bottle-washing and bottling plants in developing countries suffering high water stress, not least the Kerala province of India in 2004, Coca-Cola realised that whilst it had a monopoly on a certain fizzy drink it had no monopoly on common sense.

Since 2007, the Worldwide Fund for Nature (WWF) and Coca-Cola have worked together on water resources around the world. Their focus is conserving freshwater basins, reducing the impact of Coca-Cola's manufacturing operations and improving the company's agricultural supply chain. Together they are investing in water conservation in seven vulnerable river basins, making Coca-Cola's water use 20 per cent more efficient and bringing better water conservation and lower carbon emissions to the whole of the company's supply chain.

Whilst Coca-Cola derives commercial benefit from this arrangement it is certainly deserved as the changes wrought by the partnership are real and significant, not least in setting examples for others, including governments. Coca-Cola's enviable distribution network in Africa provides the best way of distributing medicines to the most remote and isolated communities. The young charity ColaLife, for example, has successfully designed lightweight 'aidpods', carriers for medicines designed to fit between Coke bottles in their African crates, with the company's support.

The quarrying and construction company Lafarge was WWF's first corporate partner. From 2000 they worked together to reduce carbon emissions, re-colonise barren quarries, reduce water consumption and produce sustainable building materials. WWF works with IKEA on climate change and sustainable cotton and timber and eight other major multinationals enjoy similar partnerships with them.

WWF's close relationship with leading private sector companies has not gone unnoticed and some criticism has been expressed. Toby Webb teaches Corporate Social Responsibilty (CSR) to postgraduate students at Birkbeck College, London and heads the business intelligence group the Ethical Corporation. He is cynical of WWF's performance:

> WWF has become a corporate partner, toning down its comments, particularly around business, to dangerously anodyne levels ... WWF in particular seems to be focusing more and more on corporate cash ...

> Now the former campaigner is charging NGOs and companies to attend drinks parties, presumably to engage in collective hand-wringing with the 'usual suspects', about the environmental challenges we face.

> This is not exactly cutting-edge activism and campaigning.

On his blog[6] he has given WWF the right of reply and Dax Lovegrove, Head of Business & Industry at the organisation, has taken up the challenge:

> ... To suggest we need to up our game on activism and campaigning shows little understanding of what WWF has been doing for the last 50 years ... While many other NGOs do a good job on the activism front, and we challenge various unacceptable activities ... our main focus is on working with business to arrive at sustainable solutions.
>
> Moving our economic system to being aligned with protecting the environment instead of degrading it requires a whole range of improvements to the way business is done and above all, we need new thinking. This is where WWF comes in. Our collaborative efforts ... are all about pushing business further and faster along the path towards sustainability.

The WWF message is clearly that collaboration works. The passion that motivates charities and third sector organisations does not have to be expressed as anger and businesses respect rationality more than emotion. Webb claims in the same blog that:

> Greenpeace is way out in front, leading and driving change. That's not to say [they are] perfect by any means, but they do seem to be making a significant difference.

If there are two organisations which share a reputation for diametrically opposing forms of muscular dogmatism it is McDonalds' fast food chain and Greenpeace, the environmental lobbyists most associated with sensational demonstrations.

In April 2006 an army of human-sized Greenpeace chickens invaded McDonalds' restaurants in London to ask customers if they knew that they were eating chicken fed on soy harvested from immorally and unsustainably deforested parts of the Amazon basin. Within just six hours the two sides were talking and four months later an alliance of Greenpeace, McDonalds, Marks & Spencer and the Waitrose and Asda supermarkets forced an international moratorium on soy from the Amazon basin. Four months prior to the chicken invasion the Greenpeace web site had accused McDonalds of exploiting 'cheap land, cheap labour' to the point of 'slavery' in order to destroy the rainforest.

6   See http://tobywebb.blogspot.com/2011/03/wwf-responds-to-my-blog-post-on-ngos.html

This looks to be a victory for rational, disciplined passion rather than opposition for its own sake based on sectoral apartheid.

Serco: A Turning Point

As we saw in Chapter 2, a movement which started in the 1990s and accelerated in the twenty-first century was for government and local authorities in particular to ask charities and voluntary organisations to provide services on their behalf though commissioned contracts. At the same time, groups within the public services were being asked to operate to service level agreements, a precursor of the Big Society idea of public sector workers forming mutuals and co-operatives to deliver services themselves. Elsewhere over that time a veritable giant was quietly extending his tentacles into almost every aspect of public services, ostensibly picking up the pieces where government agents had failed and creating the basis for another twist in the story.

The giant was called Serco.

Founded in 1929 as part of the RCA group to provide support services to the American cinema industry, Serco diversified and became a significant defence contractor servicing military bases on both sides of the Atlantic. Since floating on the stock market in 1988 and becoming a FTSE 100 company its web has spread further to include Northern Rail, traffic lights, Docklands Light Railway, the London-wide Barclays cycle hire scheme, immigration detention services, six prison institutions and other penal services. It has won many public sector management contracts such as three regions of Ofsted and the Business Link web site. It runs front and back office services for councils including at different times the education authorities of Bradford, Walsall and Stoke on Trent.

Today Serco manages around 800 contracts of which nine out of ten are in the public sector, each a separate business unit.

'Giant' is the right word. In 2009 Serco employed 70,000 people in 30 countries and had a turnover of almost £4 billion. Their 2009 CSR Review (Serco, 2010) touches all the right buttons: a values-led business, the partner of choice to governments and companies, principled governance, a good place to work, the trust of stakeholders and four pillars of CSR: community, people, environment and safety.

On all four pillars the record is impressive: £1.7 million invested in community projects in 2009, over 1 per cent of pre-tax profits, matched funding for employee fundraising for good causes, recruitment of young people not in employment, education or training, a high profile for employee training and engagement and award-winning environmental and safety measures. They scored 90 per cent on the BITC Corporate Responsibility Index. Of the £1.7 million, 37 per cent was cash donations to charity and community projects including a substantial ongoing commitment to the Duke of Edinburgh's Award scheme. Around 39 per cent was staff volunteering time and the rest was the donation of facilities and assets or gifts in kind. In total 443 charities and community projects benefited from Serco's largesse in 2009 compared to 250 the previous year.

This record compares well with others but why is it revolutionary? A clue is found in an objective for 2010 in the company's 2009 CSR report:

> *To capture our expertise and improve our working practices with the third sector gained through our work with our Flexible New Deals and Children's Services businesses.*

For exactly the same reasons as local authorities found it increasingly advantageous to work contractually with third sector agencies in delivering public services over the past 15 years, so do Serco today. Nowhere is this better seen than in offender management, such as the East of England Probation Service, which they run in a formal partnership with two major charities.

The Turning Point charity started life as the Camberwell Alcohol Project in 1964 and expanded both geographically and into supporting people with drug and later mental health problems. It first worked in prisons in 1997. By 2001 it had become the largest provider of into work programmes under the Progress 2 Work scheme and today styles itself as 'the UK's leading social care organisation, with more than 250 services across the country'[7] operating a successful person-centred approach for people with problems of substance abuse, mental health and learning disability.

Turning Point has been led since 2002 by the charismatic and unorthodox crossbench peer Lord Victor Adebowale who is also the Government's Ambassador for Social Enterprise and a member of the Audit Commission. It is no longer small, having a £70 million turnover.

---

7 See www.turning-point.co.uk/Pages/home.aspx

The Philanthropic Society began as a coffee-house discussion in 1788. An 1854 law allowed young offenders to be sent into their care instead of prison. In 1876 Frederick Rainer, a printer and volunteer with the Church of England Temperance Society, donated five shillings to start the London Police Court Mission which the courts recognised in 1907. In 1960 it became the Rainer Foundation and in 1997 it merged with (what was by then) the Royal Philanthropic Society and a Government initiative called Crime Concern to become simply 'Rainer'. In 2008 more mergers brought into being a charity for young offenders and those at risk of offending known as Catch 22.

The ground-breaking alliance between Serco, Turning Point and Catch 22 is well established. Not only does it deliver community-based services but it has won the contract to operate for 26 years a new £451 million Private Finance Initiative (PFI)-built prison at Bellmarsh West, currently under construction. This is by some way the largest contract ever to be won by a private-third sector partnership. Any contract in the criminal justice system is potentially fair game for this alliance which states its aim as transforming and not just transferring services, to get the best reoffending reduction outcomes in the interests of their service users.

In many of its services Turning Point boasts that for every £1 of public money invested over £3-worth of savings or benefit is produced for the taxpayer. It is clear why such an efficient delivery system makes the partnership attractive to Serco, which brings flexibility, scalability, economy of scale and the prospect of comprehensive coverage to the table.

This commercial partnership is not the first between private and third sectors and not every partnership has, of course, been successful.

Discussion

So far three theoretical models of service delivery through private and third sector partnerships have emerged:

- Businesses subcontracting elements of public sector work to the third sector (various models including Serco and Welfare to Work).

- Third sector bodies subcontracting elements of public sector work to businesses (This is rare. However, South Africa's sixth largest charity, Ma'Afrika Tikkun, commissions private sector bodies to provide comprehensive services to young people under the age of 18 in deprived communities, from womb to workplace. Its patrons, Messrs Mandela and de Klerk, no doubt approve of this innovative approach).

- Organisations from both sectors forming jointly owned legal entities to deliver public services (the special purpose vehicle model, such as Digital Outreach: see Chapter 1).

There is a fourth category:

- Businesses subcontracting work complementary to their own service mission to third sector bodies, with no public sector involvement.

Businesses must have a business case for engagement; otherwise imagination, ambition and luck together with good knowledge of the relevant community are needed. Getting the right charity partner is crucial, one that has the capacity to meet shared expectations. Table 4.1 summarises the potential risks and benefits to each partner. Reasonable questions for the business seeking a charity partner include:

1. What should this partnership achieve?

2. What community engagement/social responsibility outcomes could the project deliver?

3. Are we sustaining what is there or creating something new?

4. How can employees be engaged?

5. How long will it take to produce the desired outcomes?

6. How long thereafter should you commit to the project?

7. Which potential third sector partners have the capacity to deliver the outcomes?

8. Does the project need to be scaleable, if so, how?

9.   Start-up costs: what will they be and how do we raise the money?

10.   What is the exit strategy?

Partnerships cannot be picked up off the shelf; the work starts the moment the idea is planted and its germination requires tender care. But the mutual advantages that can be gained from a successful business–charity partnership are well worth having as local government has found.

Table 4.1   Benefits and risks associated with private – third sector partnerships

Benefits to Businesses	Benefits to Charities
Promoting activity complementary to or directly associated with business mission Marketing opportunity – improved image/reputation of company Staff developing new skills and experiences Experience assists in developing future partnerships CSR goal(s) fulfilled Preferential access to the charity's services	Enhanced opportunity to fulfil mission Sustained income over a defined period from new source Marketing opportunity – getting the message across to new audiences Access to employee skills to address specific needs of the organisation Volunteer time Assistance in developing future partnerships Likelihood of long-term personal commitments beyond partnership
Risks to Businesses	**Risks to Charities**
Reputational damage if commitments are made but not fulfilled Missed opportunities including future contracts	Failure to meet funding targets if commitments made on that basis Tied in to undeliverable contract Funding dependence on a major source

Based not least on its own experience of supporting the armed forces charity Help for Heroes, the global professional services giant Deloitte advocates a staged but bespoke development to achieve a sustainable business–charity partnership.[8]

Stage One – Understand each other:

---

8   See www.deloitte.com/view/en_GB/uk/about/community-investment/93320cad6bf9e210Vg nVCM3000001c56f00aRCRD.htm

- Have a proper structure on both sides to manage the relationship, including the regular sharing of ideas at senior levels as well as on the ground.

- Take time to understand each other's relative strengths, culture and strategic priorities.

Stage Two – Develop a plan to address strategic needs:

- Develop a long-term plan that meets the strategic priorities of both parties and utilises their key strengths.

- Remember that 'anything is possible' – a wide exploration of all options may yield some innovative new ideas outside the traditional area for support.

- Ensure you have a joint approach that can be driven together, not just the charity with business in a 'supporting' role.

Stage Three – Keep an open dialogue and monitor progress:

- Meet regularly and often, share successes and challenges and develop new ideas.

- Monitor your outcomes and evaluate how well they are meeting priorities; don't be afraid to change.

The value of Deloitte's partnership with Help for Heroes has grown at over 10 per cent a year since its inception in 2007. In 2010–11 its target was to raise £10 million. This included employee contributions (26 per cent of employees involved in payroll giving), the matched funding of Government contributions, employee volunteering time, gifts in kind (professional services) and the management of community programmes.

Deloitte has 14 other charity partners but the relationship with Help for Heroes, which generated the three stage process, has been radical and revolutionary. Tony Schofield, a Deloitte partner, describes it thus:

> Using the skills which we normally use in client engagements we have been able to make a real impact on the way Help for Heroes is working.

If the relationship were to end tomorrow Help for Heroes would not only be richer and better known than when the relationship started but it would have more and more appropriate skills available, be more sustainable and have a better understanding of the environment in which it operates.

Deloitte's focus on the service it provides to the charity, separated from the cost of providing that service, has allowed it to see its services in a new light. Its staff have been able to develop and deploy skills in a new and challenging situation, experience a new stream of motivation, improve retention and recruitment and help create 'real brand differentiation and visibility' by enhancing reputation and trust in their brand.

I defined the 'fourth sector' as the space in the middle of the triangle, where relationships between different sectors happen. That space is not static: for profit companies looking to embrace social change and third sector organisations seeking the stability and discipline of a business partnership both inhabit it in search mode, as do established cross-sector partnerships.

Figure 4.1 presents the relationship between the players in the fourth sector in another way.

		Crime	Business
MOTIVATION	*Profit*		↓ ↓ ↓
	Social Benefit	Government Charities → → →	Social investors Social enterprise
		Contributed INCOME	*Earned*

Key
→, ↓   Territorial expansion/behaviour change
Evidence for →: Partnerships built around common missions with
                        business, acquisition of businesslike skills, trading arms
Evidence for ↓ : Partnerships built around common missions with
                        charities, accountability and transparency, green
                        behaviour, ethical procurement/supply chain, triple
                        bottom line, community involvement

Figure 4.1   Another view of the Fourth Sector

The three sectors, here called 'Business', 'Charities' and 'Government', are joined by 'Social Enterprise' as a major new hybrid player and 'Social Investment', a relatively new phenomenon of people who invest their capital to bring about social change whilst bringing in a return that is smaller than an investment for profit would be whilst being large enough to justify reinvesting the proceeds. We will hear more of them in Chapter 7. A sixth player, 'Crime', is included for illustrative purposes only (profit orientated, zero social benefit, certainly not earned). The pieces are placed on the board according to their motivation (for profit or for benefit) and the way they are funded (earned income or contributed income from donation or taxation), with their position within each box nuanced accordingly.

Arrows then show not how the players have moved, but how they have expanded their territory within the last generation: some charities have taken on a business-like approach to income (but not the values) and some businesses have adopted some charitable values whilst not changing their approach to income. The 'vanishing point' where the two arrows meet (in theory: neither charities nor businesses need ever leave their respective boxes) is where social enterprise, employing business methods to bring about social change rather than make profits for shareholders, is found.

In June 2009 the *Financial Times* was quoted on the CSR Europe web site as saying:

> *Although experiencing a huge upsurge in interest and visibility globally, social enterprise is still in its nascent stages. Today it can be characterised as a fragmented sector filled with many small-scale enterprises struggling with scale. Growth and scalability are important concerns for all businesses but maybe more so for social enterprise, in that the scope of the social problem(s) it is trying to solve is so large.*

There is no doubt that social enterprise of all kinds will have a greater role to play both as a hybrid in the triangle model of the relationship between the four sectors (see Figure 1.3) and in the more dynamic model, not least because of the permission it is being afforded by the Big Society so to do. But each social enterprise, whilst a hybrid, is an integrated organisation with a single corporate entity. It is capable of taking part in relationships and partnerships, not a relationship in itself. It is a player in the fourth sector arena and not a sector in its own right as some social entrepreneurs would argue.

Business Charity Awards

In 2010 Mandate Communications (now MHPC) partnered *Third Sector* magazine to sponsor the first Business Charity Awards after they discovered that no such celebration existed. Sacha Deshmukh, Mandate's Chief Executive, praised businesses for their values and desire 'to leave a positive mark on the world' observing that these largely hidden and unrecognised charity partnerships could deliver value for business.

The 13 categories of award covered a wide range of activity, from the 80 per cent of Unity Trust Bank employees who had joined the bank's volunteering scheme to the comprehensive way in which Lambeth-based lobbying company PLMR had taken a nearby council estate under its wing. Unilever's support of the National Childbirth Trust, equivalent to an event each day over three years, was the Charity Partnership of the Year and Richard Bernstein of Eurovestech was the Charity Champion for his pioneering use of share-gifting to help fund charities. The Co-operative Group's work with Mencap on employment opportunities for people with mental health problems and the campaigning support of Beatbullying by the ill-fated *News of the World* were amongst others recognised.

For the 2011 awards the number of nominations doubled, almost certainly due to greater awareness, but the standard was no less high. I was a judge in 2011 and 2012 along with others from business, charities and the media; every nominee in the categories to which I was assigned impressed.

Michael Robson, Chief Executive of Andrews & Partners estate agents won the Business Charity Champion award in 2011 for a number of initiatives promoting employee volunteering and tackling homelessness. The imagination and determination with which Keyline Builders Merchants supported the Prostate Cancer Charity's 'Movember' campaign – raising seven times its target figure – was also recognised as were Barclays/Unicef, Lloyds Bank/British Heart Foundation partnerships. There were winners in 15 categories in all.[9]

Conclusion

Cross-sector partnerships are good for everybody. As we have seen, for the business they bring new skills, experience, markets, employee loyalty, image

---

9   Full results are at www.businesscharityawards.com

and reputation. For the charity they bring funding in cash and kind, volunteers, mentors, business advice, stability and an enhanced mission.

For public sector bodies, partnership with the third sector brings local flexibility, added value and cost effectiveness; for the service user, charity involvement brings the personalisation of services, empathy and patience.

Employees of partner companies get access to life-enhancing experiences through volunteering at home or abroad and opportunities to gain new skills, formally or otherwise. The relationship can bring purpose to their working life and in extreme cases sabbatical leave as an alternative to short-term lay-off.

For communities in developing countries, often with minimal public sector infrastructure, there is ample evidence (in Chapter 6) that Non-Governmental Organisations (NGOs) can step up to the mark, with business support, to deliver targeted services that the public sector would have provided had it had the capacity. Business finds that healthy communities enjoying child support, nutrition and health programmes and community-based training produce healthy workers with added life expectancy which costs the company less in the long run than carrying absentee or sick workers or having a high employee turnover. We can learn from that.

Here in the UK, public and third sector partnerships are seen as part of the fabric of society; even users of local authority services may not appreciate that the person who visits them regularly is employed by a charity and not the council. Where a third sector organisation alone is providing a service on a truly voluntary basis the local authority often has provided the frameworks and the support that the service needs to survive.

As for the impact of business–charity partnerships on local communities, the jury is still out. We saw how Wates employees roll up their sleeves to support local charities and social enterprises in the community, even becoming embedded in them for weeks on end. We understand that if Turning Point and Catch 22 can improve the lot of prison leavers to the extent that reoffending and chemical dependency are significantly reduced, building on infrastructure provided by Serco, the whole community will benefit.

The Co-operative Bank's policy of investing in small social enterprises that address local needs, having already been spawned by the very communities they will serve, is clearly well targeted even though in traditional terms the investment might be regarded as 'brave'. The Co-operative Enterprise Hub won the 2011 Business Charity award for Social Investment.

Too often, promising partnerships are seen as a flash in the pan. Group employee volunteering, for example, needs to be one element of the physical proximity between business and charity but it should not be the whole.

The quick in-out of the community action day, no matter how many jolly painters/gardeners/escorts are involved will not maximise benefit if it is all that there is to the partnership.

To return to the courtship analogy I have used elsewhere, a succession of one-night stands with corporate altruism can leave a community feeling cheap, unfulfilled, lacking confidence.

It's a sunny day in June.

The sales department arrives en masse for their annual volunteering outing with their tools and smiles at nine in the morning and they retire exhausted at six to the pub. Surely, they of all people know that customer satisfaction and loyalty come from creating feelings of mutual support, of awareness and care and that – unlike the brand new, brightly painted raised flower beds with wheelchair access in the community garden – Rome was not built in a day.

5

Regulating Partnerships, Taking Risks

We have seen how history has produced, for the first time, a coming together of businesses interested in running public services and third sector organisations anxious to bring and capable of bringing their inestimable qualities to the market place. Voluntary work, by its nature, is not normally a target for regulation but where public money is involved, often in large quantities, regulation is inevitable.

In this chapter we look at how relationships involving the third sector have been regulated and the challenges that have faced public–third sector partnerships in the past. We look at possible charity–business partnerships in the future, risk management and transfer, personalisation and consortium working.

The Compact

In Chapter 2 we saw how relationships between government and the third sector have matured. The introduction of the Compact in 1998 was a significant step not only towards greater co-operation but also because Compact working raised the possibility of credible partnerships between third sector and private sector bodies in the future.

As councils and government departments started to actively seek cost effective, flexible partners to deliver services some form of discipline was required to create a level playing field. The demand for this was crystallised by the Deakin Commission on The Future of the Voluntary Sector in 1996. Professor Nicholas Deakin, subsequently the winner of a lifetime achievement award from *Third Sector* magazine, called for a number of innovations: the Compact,

Change-Up and the Office of the Third Sector (OTS) were all introduced over time by the incoming Labour Government.

The Compact would be a memorandum of understanding governing working relations between the voluntary sector and government in its widest sense, whilst Change-Up would be a capacity-building programme within the third sector involving bespoke organisations like Capacitybuilders. The capacity in question is that of organisations to think and act strategically, to scale up solutions and activities, to innovate and partake in partnership working. All this would employ established good practice and high standards of management and financial probity. In the OTS from 2004 the responsible minister would oversee all aspects of co-operation with voluntary organisations, volunteering and the wider third sector.

Alun Michael MP, to become the Minister responsible for the Home Office's Active Community Unit in May 1997, led the Labour Party's parallel enquiry to Deakin. His 'Building the Future Together' report, calling for greater engagement between politics and the voluntary sector on all fronts, was published in February 1997. As a Labour candidate I worked closely with him. Thirteen years later, my Parliamentary career and Alun's ministerial time both over, he succeeded me as Chair of the All Party Group of backbench MPs which takes a special interest in the sector.

The Compact was the most urgent of the Deakin innovations. In July 1997 the National Council of Voluntary Organisations (NCVO) proposed to a meeting of third sector umbrella bodies that it was worth having and got their backing. Sir Kenneth Stowe led the process of drawing it up and there was a four month consultation from October 1997. One of the principles espoused by the Compact was that government consultations involving the third sector should include a reasonable time for public discourse. This was particularly important when the consultees included thousands of organisations and millions of individuals, as the third sector does. There were 25,000 responses to this consultation.

Sir Kenneth had, amongst other roles, been Principal Private Secretary to Prime Minister James Callaghan (1977–79). On retiring from the civil service he had become a trustee of Cancer Research UK.

The Compact was launched with great fanfare in November 2008. Invitations announced that Sir Kenneth would sign the Compact in the presence of Minister

Alun Michael and Phil Hope as the Chair of the All Party Parliamentary Group on the Voluntary Sector and Charities (as it was then called).[1] When neither politician could make it, at the last minute Alun's Home Office teammate Paul Boateng and I substituted.

The Compact recognises the values, principles and commitments that government and third sector share and lays down guidelines for working together. It is built on trust and goodwill but cannot be legally enforced, its authority being derived from its endorsement by both government and by the voluntary and community sector (VCS) through the consultation process. This was not a weakness; legalistic solutions tend to generate antagonism, bureaucracy, cost and delay.

It was the start of a process in which the private sector had no role. However, the improvement in relationships between the private sector and the third in the early 2000s, leading in some cases to genuine win–win partnerships, could not have happened without the experience of the Compact that VCS organisations gained from 1998 onwards.

The Compact was a milestone, not a finished product. It was followed by a Funding Code (2000, reissued 2006), a Consultation and Policy Appraisal Code and Local Compact guidelines (2000) and more codes on Black and Minority Ethnic Groups, Volunteering (both 2001) and Community Groups (2003). 2005 saw a consultation on strengthening the Compact which led to the appointment of a Compact Commissioner as a sort of Ombudsman (John Stoker in 2006) and a full Commission for the Compact (2007). In 2008 Sir Bert Massie, former head of the Disability Rights Commission, took over from Stoker as Chair of the Commission for the Compact.

By 2002 every top tier local authority had drawn up a Local Compact with its local VCS. Dorset did so in 1999 in advance of the guidelines.

THE BENEFITS OF THE COMPACT …

Local Compacts have had a mixed press but in their 2010 report on the Social and Economic Benefits of Compact Working (Thornton and Jenkins, 2010) the Commission was unequivocal. Even, perhaps especially, at a time when local authority budgets were coming under stress the benefits of Compact working were too good to miss, they said; those local authorities who argued that the

---

1   Phil Hope was later Minister for the Third Sector, June 2007 to October 2008.

business case for full Compact compliance had not been made were simply wrong. The Commission cited many examples of successful Compact working, including:

1.   reduced administrative costs;

2.   better use of officer time by reduced duplication of monitoring;

3.   improved partnership working with voluntary organisations;

4.   improved understanding of the outcomes delivered;

5.   more and better quality tenders and funding applications.

In Worcestershire, they reported, a combined county council and VCS project received over a million pounds in grants which neither partner could have achieved alone. In Calderdale, six council departments funded the same VCS body for different purposes. Through better co-ordination by a single lead officer a huge duplication of monitoring was avoided. In Birmingham, use of the Black and Minority Ethnic Code within Compact guidelines led to improved provision of care services in a cost effective way.

A general benefit of Compact working in both local and central government was the move away from annual to three-year funding agreements as the norm, allowing organisations and projects time to bed in before embarking on re-applications for funding whilst reducing bureaucracy. The Government introduced three-year budgets for councils at the same time, making it easier for councillors to make those longer-term commitments.

... AND ITS WEAKNESS

There was a major weakness in the original Compact which is all too clear with hindsight. It was not anticipated quite how fast and to what extent new sources of funding would come into the sector through the commissioning of services by contract and many VCS organisations were simply not ready: too many did not know how to properly calculate the cost of a project.

'Full cost recovery' means getting back all of the costs of providing a project or service through the contract to deliver it. It is relatively easy to measure the costs directly associated with a project but fulfilling a contract will also call upon back office costs, management time, wear and tear of equipment and the use of IT systems. The full cost of any project must therefore include all overheads, the cost of which should be allocated on a comprehensive, robust and defensible basis.

There was political sympathy for the position that third sector organisations found themselves in, though a short-term fix was difficult to envisage. Fiona Mactaggart MP, one of a rapid succession of Home Office ministers with responsibility for communities policy (and a former NCVO press officer) told the sector not to take things lying down. 'Just say no' was her advice to any organisation which felt that the terms of a proposed contract were unacceptable on the grounds of either the absence of full cost recovery or mission drift.

Both issues raised concerns in the sector that in pursuing income with strings attached charities might find themselves either subsidising the very service they were supposed to be providing or compromising their historic aims.

'Mission drift' refers to the accidental change in priorities, strategies or goals that an organisation might find itself making as a result of short-term, short sighted, successive or simply pragmatic decisions. A deliberate tactical rethink of missions, goals and priorities may be necessary from time to time to ensure that they remained relevant, achievable and appropriate. Drift and revision should not be confused. As John Maynard Keynes might have said to the charity world, 'When the facts change, I change my mind; what do you do, sir?' But when the facts which informed the mission had not changed there was no reason to change it.

The Minister's advice was sound. Third sector bodies like the Association of Chief Executives of Voluntary Organisations (ACEVO), the chief executives' union, were on the case and the Government was ready to listen. By 2002 the Government and the third sector had reached agreement in principle on overhead costs:

> *Funders should recognise that it is legitimate for providers to include*
> *the relevant element of overheads in their cost estimates for providing a*
> *given service under service agreement or contract.*

Sir Peter Gershon's Efficiency Review of July 2004 urged the Government to ensure that 'publicly-funded services are not subsidised by charitable donations or volunteers'. The Government committed all departments to fund projects accordingly by April 2006.

In 2004 ACEVO produced a toolkit to give the sector practical measures of obtaining full cost recovery. In 2006, with support from the Big Lottery Fund, they began a three-year programme of education and training for 15,000 third sector organisations alongside the National Association for Voluntary and Community Action (NAVCA), the co-ordinating body for Councils of Voluntary Service.

REFRESHING THE COMPACT

In early 2009 the Government invited its partners in the Compact to refresh the document and bring it up to date. The new agreement retained the key points of the original, taking into account developments in law, policy and practice. It was divided into three areas: involvement in policy development, the way resources are allocated and new legal duties under the 2010 Equality Act.

The refreshing process and its outcome were welcomed by the sector, though as the weeks before its December relaunch ticked away the Government was accused of a major breach of Compact principles within the Cabinet Office itself. The Campaigning Research Fund was intended to help smaller, less professional organisations hone their campaigning techniques and develop new ones. It was only seven months old when Minister Angela Smith announced its immediate demise. Grant offers totalling £750,000 to 32 organisations were withdrawn and the cash was reallocated to the £17 million Hardship Fund for charities in financial difficulty.

Smith quickly acknowledged that neither the speed nor the unilateral nature of the decision were Compact compliant. The Cabinet Office pointed to a get-out clause in the Fund's constitution that appeared to allow either signatory to walk away. This probably saved the Government the ignominy of a judicial review in the absence of any legal powers to enforce the gentlemen's agreement that was the Compact.

The Minister's line was that voluntary organisations hit by the recession had convinced her that the money would be better spent through the Hardship Fund. Speculation amongst charities was that this was more likely traditional pre-election housekeeping whereby a government stops people spending its money in ways which might prove embarrassing during the campaign, such as on travellers or refugees. The probable explanation is that one or more of the organisations was intending to use the cash to campaign rather than to develop campaigning techniques. Exposing a charity for a technical abuse of the fund would have put the Government in a bad light for both careless management and undermining a 'good cause'.

Barely was the ink dry on the refreshed Compact when the next revision started. The incoming Coalition Government clearly saw the Compact as important in their Big Society vision. Within two weeks of the election the OTS had been renamed as the Office for Civil Society (banishing 'third sector' to a lexicological gulag) and the Compact Review had been announced.

New elements, said the new Minister, Nick Hurd, would include commitments to give communities more powers, strengthen the role of local government in decision-making and make government data more readily available.

The announcement was heard with trepidation by some. An acceptable refresh had only just been agreed. The Government had firm (if not yet very transparent) views on 'Big Society' – but would they dictate or negotiate the new Compact? Would a government committed to deregulation wherever possible see full cost recovery as a constraint on market forces and omit it?

They need not have worried. Hurd launched the Renewed Compact[2] at the Christmas 2010 reception for the All Party Parliamentary Group on the Civil Society and Volunteering[3] to a warm welcome: peppered with the term 'Big Society' the new document was slimmer and more succinct than its predecessor. It had a welcome new feature, that of scrutiny by the National Audit Office (NAO) followed by a report to Parliament. Simon Blake, Chair of Compact Voice, launched the document together with Hurd, saying:

> *The sector has wanted a Compact with teeth for a long time. This new Compact with greater accountability provides just that. With major changes in relationships and funding across the country, more than ever both parties need to know, and stick by, the 'rules of the game'. I call on the voluntary and community sector and government to get behind and use this Compact now as a compass for effective partnership.*

---

2   See www.compactvoice.org.uk/sites/default/files/the_compact.pdf
3   As I had previously, Alun Michael began his Chairmanship of the APPG by changing the name of the group. I had called it APPG for the Community and Voluntary Sector.

The new Chair of NCVO, speaking at the same Parliamentary reception, was the former newsreader Martyn Lewis. He was more circumspect, reminding the audience that progress towards achieving the Government's vision of the Big Society contained threats for the sector as well as opportunities; proposed spending cuts could not be ignored.

The 2011 Compact includes 32 undertakings by Government and 16 for Civil Society Organisations (CSOs). The right for CSOs to campaign, so controversial under previous Conservative Prime Ministers, was explicit in the very first clause.

One undertaking explicitly mentions full cost recovery. In paragraph 3.8 the Government agreed to:

> *Recognise that when CSOs apply for a grant they can include appropriate and relevant overheads, including the costs associated with training and volunteer involvement.*

The same criterion must surely apply to a contract bid, subject to commercial considerations. The lowest cost service is not always the right choice and few charities can afford to run a loss leader in the way that companies might, due to their small scale, aversion to risk and frequent paucity of financial reserves.

Looking to the future, a most significant form of words is used in paragraph 2.1. Under 'Effective and transparent design and development of policies, programmes and public services' the Government undertakes to:

> *Ensure that social, environmental and economic value forms a standard part of designing, developing and delivering policies, programmes and services.*

This is a fascinating form of words. 'Social, environmental and economic value' is known in corporate responsibility circles as the 'triple bottom line' (see Chapter 3). The phrase is the key to involving private sector partners – who have played no part in evolving the Compact – in future partnership agreements.

Not everyone regarded the renewed Compact in glowing terms. The words were one thing, argued Colin Rochester's team in an independent valedictory review for the Compact Commission published in March 2011 (Zemmeck et al., 2011):

> *Despite widespread belief that the Compact is a 'good thing', at least in principle, the substantial effort devoted to translating it into reality, and its positive impact, the Compact is currently at low ebb and is in danger of being ignored to death. Recent developments – the thicket of newer and higher-profile initiatives that bypass it; the new text scrabbled together to reflect the Coalition's emerging policy agenda; the 'cull of the Quangos' that terminated its principal guardian, the Commission for the Compact; and the government's somewhat cavalier approach to the resourcing (and even existence) of the organisations required to deliver the Big Society agenda – testify to its parlous state.*

They also criticised the new Compact's frequent references to 'Big Society' as being blatantly political and claimed that the Government had downgraded the Compact by not publishing it as a Command Paper. It focused too narrowly on service delivery, they said, rather than specifically including volunteering and community groups as it had previously done.

The NAO audit of the Compact proved to be a double-edged sword. 'Why ask them to do the Compact Commission's job?' asked some. The Commission had itself been lobbying for the right to place before Parliament an annual report on the state of the Compact. Even before the scrutiny had got into gear the NAO was no doubt causing ministers to wonder what they had done: they had no reason to pull their punches.

The Office of Civil Society (OCS) 'seemed to have observed the Compact in the breach more than anything', observed John Hoadley, whose team was due to carry out the NAO audit, at a Compact Voice conference on 10 March 2011.

He went on:

> *If the Compact is going to be effective, it does require leadership. It's not there. The OCS is consistently not Compact-compliant.*
>
> *One would expect it to lead by example across government to ensure the Compact is the force it could and should be. If there's no leadership at national level, I don't see how that can impact at local level other than negatively. (Plummer, 2011)*

As if to make the point, three months after the refreshed Compact had proposed that the sector should have 12 weeks notice of major policy changes affecting them the Government launched a 17-day consultation on the Modernising Commissioning Green Paper.

Although a Government spokesman described Hoadley's comments as 'nonsense' at the time the NAO view was vindicated by the report when it was published in January 2012. It found that whilst most government departments were well disposed to the Compact in principle, leadership on the issue within the Government was 'not always visible' and a staggering 40 per cent of government consultation exercises were not Compact-compliant (NAO, 2012).

OTHER COMPACT BODIES

The original third sector working group to draw up the Compact was not disbanded but re-formed as Compact Voice, the representative body for the VCS in all matters related to the Compact. Housed within NCVO headquarters but operationally independent this alliance has national, regional and local members to ensure that all levels of the VCS are represented. Compact Voice speaks to government and spoke to the Commission for the Compact on a regular basis.

Compact Advocacy is a Big Lottery Fund funded programme also based within NCVO. It advises and supports third sector groups who feel that they have been victims of a Compact breach. A breach might be that either the quantity (under 12 weeks) or quality of a consultation on government proposals for a significant change to a contract were at fault; or funding was withdrawn at very short notice; or unreasonably stringent monitoring procedures had been imposed.

The Commission for the Compact was established to oversee the operation of the Compact and its codes of practice. It was an independent public body whose work included promoting awareness and implementation of the Compact, undertaking research and exploring key themes that affect the relationship between statutory and voluntary sectors. It was not a regulatory body and had no legal powers.

The idea of a Commission had been floated in the initial discussions around the Compact but instead a single Commissioner was appointed in 2006, as we have noted. In 2004 there was an opportunity to create a statutory Commission through a Local Government Bill but the Treasury blocked it. So, when the Commission came into being in April 2007, with 15 staff in Birmingham and a board of directors, costing over a million pounds a year, it had no legal status. On 19 May 2009 my 'Commission for the Compact Bill' sought to address this anomaly.

My Ten Minute Rule Bill would have made the Commission for the Compact statutory. It would have given the Commission powers to investigate claims of Compact breaches, to access relevant information and to impose a duty on others to co-operate with its investigations.

Introducing it in the Commons, I said:[4]

> *To fulfil the role, the Commission needs to act independently and be seen to do so, but the current legal structure does not ensure that. The Minister created the Commission and decides on 100 per cent of its membership himself, as well as having full powers over its constitution and existence. In practice, successive Ministers have allowed the Commission full operational independence, but there is no guarantee that future Ministers would do the same, in which case both the Commission's status and its credibility could be undermined. The Commission is not a regulatory body and has no powers beyond those of any private citizen.*

> *With this Bill I propose to place the Commission for the Compact on a statutory basis and confer a very limited range of legal powers to enable it to promote better implementation of the compact. Having the Commission established by Parliament, with a constitution and powers determined by Parliament and a duty to report to Parliament, would make a great difference, lifting the Commission out of direct Government control and making it inherently and visibly independent.*

I had the backing of the Cabinet Office, the Treasury and the Department of Communities and Local Government, but the Parliamentary timetable was against me. Although my initial speech had its allotted ten minutes at prime time, the important second reading on a Friday morning never got called, despite being scheduled several times, and time ran out.

---

4   See www.publications.parliament.uk/pa/cm200809/cmhansrd/cm090519/debtext/90519-0004.
     htm#09051970000001

It was therefore with a sense of irony that I heard of the Coalition Government's plans not to make an honest Commission out of Bert Massie and his team but to get rid of them. The Public Bodies Bill sought to abolish over 100 allegedly unnecessary bodies in a process dubbed 'the bonfire of the quangos'. Ostensibly a cost-and-red-tape-cutting measure, critics were not impressed. Several bodies with quasi-judicial functions had to be withdrawn from its scope and many of the abolitions would save little in cash terms when redundancy payments and the transfer of essential functions to government departments or other bodies were taken into account.

Some of the Commission for the Compact's duties were transferred to the Local Government Ombudsman. The headline saving of just over a million pounds is likely to be a huge overestimate. Bernard Jenkin MP, Conservative Chair of the Commons Public Administration committee, speaking about the Bonfire of the Quangos, told *The Guardian* in January 2011:

> *The whole process was rushed and poorly handled and should have been thought through a lot more. This was a fantastic opportunity to help build the Big Society and save money at the same time, but it has been botched. I suspect that in the short term the reorganisation will now cost more than it will save. This was put together on the hoof and can be much improved for future reviews. (Curtis, 2011)*

The Commission for the Compact no longer exists.

THE FUTURE OF PARTNERSHIPS

The Compact is strictly an understanding between the third sector and government, its departments, agencies and local government, whereby each will respect the rights, dignity and purpose of the other. To date there has been no formal memorandum, contract or Compact to regulate relationships and partnerships between voluntary organisations and the private sector. Perhaps this is because such arrangements are relatively few, new and informal; perhaps because the private sector is so diverse it cannot speak with one voice on the matter, especially where matters of regulation are concerned; perhaps the world is simply not yet ready.

Or is it?

As we see elsewhere, social responsibility is taking root in Britain's boardrooms. Pursuit of that triple bottom line is increasingly seen not just as the right thing to do but the right thing to do for business. Recognition that the planet's life-sustaining climate demands urgent remedial action through what they call the 'internalisation of externalities' has opened the private sector's eyes to other roles too. The third sector provides a wealth of partners who can help business discharge its responsibilities towards the environment, our communities and the poor in distant and disadvantaged countries who produce the raw materials for our supply chains.

As the Big Society rolls out and more services are delivered within communities by voluntary organisations so individual groups may find scaling up what they do a challenge too far. But growing may not be the only answer to scaling up: an anticipated era of charity mergers has not yet reached the pace many expected. In terms of scale nothing yet rivals the merger of Age Concern and Help the Aged to create Age UK, with all its local difficulties.

Throughout the period of the Labour Government, from the New Deal onwards, the Department for Work and Pensions (DWP) and its predecessors developed plans and strategies for creating jobs. Much of this work was outsourced and won by private sector companies as no third sector body was large enough to compete alone for the contract. One of the winners – the recipient of the single largest job creation contract ever awarded in the UK – was A4e, which started life re-skilling Sheffield's redundant steel workers 20 years ago. It is now an international employment and business support operation in 11 countries employing over 3,000 people.[5] The only way charities and voluntary organisations could get in on this act was through coming together as consortia.

A few were successful; some hooked up with private sector partners and some, like the Shaw Trust which provides training and job placement for people with disabilities, were big enough to go ahead on their own. But many could only get into this market by working with like-minded others. Consortium working is complex. It involves forging common goals and strategies, recognising relative strengths and weaknesses, managing contracts in a way which is not subject to the worst aspects of management by committee and keeping multiple partners 'on board' all the time. It can be very stressful!

Following the 2010 Comprehensive Spending Review local authority services will never be the same again. A 25 per cent cut in spending over four years, front-loaded, is having devastating effects on some services including

---

5   In early 2012 A4e was the subject of allegations of corruption around these contracts, prompting the resignation of its high profile founder.

many provided by third sector bodies. A good thing, some might say, they needed a shake-up; others will pray in aid the Big Society in which people power, the resources and consciences of our communities, will somehow provide a new generation of localised and nuanced grass roots services.

And so it might. But the planned time scale, accelerated so that the ship is steady in time for the next election, is creating mayhem in the short term. Not only is money being withdrawn from the sector and jobs lost but confidence will be shattered as communications break down because of local authority contacts disappearing. People of goodwill will be traumatised as they survey a landscape containing little immediate hope or certainty.

The Communities Secretary, Eric Pickles, addressed the 2011 NCVO annual conference as many local authorities were setting their budgets for the financial year which was to start just five weeks later. Across the land budget setting meetings had been lobbied by organisations facing knock-on cuts to little avail. Mr Pickles tried to cheer delegates up: Tendring (one of the smallest district councils in the country) was increasing its funding to the sector ten-fold, he said, and Reading showed a slight increase, too. He called on councils to be 'reasonable' and not inflict 'disproportionate' cuts on the sector. In a remarkable passage from a Government committed to localism he said that he would be the final arbiter of reasonableness and proportionality.

Was it all too late? With budgets already being set the Minister admitted that he did not yet have the legal power to make such judgements. He had opened up a can of worms in which lawyers and judicial reviews would undoubtedly thrive. If a council faces a 10 per cent cut in its budget, is any cut of over 10 per cent by definition disproportionate? If the council finds that it cannot cut those services which it has a legal duty to provide without being in breach of its statutory duties, might not a larger percentage cut inflicted on its smaller discretionary budgets actually be deemed reasonable?

With decisions already being made, a new financial year about to start and local elections pending in many areas, Mr Pickles called for councils to give up to six months' notice of major funding changes to charities. How and when was he going to resolve the multiple conundrums he had created?[6]

---

6   CLG guidance in autumn 2011 failed to address the problem directly, advising only that the total amount of funds councils gave to the voluntary sector and small businesses (together) in future should not be cut disproportionately.

The outsourcing of services to third party providers, whether in the private or third sector, involves the transfer of risk.

The Management of Risk

In late 2010 a remarkably hard hitting and perceptive report was produced by Zurich Municipal – the insurer of choice of both local government and the third sector – and Ipsos-MORI. They outlined the 'Tough Choices' ahead for public services (Zurich, 2010). Their conclusions can be distilled to just three:

1.   Short-term spending decisions which are rushed will produce long-term consequences, anticipated and otherwise, at such a pace that proper planning is unlikely to happen.

2.   Neither the third sector, nor the public sector, have ever experienced a level of risk transfer of the size and nature that is proposed, with little evidence that this is being acknowledged.

3.   Such seismic changes will lead to problems of staff morale; downsizing could prompt industrial unrest and service failure followed by possible social unrest.

As has been said, our three sectors reflect their characters in their approach to risk. The private sector thrives on it, risk being at the heart of the capitalist ethos. The public sector is uneasy about it but, hey, if it all goes wrong I could still have a job. To smaller, community-based organisations of the third sector risk is anathema: we cannot put charitable funds at risk, full stop.

It is the second conclusion that is the most interesting because risk transfer is not only a function of the cuts but is found in other policy areas too.

The Building Schools for the Future programme, Foundation Hospitals and Academy schools all involved the transfer of financial risk away from the public sector. Where 'We, the local authority, retain the responsibility for providing this service but you, a charity or community organisation, will help us deliver it', the previous principal commissioning model, there is no risk transfer: the consequences of failure stay with the public body. But if they say, 'This contract means it is now your responsibility to deliver this service' there is a risk transfer with which the charity may not be able to cope either psychologically or physically. They may not even recognise that it is happening.

The increasing trend in Government policy towards payment by results is another way of saying, 'Your payment will be both end-loaded and dependent on outcomes'. It is clearly risk transfer. Right up to the day a job is complete the charity may have to meet its costs 'up front' with no guarantee that they will be paid for; a repudiation of the principle of full cost recovery. More realistically, interim payments may be made as the work is carried out with the end-loaded final payment at risk if the desired outcome is not achieved.

Payment by results is dangerous new territory and no such contract should be entered into unless the third sector contractor's eyes are fully open and the brain engaged. The questions they should ask include:

1.   Do we agree on what we mean by 'results'?

2.   Is the risk of failure tolerable?

3.   Will we be able to renegotiate the contract if necessary?

4.   What is the baseline against which results will be compared?

5.   Is there a simple correlation between our inputs and the desired outcomes?

6.   How do we minimise the risks posed by factors outside our control?

7.   What are the milestones along the way of delivering the desired outcomes?

8.   Is there an alternative way of funding this project so the risk is not transferred to us?

If the answer to any of the first three questions is 'no', stop immediately! The answer to the final question may increasingly be 'yes'. Innovative means of financing service delivery are discussed in Chapter 7.

The very first paragraph of the Zurich report uses the words 'unprecedented', 'drastic' and 'dramatic' in relation to local authority, health, fire, police and third sector services. The first page says that, cuts and risk transfer aside, difficult choices will be made much tougher by the economic downturn, demographic change and structural reform within services.

In short, any provider who manages or takes on responsibility for public services at any level should read 'Tough Choices' – urgently.

Government Action on Third Sector Commissioning

The capacity of the third sector to deliver on its contractual obligations will be crucial to the success of any future regime in which the private sector commissions services from the third sector either in the delivery of quasi-public services or for its own purposes. Understanding the recent history of the relationship between government and its agencies with third sector contractors is crucial to surviving the future.

By 2006 various government departments, with the new OTS in the Cabinet Office at the centre, had realised that a level playing field did not exist between private and third sector bidders for contracts for delivering public services. Seven Government departments tried to address this with the Department for Communities and Local Government (local government), Health (Primary Care Trusts), DWP (Welfare to Work) and the Department for Trade and Industry (later to become BIS) leading the way.

The local government Improvement and Development Agency (IDeA) was asked to co-ordinate work on making sure that public sector contracting procedures ensured that third sector service providers got a fair 'crack of the whip' and to implement The National Programme for Third Sector Commissioning. From 2006 the Advisory Group overseeing the process was chaired by Baroness Glenys Thornton, whose background in the Co-operative movement and as a former chair of the Social Enterprise Coalition made her a strong choice. I took over when she became a Government Whip in the House of Lords in 2008, relinquishing the post in 2010.

The National Programme was key to implementing the Labour Government's 2006 policy 'Partnership in public services: An action plan for third-sector involvement'. It envisaged training 2,000 commissioners to create the capacity to run public services and the harmonisation of commissioning strategies across government. Its intended outcomes were increased awareness and understanding of commissioners' needs by contractors and vice versa, more third sector involvement in commissioning and improved bidding practices.

Eight principles of good commissioning were drawn up to guide the way public sector commissioners should engage with TSOs:

- Understanding the needs of users and other communities by ensuring that consultees engage with third sector organisations, as advocates, to access their specialist knowledge.

- Consulting potential provider organisations, including those from the third sector and local experts, well in advance of commissioning new services, working with them to set priority outcomes for that service.

- Putting outcomes for users at the heart of the strategic planning process.

- Mapping the fullest practical range of providers with a view to understanding the contribution they could make to delivering those outcomes.

- Considering investing in the capacity of the provider base, particularly those working with hard-to-reach groups.

- Ensuring contracting processes are transparent and fair, facilitating the involvement of the broadest range of suppliers, including considering subcontracting and consortia building, where appropriate.

- Ensuring long-term contracts and risk sharing, wherever appropriate, as ways of achieving efficiency and effectiveness.

- Seeking feedback from service users, communities and providers in order to review the effectiveness of the commissioning process in meeting local needs.

The package was designed not as a sop to the third sector but as a way of ensuring that the public sector obtained the optimum service for its users in a cost effective way and that service qualities were taken in to account as well as measurable outcomes. The principles accepted that the sector could be a voice for the public as well as a provider of services; and that the best people to provide a particular service (such as one to a hard-to-reach group) may need help in developing the capacity to deliver the scale or the cost effectiveness required. Otherwise, the principles embody common sense and fair play.

The principles were necessary because the existing architecture was proving insufficient. The Compact had been designed for simple public-third sector relations but was clearly inappropriate when the third sector was competing in the market place with the private sector. The baseline evaluation of the National Programme found (Shared Intelligence, 2008) that only a quarter of CSOs responding to the survey agreed that 'the Compact has been helpful in improving working relationships between the third sector and the public sector' while over a third disagreed. This was a ten-year old Compact by then: its re-write to take into account the demands of commissioning was still a year away.

The baseline research contains other interesting findings: only one in five CSOs and two in five commissioners were aware of the commissioning principles whilst three CSOs in five had seen their public sector funding move away from core or grant funding and towards commissioning. Two in every three larger CSOs were involved in service delivery and planning compared to one in three smaller ones. Most potential commissioners said that they valued what CSOs had to offer but only one CSO in five appeared to believe this.

Three-quarters of CSOs thought that commissioning would grow in importance yet two in five saw it threatening their independence or compromising their advocacy role.

Two in five CSOs believed that commissioning was not a fair and transparent process (especially amongst those with most experience of it) whilst only one in five believed that it was. A belief was identified that Councils for Voluntary Service (CVS) should play a greater role, pre-empting the Consortico approach discussed below, though it was also clear that CVSs generally did not have the comprehensive capabilities that the role would demand.

Commissioners shared a common understanding that:

1. the third sector brings something unique to public service delivery (83 per cent);

2. the third sector can provide niche services (80 per cent);

3. the third sector is a source of innovation (70 per cent);

4.   a broad provider base made it easier to commission high-quality services (82 per cent);

5.   a thriving third sector was beneficial for their organisations (90 per cent).

But commissioners were less confident about their third sector partners' capacity to deliver, believing that CSOs:

1.   'often don't have the resources or capacity to successfully manage public sector contracts' (51 per cent);

2.   needed to 'be more professional' (37 per cent);

3.   were 'more effective as advocates than service deliverers' (34 per cent).

Old habits die hard: there was evidence of pre-Compact stereotyping as two-thirds of CSOs said that commissioners regarded them as 'amateur' whilst only one in nine commissioners actually thought that.

One-year contracts were the norm with all their associated difficulties of continuity, economy of scale and worry about future planning, except in the case of local authorities which were moving towards a norm of three years. Half of all CSOs said that the level of risk they were expected to take on was unmanageable and seven in ten said that in 2008 the need for full cost recovery was not respected by commissioners. Where CSOs fed back information and advice to commissioners based on experience it was generally not clear what happened to that advice.

Only a minority of commissioners had received commissioning training. Those within central government reported that training was expected to rise – from a zero base.

From this baseline study it was clear that there was a lot of work to be done. Phase two of the advisory group's work from 2008 was to build on the above, oversee the design and content of the training, establish an online Community of Practice and commission Chartered Institute of Public Finance Administration (CIPFA) and others to deliver the training nationwide.

Since 2010, the work of the National Programme has stalled. IDeA has merged with the Local Government Association and lost three in five of its employees in the process. The third planned stage – producing a third sector more capable of standing on its own two feet when dealing with commissioners and partners – may never happen.

In 2010 NCVO published a 'Third Sector Commissioning Guide' aimed at both contractors and commissioners, based on the experience of Voluntary Norfolk.[7] It is a comprehensive and valuable checklist for the commissioning process covering Analysis, Planning, Sourcing and Monitoring and Reviewing.

The NAO's parallel 'Successful Commissioning Toolkit'[8] describes the commissioning process as a wheel with principles at its hub and a five stage commissioning cycle (Assessing needs, Designing services, Sourcing providers, Delivering to users, Monitoring and evaluation) generating interaction between public and third sector bodies at all stages.

MERLIN TO THE RESCUE

The DWP's approach to commissioning, the Merlin Standard, is not to be confused with George Osborne's plan of the same name to get the banking community to behave itself. DWP has one of the better established contracting links with the third sector even though the sector's involvement is less than many had hoped to see by now. Nevertheless, private contractors have recognised the value of the third sector through their subcontracting practices. It is excellence here in the supply chain that Merlin seeks to promote.[9]

Throughout much of 2009 and 2010 members of the Government's Advisory Group on Third Sector Commissioning waited with anticipation for Merlin to appear. DWP was a major recruiter of private and third sector partners through Welfare to Work and it had a wealth of experience of commissioning, contracting and subcontracting.

The Standard is essentially a Code of Conduct based on four integrated principles – Supply Chain Design, Commitment, Conduct and Review – together with an overview on Commissioning, all subject to elaborate feedback

---

7   See www.ncvo-vol.org.uk/sites/default/files/Third_sector_commissioning_checklist_FINAL 1.pdf
8   See www.nao.org.uk/help_for_public_services/third_sector/successful_commissioning/toolkit _home/introduction/nao_model_of_commissioning_and.aspx
9   See www.merlinstandard.co.uk/downloads/merlin-standard.pdf

mechanisms. Prime contractors are responsible for upholding the Code, collecting feedback and identifying best practice which is then made available to others. Supply chain members are invited to validate the prime's findings and comment on any element of the prime's practice that affects the commissioning process, especially if resulting from contract design or procurement activity.

The Code requires the prime to use certain criteria for designing the supply chain including being open to applicants from all sectors. Under 'Commitment', it requires them to 'collaborate, co-operate and communicate' with others, not least to show how subcontractors' experience feeds back into supply chain re-design, and encourage the development of smaller and more specialist providers in the voluntary sector. The Code promotes 'Review' as a continuous and inclusive feedback process.

The 'Conduct' element of the code comes close to saying, 'We require you to exhibit social responsibility'. In particular it requires the prime contractor to:

1.   work to business principles including customer service values;

2.   have a clear and effective strategy to deal with TUPE[10] where necessary;

3.   ensure the supply chain is legislatively compliant;

4.   manage risk in a fair, transparent, equitable and proportional manner;

5.   ensure proper health and safety standards throughout the supply chain;

6.   behave in a transparent manner and promote good practice;

7.   have an effective dispute resolution process and be bound by external mediation and arbitration where necessary;

8.   promote equality and diversity including within the supply chain.

Today the Merlin standard is established and DWP anticipates that other Government departments and agencies will take it up. Merlin accreditation of

---

10   TUPE is the Transfer of Undertakings (Protection of Employment) Regulations 2006.

prime contractors who ensure that their supply chains adhere to the Code was introduced in 2011.

Merlin is a sincere attempt to ensure that commissioner–contractor conduct is fair whilst obtaining the best possible service for the commissioner. It is not a Compact: its policing sanctions are stronger. Nor does it treat private sector and third sector (sub)contractors equally: rather it recognises that those with something valuable to offer but without the weight necessary to bring them to the table do need encouragement and help. As we shall see in Chapter 7, early experience of Merlin has not yet resulted in greater numbers of third sector prime contractors.

In the longer term, and outside the DWP context, help to create business-like capacity used to be available from Futurebuilders.

FUTUREBUILDERS

In 2003 the Treasury put out a tender to run a £125 million initiative to strengthen the third sector's role in public service delivery. The money was to be invested in schemes to demonstrate the added value that the sector can contribute to improving public services, principally using a concept alien to the third sector: loan finance. Key to its success would be transparency, thorough evaluation and the sharing of good practice. The tender was won by a consortium of Charity Bank, Unity Bank, NCVO and the Northern Rock Foundation. A non-profit company, Futurebuilders (England) was born.

In the first three years one loan was made on average each day, with about a quarter of all applicants being successful, many for capital projects. The Chief Executive from 2004 to 2008 was Richard Gutch who already had a long career behind him as a town planner, local government official, charity leader (with Arthritis Care) and a funder as Chair of the Community Fund, a predecessor of the Big Lottery Fund. Defending the practice of imaginative funding, he told *The Guardian* (Benjamin, 2007):

> *People are surprised that we often invest more than they ask for. We tell them: 'You must get a finance officer in place, otherwise how are you possibly going to run the service?'*

One of the purposes of Futurebuilders was to loan to charities where commercial loan providers feared to tread. During Gutch's regime only two loan recipients defaulted.

The right to administer the £200 million second phase (2008–11) was won by the Social Investment Business under the Chairmanship of Stephen Bubb, Chief Executive of ACEVO. In 2008–09 recipients of their loans won £23 million-worth of public sector contracts and this doubled the following year.

Despite its modest capital, Futurebuilders made a real difference to the capacity of hundreds of organisations not only to compete for local authority or government contracts but to behave in a business-like way in a society that was more like a market place than at any previous time in history.

By January 2010, all Futurebuilders' capital had been loaned out and despite £90 million-worth of applications arriving on its doormat each month, due to a combination of growing need and growing awareness, it closed its doors to new applications.

Soon after the 2010 general election Civil Society Minister Nick Hurd announced that Futurebuilders was to close. It was insufficiently targeted on community groups, he said, an argument Bubb strongly contested. There would be no phase three; repayments from its loans would go to the Big Society Bank which, for legal reasons, was re-named Big Society Capital.

WORKING IN A CHARITY CONSORTIUM

Consortico[11] is a special purpose vehicle (SPV) identical in purpose to that which we met in the context of Private Finance Initiative (PFI). It is a professional, all purpose, consortium hub developed by Bedford CVS. It is not a charity but a company limited by guarantee, not for profit, wholly owned by its members who are nine voluntary bodies from the local area. Their prospectus says that:

> Consortico will act as a Super Contractor, identifying public service contract opportunities. Our goal is to secure these contracts and deliver them through sub-contract arrangements with local, not for profit, sector three organisations, for the benefit of local communities.

Knowing that the Consortico hub exists will help prevent the third sector trying to re-invent the wheel. It is an effective model, replicable and scalable.

As an SPV Consortico sits at the centre of a network of three or more collaborating organisations of a variety of size and experience to negotiate

---

11   See www.consortico.com

with a public sector commissioner on their collective behalf initially (at least) in the Bedford area. It appreciates that the commissioner saves costs by having only one contract rather than many; any risk associated with providing the service is carried by the hub and not by its directors personally or its possibly vulnerable members. Where no single charity has the capacity to take on the contract so the consortium becomes the only medium through which third sector involvement in that service, together with its distinctive blend of locally appropriate or personalised delivery, can be delivered.

The consortium saves its members money through the central procurement of goods and services, takes responsibility for legal compliance and has its own costs built in to the contract rather than top-slicing for that purpose. Any surplus it makes can be re-invested in the hub at the discretion of its directors who are accountable to the members.

The challenge of establishing itself at a time of severe local government spending cuts has proved too much for Consortico: despite investment from Futurebuilders the organisation collapsed early in 2012. The idea still survives elsewhere as both larger and smaller CVSs, not least in rural areas, realise the value of providing such a risk-sharing service to their local third sector partners.

Meanwhile 3SC is an offshoot of Futurebuilders itself, the brainchild of Ian Charlesworth of The Social Investment Business and Richard Lichfield of Eastside Consulting. Charlesworth was previously with the Shaw Trust, the disability charity which is, by third sector standards, a highly successful bidder for public sector contracts. Before that he was both a manager providing local authority services and a commissioner of out-sourced services.

3SC intends to be a national version of Consortico. It is an independent not-for-profit company owned and run by ten constituent third sector organisations including the National Youth Agency, National Housing Federation and the Eden Project. Since 2009 it has recruited over 1,300 charity partners, initially to bid for Welfare to Work contracts, all anxious to get involved in consortia which 3SC would then manage. By this means, its employment service alone has delivered over 5,000 placements in contracts worth over £36 million.

Ultimately 3SC seeks to establish such consortia involving 10,000 service-delivering charities some of which will be capable of running regional or national contracts (Ainsworth, 2011).

So, the hub idea is catching on and the third sector is getting smart. This doesn't mean that commissioners are up against worthy opponents. Rather, commissioners and third sector contractors can in future look each other in the eye and talk the same language, to the advantage of both them and their service users.

There is no doubt that if the commissioning of services from the relatively fragmented third sector by the relatively coherent private sector becomes established then consortium hubs will need to play a major role.

PERSONALISATION

The personalisation of care services has been a real challenge to traditional providers of domiciliary social care although few doubt that tailoring provision to people's individual needs is better than the one-size-fits-all approach of the past. Nor is there doubt that in many cases the third sector is well placed to deliver: their caring voluntary ethos, infinite corporate patience and low unit cost can all contribute to efficiency. User satisfaction has risen with personalisation and there has been a widespread feeling of surprise in some quarters, relief in others, that budgets have not spiralled out of control.

Success stories are rife. They include that of the man with multiple sclerosis who was given a £14,000 service to help him dress each day when what he really wanted and got, thanks to personalisation, was a £4,500 ironing service instead. Or the man in a wheelchair who suffered from depression until he realised he could spend his new allowance on a season ticket to his local football club, which turned his life around.

Whilst there are still concerns that personalisation is but a euphemism for privatisation and cost-cutting these are abating as a body of good practice is established. Some local authorities are nearing completion of the rollout of bespoke care. Others wonder what the limits of personalisation will be – will domestic carers employed in this way find unreasonable demands are being made, such as antisocial hours, or will some disabled people simply not want to hire and fire their carers?

Any financial risk associated with lack of take-up remains the council's responsibility. They may find both that some clients don't want to change their provider (the commissioning council) and that it may be necessary to stimulate the market to ensure that a full range of personal services is available locally.

Many major charities serving the interests of people with disabilities are involved with this process which has turned, in the words of one charity leader, from a wholesale operation to a retail one. Having only just got used to selling their services en bloc to commissioners TSOs are having to work on a new front, selling to individual customers, sometimes in competition with other TSOs. This is a challenge that some have met with gusto but inevitably others are not so sure. Concerns have been expressed that personalisation opens vulnerable clients up to exploitation or that hard earned working conditions may suffer. Neither of these is inevitable and with good governance both can be avoided.[12]

A Compact for the Private Sector?

Will there be a Compact to regulate private sector relations with the third sector? Possibly, but it is neither inevitable nor imminent. Whereas the public sector seems to thrive on regulation many in the private sector abhor it, preferring the touchstone of market forces. With Government pushing hard on de-regulation to assist the third sector exploit new-found 'freedoms' the environment will not support new regulation. And whilst many umbrella bodies exist within the private sector, none could speak with sufficient authority for the sector, for Small and Medium-sized Enterprises (SMEs), foreign-based multinationals and a plethora in between, to be able to deliver either comprehensive buy-in or conscientious observance. On top of all this, although the good practice necessary to inform any such Compact does exist it does so in many different contexts and not in sufficient quantities to be regarded as normal.

In short, private-third sector relations will continue to be driven, from the private sector point of view, by a mixture of carrots and enlightened self-interest for the foreseeable future; whilst charities will continue to get what they can, where they can, through sophisticated means of persuasion and the lure of a common mission achieved.

The best chance for decency in cross-sector partnerships of this nature will come from a new atmosphere in which the triple bottom line is upheld by Corporate Social Responsibility (CSR) policies which uphold the dignity of partners.

---

12 See www.knowhownonprofit.org/funding/service/getting-ready-for-contracts/personalisation

6

Partnerships in the Developing World

The private sector represents the greatest presently unrealised potential to bring about the needed systemic change at the pace and scale demanded by the urgency of global poverty.

So says the ethical business think-tank Tomorrow's Company in their report 'Tomorrow's Force for Good' (2011).

It is generally accepted that within developing countries economic development is the key to a sustainable rise out of poverty. Thirty years ago business was regarded as contributing more to the problem of poverty than to its solution. With China and India rapidly developing 'second world' status there is a widespread belief that the new markets of the future will principally be found in Africa. As the former South African President FW de Klerk, the man who woke up to the need to end apartheid, reminded us in 2010 in a speech in London:

Africa has had a positive economic growth rate for 15 of the last 17 years – and you can blame northern bankers for the other two.[1]

Markets require consumers to have two basic qualities: purchasing power and choice. Neither of these are present in sufficient quantities in enough African countries to make the leap to sustainable prosperity; too many people there (and even more amongst the vast populations of China and India) lack both. Working markets do not guarantee the relief of poverty: many people in the world (including, in relative terms, too many in the UK) are classed as the working poor. To become sustainable there has to be access to skills and a

---

1   I heard De Klerk speaking at an event for Ma'Afrika Tikkun, the South African charity of which he and Nelson Mandela are co-patrons, 14 October 2010.

diversity of markets, both geographically and in terms of labour, goods and services, accompanied by good management and good governance.

Markets generate taxation which provides governments with the wherewithal to provide services; services stimulate greater public involvement and more pressure to adopt good governance standards. Where neither corporate nor government frameworks exist, civil society in developing countries will try to meet community needs. However, the same poverty of opportunity that is so limiting economically also restricts the power of communities to develop the capacities to meet their own needs. Civil Society Organisations (CSOs) within developing countries are as likely to be campaigning for civil liberties, striving for those fundamental rights which westerners take for granted, as on bread and butter community welfare ones.

Aid from major donors is helpful, of course; but project funding is of little value if, once the project is over, no development gains are evident. Budget support relies on host governments being both capable and clean; hence the reason why many donor governments, especially Britain, often use well-established Non-Governmental Organisations (NGOs) as their preferred means of delivering development programmes. In only one major case prior to 2010 had the UK Government funded a private sector company to deliver a development programme: the ground-breaking work of Vodafone in the mobile telephony revolution that has enabled Africa to develop sophisticated market access and financial inclusion.

The private sector can help African development in a number of ways:

1.   creation of local markets by local companies, principally Small and Medium-sized Enterprises (SMEs);

2.   local companies exploiting new trading and exporting opportunities and generating taxation revenue;

3.   multinationals operating as good corporate citizens;

4.   UK-based companies following the ISO26000 call to reinforce the Millennium Development Goals (MDG) in their supply chains.

The eight quantifiable MDGs were identified and adopted by the United Nations (UN) in 2000 as being necessary to achieve by 2015. They cover Ending poverty and hunger, Universal education, Gender equality, Child health, Maternal health, Combating disease, Environmental sustainability and Global partnership. They received a boost from promises made by world leaders at the G8 summit of 2005 at Gleneagles, the culmination of the Make Poverty History campaign.

Unfortunately, international nerves have not held, promises have not been kept and most of the world's poorest countries will fail to achieve most of the goals on schedule.[2] Most African businesses are very small, one man or one family, farmers and street traders. Many operate in the informal economy and thus cannot readily be reached through formal supply chains or partnerships. There are few major African corporations; SME and other local markets will probably fare best when other players are established and healthy.

A President of the United States has said:

> *Never before has man had such capacity to control his own environment, to end thirst and hunger, to conquer poverty and disease, to banish illiteracy and massive human misery. We have the power to make this the best generation of mankind in the history of the world or to make it the last.*

The President was John F. Kennedy, the occasion his final address to the UN in September 1963. The capacity to which he refers has proved inadequate without the means or, evidently, the will; neither his hopes nor, fortunately, his fears have come to pass. Kennedy passed legislation in 1961 to establish USAID, the American equivalent of Department for International Development (DfID), the first government agency to focus on international development in the world's poorest countries. In 1964 Britain followed suit with its Overseas Development Administration which subsequently spent several periods within the Foreign Office. Not until the creation of DfID in 1997 was International Development afforded full Cabinet status.

In the two generations since Kennedy's words several hundred UK international development charities have played their part. Over half were created in the 1990s and a quarter in the two decades before that.

---

2   The charity ONE reports (May 2011) that whilst considerable development has taken place in Africa since 2000, there was a $7 billion shortfall on commitments made at Gleneagles since 2005. Germany and France failed to meet their undertakings and Italy reduced rather than expanded its commitment. UK almost achieved its very ambitious target whilst the US, Canada and Japan met or exceeded more modest ones.

In 2005 Tony Blair set up a Commission to report on the way forward for Africa. Half its membership were current or former African statesmen plus Bob Geldof, the then Chancellor Gordon Brown, International Development Secretary Hilary Benn[3] and experts from several disciplines. The conclusions of 'Our Common Interest' were wise and practicable, an appropriate blend of optimism and disappointment. The role of business as the driver of wealth creation merited a mention principally in the context of African industry, small enterprises and infrastructure:

> ... investors, domestic or foreign, will place their money only where they feel that risks are acceptable in relation to returns. Where governance is weak, corruption is prevalent or infrastructure is poor, investors are reluctant to risk their resources. Change this, and growth will soon be underway.[4]

It called for barriers to trade to be relaxed, reporting:

> Africa has seen its share of world trade fall from six per cent in 1980 to less than two per cent in 2002. If sub-Saharan Africa could manage to increase its share of world exports by just one per cent, it would generate over US$70 billion – treble the amount it gets from all its current aid flows and nearly a quarter of its total annual income.

A follow-up report, 'Still Our Common Interest' came in September 2010, exactly five years before the MDGs fell due.[5] It allowed itself some satisfaction with progress on some counts but considerable alarm at its lack on others. As to the private sector:

> The Commission's recommendations had considerable influence. It contributed to the agreement at Gleneagles to double aid to Africa and provide 100 per cent debt relief to eligible countries. It contributed to the creation of the Investment Climate Facility for Africa, the Infrastructure Consortium for Africa and Business Action for Africa.

African development in the late twentieth century was a road paved with good intentions. Project aid from taxpayers and donors was too often spent on projects that ceased when the spending stopped. Budget support was unreliable

---

3   I was Parliamentary Private Secretary to Hilary Benn, 2003–07.
4   See http://webarchive.nationalarchives.gov.uk/20050606200944/http://www.commissionfor africa.org/english/report/thereport/english/11-03-05_cr_chapter_2.pdf
5   See www.commissionforafrica.info/2010-report

with levels of transparency and accountability too low and corruption too high. Diversity of funding was less effective than it should have been as donor countries sought often incompatible political ends and charities and foundations pursued inconsistent practical and even spiritual outcomes. Short-term thinking instilled by electoral cycles, changing leaderships, the traditional capitalist ethos and crisis management worked against sustainability. War and political instability frightened donors – let alone investors – away from many countries and it took years for UN members and agencies to start talking seriously about outcomes rather than inputs and the need to co-ordinate aid programmes.

Against this background the continent achieved an average of 6 per cent economic growth each year from 2003 to 2008. This is well above the global norm but less than the 7 per cent the World Bank estimates is required simply to stop poverty getting any worse.

Historically, land routes across Africa connect places where riches in the form of precious metals and gems, and then cash crops, were found to the nearest port. The resources may have been African but the wealth they generated most certainly was not.

The extractive industries could not choose where to situate themselves but had to literally follow seams until they found the best spot. They were amongst the first to substitute responsibility for ruthlessness as we saw in Chapter 1. Today 500 multinational companies trade in Africa and most of these acknowledge the benefits which come from sustainable growth and the emancipation of markets. They dominate the food (Nestlé, Kraft), household (Unilever), soft drink (Coca-Cola), alcohol (Diageo, SAB Miller) and telecoms (Vodafone) markets. These companies now excel in humanitarian work, something which could not be said a quarter of a century ago. But the real African economy, of family farms, small shops and manufacturers, is still underdeveloped; the streets look very similar to how they looked a quarter of a century ago, though the cars are now second-hand Toyota Landcruisers rather than unrecognisable wrecks – and mobile telephones are now ubiquitous.

Thirty eight of the 50 largest indigenous African companies are based in South Africa and ten others are on the Mediterranean coast.[6] The other two are an Angolan oil company and a Nigerian Telecoms giant.

---

6   See www.theafricareport.com/index.php/20090527617/top-500-companies/top-500-companies
     -in-africa-617.html

The secret is getting this lot to work together in a socially responsible way, to combat poverty and develop markets at one and the same time and to ensure that wealth so created is distributed in a fair way that makes a difference. Distribution is a real issue: Equatorial Guinea, for example, ranks 100 places lower on the international scale of deprivation than on the scale of wealth. Its massive oil revenues are not helping the poor whereas in Ghana and Uganda an improved economy has led directly to improved living standards.

'Still Our Common Interest' updated the figures for potential benefits of trade cited five years earlier, pointing out that 1 per cent of global trade is now worth $195 billion a year. If Africa could win an increase of this size it would be worth five times the 2010 aid budget. Many African countries today show a high percentage growth rate by world standards, albeit building on a very low base.

'Our Common Interest' says that both international and African businesses:

> ... must sign up to leading codes of good social and environmental conduct, including on corruption and transparency, and focus their efforts on co-ordinated action to tackle poverty – working in partnership with each other, with donors, with national governments, and with civil society, including trade unions. In support of this, developed countries should support the UNDP Growing Sustainable Business initiative in the region. For their part, donors and African governments must develop more effective partnerships with the private sector.

One way to make development sustainable is through third sector partnerships.

The Nestlé Story

Teaspoon was nine years old and tiny, hence her name. She was HIV positive from birth but full of life. An only child, she had never known her father and had recently lost her mother to AIDS. She was bright and dressed in a smart school uniform. 'Thank you for what the British people do for us', she said, smiling the most captivating, charming and sincere smile I had ever seen and giving each of her visitors a great hug.

This was February 2008, Soweto, South Africa, at an after school club for AIDS orphans run by the American charity, Hope Worldwide. I was there as a guest of Nestlé, the global food and nutrition company, one of the corporate sponsors of this vibrant facility which was literally bringing hope to children who had none.

The eponymous founder of Nestlé 100 years ago left the company with a logo depicting a nest which embodies care, motherhood, family, food and social responsibility. There is clear corporate pride in their record of 'Creating Shared Value' for customers, communities, staff and shareholders alike, as we saw in Chapter 3.

The company's indiscretions of a generation earlier, when the over-enthusiastic marketing of baby milk substitutes led to premature weaning in countries without clean water, have not been forgotten but they have been learned from and they are a thing of the past. For 30 years Nestlé has been amongst the most ethical producers of infant formula, still necessary given poor standards of maternal health and the risk of HIV transmission from mother to baby in much of the world. Nestlé's web site promotes breast feeding as best wherever possible; they have been a major driver of the World Health Organisation's (WHO) global standards on the marketing and use of infant formula milk.

Ninety years of Nestlé activity in South Africa, providing a wide range of affordable and wholesome foods, was celebrated in 2006 when the country's Health Minister, Geraldine Fraser-Moleketi, said:

> Nestlé has come forward to be counted among those who are part of the struggle for development, the struggle against hunger, the fight against poverty. It is a fight that needs everyone. It needs government, it needs the private sector, it needs civil society and it needs communities with empowered people.

During the week I spent with Nestlé in South Africa[7] I saw many examples of how a corporate partner can make a real and positive difference to the lives of the poorest people and the development of a disadvantaged country. This is especially pertinent where public sector services are weak, patchy or non-existent as in much of the Cape Town and Johannesburg areas that we visited.

7   My former parliamentary constituency includes Buxton. Buxton Water is one of Nestlé's best known brands. In February 2008 Nestlé invited four MPs with connections to the company to South Africa to look at their CSR activity.

The company's corporate social investment programme operates in the fields of nutrition and water, primary health care (especially AIDS), environment, early learning and vocational education and job creation.

The day we spent at Harrismith in Free State Province was particularly impressive. A few years previously, concern had been expressed at corporate HQ in Switzerland that staff training costs here were too high relative to turnover. The reasons for this were clear: young people joining the workforce at 16 or 17 years old were receiving training and work experience at a cost to the company. After a couple of years they had become more productive and less demanding of training so part of the value that they were adding to the manufacturing process was paying back the training 'debt' that they had built up. A couple of years later they had become a net asset to the company earning not just real wages but a profit for the shareholders too. And a couple of years after that there was a high chance that they would be dead from AIDS or tuberculosis so the investment cycle would have to start again.

The company decided to tackle the problem in a constructive and humanitarian way. Rather than take their investment away and reinvest in a more profitable community they decided to tackle deprivation in the early years of children's lives and promote economic emancipation, community health and employee 'wellness'.

Through investing in Project Head Start with the University of Pretoria and a CSO called the Early Childhood Development Project they help healthy and better educated infants improve their life chances and life expectancy. Through cash for the WARMTH programme elsewhere they help to promote soup kitchens as small businesses serving the young, elderly and frail and working with Soroptimists International they sponsor awards for women working to promote high standards of community nutrition. Nestlé started the Agri-BEE (Black Economic Empowerment) programme in the Harrismith area taking a microfinance-style approach to helping 140 small farmers become more diverse, productive and profitable in their operations.

We visited a woman whose farm had allowed her and her two sons to scrape a living with a dozen cows. By giving her advice and loaning her money on very reasonable terms Nestlé enabled her to have a new milking parlour, more than double her number of cows, employ an extra person and plant a field of maize to feed both her cows and her family.

Within a relatively short time the combination of measures inside the workplace and the Harrismith community paid off with a measurable increase in the life expectancy of new recruits to the workforce; and the training budget fell. The return on investment justified the diversification of funds and the shareholders were happy.

The investment in small farmers proved not entirely altruistic as Nestlé is the biggest purchaser of milk in South Africa. More productive farmers close to the factory meant more efficient logistics, more reliable supply and more cost effective collection and production. And the healthier workforce did not just live longer but were happier and more productive. To cap it all the community and civil society held the company in higher regard so levels of trust went up and, who knows, brand loyalty may well have increased.

Nestlé's practices are a fine example for others to follow and a number of lessons can be drawn:

1.   Where the public sector is absent or ineffective, the opportunity to organise pro-poor services falls on the player with the best reach and capacity to invest. Where one employer dominates a community that opportunity becomes a moral obligation.

2.   It is important for the company to know what it is capable of doing and only to do alone what it knows it can deliver alone. Where it needs help in providing a service an appropriate partner must be found. Investing in small businesses, such as the Harrismith dairy farmers or armies of self-employed ice cream salesmen elsewhere in South Africa, is something that the company can do on its own; preschool support for children is not.

3.   Where partners do not exist on the required scale they will need help developing their capacity. The company can provide help and advice.

4.   Partners should be chosen according to circumstances; the above examples include the local NGO WARMTH, the international NGO Hope Worldwide and a national affiliate of an international NGO, the Soroptimists.

5.   NGOs and shareholders of private companies have different expectations of what constitutes a return on investment, in quality, quantity and time scale, which needs to be understood by all sides.

Chairman of Nestlé, Peter Brabeck-Letmathe, is adamant that 'shared value' is the secret to triple bottom line sustainability. Speaking to Shivvy Jervis of IBLF he says:[8]

> The old corporate responsibility concept was rather defensive. You know, this 'giving back to society' implicitly means that I have taken away from society something that doesn't belong to me. I don't believe that. I think if you run the company responsibly in the long run, if you comply with the laws, if you ensure that the company is sustainable and if you create value for the society at the same time as the shareholder you don't have to give back anything, because you are creating constantly. If you make a profit part of this profit will create future actions and therefore again create value. So I think it is a much more constructive approach than corporate social responsibility.

Fortunately Nestlé is not the only corporate citizen with a good story to tell about its work in developing countries.

The International Corporate Citizen

The work of the UN and bodies like the International Labor Organisation (ILO), whilst universal in principle, relate mostly to poorer, less developed countries. The rules on child labour, for example, inherent in the social responsibility standards for supply chains embodied in ISO26000, apply across the world but compliance is an issue in Burkina Faso, not in Belgium.

There is no shortage of ways in which like-minded businesses and others with an interest in international development can come together and share good development practice but there is no obligation on them so to do. At the same time as western companies are taking a more enlightened view in Africa, Chinese investors are coming in and taking a more exploitative approach.

---

8   See http://vimeo.com/channels/iblf#21448860

A veritable alphabet soup of business organisations is involved in development: the UN's own Global Compact (UNGC, see Chapter 1), Business Call to Action (BCtA), International Business Leaders Forum (IBLF), Business Fights Poverty (BFP), Business Action on Africa (BAA) and British African Business Association (BABA) to name but a few.

THE UNITED NATIONS GLOBAL COMPACT

Three thousand businesses from over 100 different countries have signed up to the UNGC (2010) since Kofi Annan created it in 1999. In 'the world's largest voluntary corporate citizenship initiative' companies commit to business practices which 'contribute to a more stable, equitable and inclusive[9] global market and help build prosperous and thriving societies'. Its principles reflect those of the MBA Oath and the ISO26000 social responsibility standard, explicitly supporting the MDGs. The principles relate directly to existing international declarations and conventions in the fields of Human Rights, Labour, Environment and Anti-corruption:

- Businesses should support and respect the protection of internationally acclaimed human rights; and

- make sure that they are not complicit in human rights abuses.

- Businesses should uphold the freedom of association and the effective recognition of the right to collective bargaining;

- the elimination of all forms of forced and compulsory labour;

- the effective abolition of child labour; and

- the elimination of discrimination in respect of employment and occupation.

- Businesses should support a precautionary approach to environmental challenges;

- undertake initiatives to promote greater environmental responsibility; and

---

9   In this context and throughout this chapter 'inclusive' is taken to mean pro-poor. In other contexts it may mean 'cross-sector' or inclusive in an equalities sense.

- encourage the development and diffusion of environmentally friendly technologies.

- Businesses should work against corruption in all of its forms, including extortion and bribery.

The first Global Compact Leaders' Summit was in New York in 2004. At the second, in 2007, the Geneva Declaration on Corporate Responsibility was signed. Sir Mark Moody-Stuart of the mining giant Anglo American – the world's largest private purchaser of anti-retroviral drugs to fight HIV/AIDS – chaired it. The meeting was vocal in its call for action on climate change and it launched 'The CEO Water Mandate' to help companies manage this increasingly rare resource both in their businesses and their supply chains. Nestlé, Coca-Cola, SAB Miller and Levi Strauss were amongst the first signatories to this initiative.

The summit also saw the launch of the UN's Principles for Responsible Investment (UNPRI) which is discussed in Chapter 7.

Some 400 CSOs are involved in Global Compact assessment and monitoring. As the UNGC web site[10] says:

> ... civil society organisations are an important and integral part of the UN Global Compact and its goal of embedding economies with universal principles and values. Civil society organisations contribute much needed perspectives and expertise that can complement those of other participants and stakeholders.

When a company makes a declaration of support for Global Compact principles it is asked to make an annual statement on how its work is compatible with and supportive of the principles. At the tenth anniversary summit it was reported that 8,000 signatories had been acquired from 135 countries, of whom well over half were businesses and the rest NGOs and government agencies.

In 2008 it was decided that any company that was a year late in publishing its Communication on Progress should be de-listed and 951 were accordingly removed from the register in 2009. Campaign groups also target companies for de-listing, such as Petro China for alleged complicity in human rights violations in Sudan. In 2009, 127 more businesses joined the list but in February 2010 it was announced that a further 859 were being de-listed including five from

---

10 See www.unglobalcompact.org

UK. In the absence of enforcement mechanisms de-listing has strengthened the reputation of the Global Compact.

There is a UK support network of businesses for the Global Compact[11] which operates under the auspices of the IBLF. The IBLF representative Graham Baxter says in an excellent June 2010 summary of the booklet 'The Impact of UK Companies on the Millennium Development Goals':[12]

> ... *business cannot tackle these enormous challenges alone. As MDG 8 highlights, partnership is an essential part of the development process, especially if progress is to be made on the scale required to meet the MDG targets by 2015. Companies need to work together with governments and civil society to maximise the effectiveness of their combined impact.*

The publication, sponsored by the Department for Business, Innovation and Skills (BIS) is an encouraging and accessible introduction to international business/charity partnerships for anyone wishing to take their study further.

ISO26000 advocates that the MDGs should be part of community engagement and development policies within socially responsible businesses where supply chains or other activity makes this appropriate. KPMG International, led by Lord Michael Hastings, is one company which has integrated the MDGs into its existing governance and management processes already.

INTERNATIONAL BUSINESS LEADERS FORUM AND PARTNERING

The IBLF is a leading authority on cross-sector partnerships in developing countries. It is committed to a broad definition of sustainability and an inclusive or pro-poor business model not only in business operations in developing countries but also in cross- and intra-sector partnerships and broader supply chain issues. Business, they say, should be at the heart of sustainable development.

IBLF has over 100 corporate members, a roll call of the great and the good of international corporate citizenship, and an even longer list of non-corporate supporters. Within the UK these include several government and university departments, Oxfam, Volunteering England and the RBS Foundation. The

11 See www.ungc-uk.net
12 See www.iblf.org/~/media/Files/Resources/Publications/Impact_UK_companies_MDGs.ashx

international anti-corruption charity Transparency International and several umbrella groups such as Business In The Community are also on the list.

The Partnership Brokers Project started life in 1996 when IBLF co-ordinated a programme involving 100 people from six countries who focused on central and eastern Europe. In 1998 they published the first book on the subject, *Managing Partnerships* by Ros Tennyson (Tennyson, 1998), who has been associated with this work throughout and now leads the project. The work took off, especially in the extractive industries, and in 2003 the Partnership Brokers Accreditation Scheme was launched in association with the Overseas Development Institute (ODI). A further book followed, *The Brokering Guidebook – Tools for Navigating Cross Sector Partnerships*, now recognised as an authority on the subject (Tennyson, 2004). In 2010 all of the various partnership initiatives were brought together as the Partnership Brokers Project.

The initial phase was financed by British Airways, the British Council and the Mott Foundation and during the last decade the project was kept going by Microsoft, Nike, Rio Tinto and Shell. Today it is truly global in operation and largely self-funding such is the demand for its services.

Brokering is central to the success of such partnerships. Through brokering a third party can identify strategic partners using objective and informed criteria. A trained and experienced person helps design a partnership bringing together elements of the roles of planner, architect, counsellor, midwife, wet nurse and guide. IBLF identifies four key phases of partnership working: Scoping and building, Managing and maintaining, Reviewing and revising and Sustaining outcomes.

Partnerships, says IBLF, should be based on equity, transparency and mutual advantage. Business needs to be convinced of the latter as they are not at heart motivated by either philanthropy or development:

> *We are convinced that it is important that partnership means something specific and can be differentiated from other forms of cross-sector engagement and collaboration. Above all, we believe that it is important that the partners themselves in any partnership work through, agree and document a shared definition of their understanding of their partner relationship.*[13]

---

13 See http://thepartneringinitiative.org/what_is_partnering.jsp

In the first year of an intensive three-year programme the partnership brokers training programme attracted over 300 individuals from a wide variety of business, third sector, public sector and international organisations.

As an example of IBLF's work I recommend their primer on 'Investing in Women and Children's Health'[14] which makes the business case for doing just that. Essentially, the case is that such investment:

1.   reduces poverty (healthy women are more productive and earn more throughout their lives);

2.   stimulates economic productivity and growth (maternal and newborn deaths cost the world $15 billion in lost global productivity annually);

3.   is cost effective (essential health care prevents illness and disability saving billions of dollars each year in treatment costs);

4.   helps women and children realise their human rights (people are entitled to the highest attainable standard of health).

The questions a company should ask itself are:

1.   are we in a position to intervene, directly or indirectly?

2.   does the initiative involve new and/or old products, services, markets and customers?

3.   is the initiative a one-off, is it scalable or replicable?

4.   what financial incentives for investment exist?

5.   will the return on investment be measured in commercial/economic or social development terms?

6.   are the benefits to women and children's health (or another of the MDGs) measurable?

---

14 See www.iblf.org/latest-news/2010-Dec/%7E/media/3C91889BED3946519E0AB89B13DC955E.ashx

Many examples are given in the booklet of companies which have accepted the business case for investment in women's and children's health, such as:

> Johnson and Johnson: 15 million expectant mothers in six countries to receive regular text messages on pre-natal care; 200 million free doses of a drug that kills intestinal worms in children; roll-out of good practice in combating the prevention of HIV transmission from mother to foetus, total $200 million over five years.

> Body Shop: $2.25 million on a campaign with an international charity to fight sex trafficking of young people.

> Pfizer: £2 million over five years to promote infant immunisation and measures to improve the health of pregnant women.

Many of these initiatives can only be delivered on the ground through the use of cost effective, committed partners involving significant numbers of people based within the target communities: a neat description of the third sector.

The American charity Care International currently has partnerships in Africa with Cadbury's, Allianz, Barclays, Danone and the Ethical Tea Partnership. Whilst Care has a strong philosophy of working with and building up the capacity of local NGOs in developing countries there is concern that this outlook is not as widespread as it could be amongst companies and large INGOs.

The Director of Global Programmes at IBLF, Graham Baxter, is sceptical about the value of having a global ISO standard on social responsibility.[15] Essentially, he believes that without enforcement the standard will be toothless and weak with little incentive for business to comply. With enforcement it would be resented by business and give rise to a minimum response of a box-ticking rather than of a programmed nature. Far better, he says, is the IBLF way of demonstrating the business case for engagement through partnership – shared value – and lead by example. His organisation represents over 100 of the world's 80,000 multinational companies. Of course, in principle, he is right. I wish him luck.

TRADE UNIONS IN INTERNATIONAL DEVELOPMENT

Trade unions play a distinctive role in civil society both in Britain and abroad. In South Africa, COSATU has been a major player in politics over a long period.

---

15 Private conversation, March 2011.

In the UK unions have recognised that the achievement of better pay, working conditions and civil rights for working people is not confined to one country alone and is rightly the subject of global campaigns: we saw in Chapter 1 how unions were influential in establishing the Ethical Trading Initiative (ETI).

In 2007 DfID provided funding to develop education and action around the MDGs within and between trade unions. As Prospect, the white collar union, explains on its web site:[16]

> *This work is core to our union because it springs from the values of fairness and equality that underpin everything we do and we are proud that Prospect members choose to contribute to civic society, human rights at work and the United Nations Millennium Development Goals in this way.*
>
> *By engaging with business practices such as corporate responsibility, sustainable development, supply chains and charitable works the Prospect Development Advocates have, via bargaining agendas, brought about change that alleviates extreme poverty and addresses global workplace injustice.*

As far as taking up the MDGs as an achievable campaign within its members' workplaces is concerned, no union has done more than Prospect. The union voted at its 2006 conference to raise the profile of the MDGs amongst its members. Its subsequent 'Think Global, Act Union' campaign on reducing global poverty, achieving trade justice and promoting labour standards received some DfID funding via the Trade Union Congress's (TUC) Bargaining for International Development (BID) programme. Their excellent *Negotiator's Guide to CSR* (Prospect, 2008) is a handbook on how MDG principles can be incorporated into workplace activity. The union has also published a report on its BID activity with impressive stories of how employees in the UK have made a real difference, usually with their employers's support, to the lives of people in developing countries.

Clare Hawkes, an inspector with the Health and Safety Executive (HSE) and a Prospect member travelled to Honduras to participate in a conference organised by War on Want and a local women's collective. She met women who were suffering from physical disability caused by 'abysmal' working conditions. Amongst other outcomes Clare's visit led to greater awareness

---

16 See www.prospect.org.uk/campaigns_and_events/international/key_issues/index?_ts=1

amongst union members and HSE staff of sweatshop conditions in developing countries and work with HSE itself to use both procurement policies and its own expertise to improve the lives of women workers in the developing world.

OTHER INTERNATIONAL INITIATIVES

The IBLF was one of the founders, along with British Prime Minister Gordon Brown, of the BCtA in May 2008. Presidents Kagame of Rwanda and Kufuor of Ghana attended the launch. BCtA challenges companies to develop innovative business models that achieve commercial success as well as pro-poor development outcomes. Housed within the UN Development Programme (UNDP) in New York, BCtA provides a way for companies to share the skills, tools and resources required to capture development results and report annually.

The Cadbury Cocoa Partnership,[17] a £45 million investment in Ghanaian cocoa which we met in Chapter 2, was launched under the BCtA by one of its founding members. Over a five-year period this investment in people, communities, co-operatives and new cocoa trees is expected to generate new revenue of up to $350 million by doubling cocoa yield and quadrupling fair trade cocoa yield. Ten thousand farmers in 100 communities and 55,000 people in the Kuapa Kokoo farmers' co-operative are already benefitting; Care, World Vision, Voluntary Services Overseas (VSO) and local NGOs are amongst partners also seeing improved outcomes to their work through the partnership.

Other BCtA initiatives include M-PESA, the Vodafone mobile telephone money transfer scheme pioneered in Kenya, through which 10 per cent of the country's financial transactions now pass; Anglo American's undertaking to develop 12 hubs of local economic development in South Africa, based around its own enterprises; Coca-Cola's franchising of distribution networks in Africa; Diageo's investment in sustainable sorghum in Cameroon and SAB Miller's similar operation with barley in India.

In 2011 DfID launched its Business Innovation Facility (BIF) in line with the new Government's conviction that the development of local markets was the most sustainable way of generating wealth and alleviating poverty. BIF is managed by a partnership involving DfID, IBLF, Price Waterhouse Coopers and Accenture Development Partnership (ADP).

---

17 See www.businesscalltoaction.org/wp-content/files_mf/1286825168BCtACadburyCocoaPartn ershipCaseStudy.10.10.2010ForWeb.pdf

BIF identifies projects which are 'pro-poor', whether employees, suppliers, distributors, consumers or potential consumers. The project could be a small business or social enterprise in a developing country that needs help in growing to scale, accessing new markets or making its product more accessible; or a UK company with an innovative idea involving its supply chain. Proposals should be climate-friendly and unlikely to receive investment from traditional sources. BIF is currently a three-year pilot in Nigeria, Zambia, Malawi, India and Bangladesh. Although it does not provide investment funding BIF can point projects in the right direction having counselled, advised and coached them about their plans.

BFP and BAA are initiatives which stem from the Africa Commission's initial report. BAA has over 100 members, largely corporates but also government agencies, foundations and academic, umbrella and trade bodies as well as a handful of charities such as Comic Relief and Traidcraft. BAA trades as a not-for-profit organisation advocating pro-poor policies and business engagement in Africa as well as facilitating business to business partnerships.

BFP is an online community of almost 8,000 business people and other interested groups which shares ideas about how business can fight poverty in developing countries. It acts as a clearing house for events and ideas with occasional conferences of its own.

In 2009 the ODI proposed a 'Good for Development' label[18] which would recognise companies whose activities supported the aims of the MDGs, going beyond simply 'fair trade' although it has not yet seen the light of day.

BABA is a small grouping focused on SMEs and African diaspora businesses in Britain. They look for business opportunities in Africa, sharing leads and experiences.

AFRICAN NON-GOVERNMENTAL ORGANISATIONS IN PARTNERSHIP

AMREF, the African Medical and Research Foundation, was founded by three British physicians in 1957 as the East Africa Flying Doctor service. Today it is a charity providing health services across Southern and Eastern Africa. Based in Nairobi, its principal purpose is to make primary health care readily available to more communities. It is also a major recipient of money from the Global

---

18   See www.makingitmagazine.net/?p=1609 [and] www.odi.org.uk/resources/details.asp?id=3296 &title=good-development

Fund to fight HIV/AIDS and malaria in Kenya. Mobilisation in support of this cause involves working with local CSOs.

Katine in Uganda is one of the poorest communities in Africa. From 2007–10 AMREF carried out intensive development work there thanks to £310,000 raised by readers of *The Guardian* and *The Observer* and Barclays Bank. The rest of a £2.3 million pot was divided between water, education, livelihoods and governance.

In July 2009 Andrew Whitty, CEO of the pharmacy giant GSK visited the area. GSK's web site records his reactions to the paucity of health provision there:[19]

> *One of the things you will find in countries like Uganda is big warehouses full of medicines at the port and nothing on the shelves in places like Katine – and that's one of the things I think we could put our minds to.*

Since Whitty saw the situation in Kenya and Uganda GSK has raised the profile of neglected diseases in the pharmaceutical community and proposed pooling patents to make drugs more widely available. GSK has cut the price of medicines in 49 of the least developed countries by up to 75 per cent which also protects their patents against cheap copies. They have reinvested 20 per cent of GSK's profits in those countries into health care infrastructure and created new initiatives on HIV, education and children's medicines. GSK has also launched a £50,000 challenge fund which goes directly to AMREF. Whitty says:

> *Progress is being made but it's only going to continue being made if people like GSK people and GSK as a company continue to be restless about what more we can achieve.*

He goes on to say:

> *As CEO I want this company to be a very successful drug company but not by leaving the population of Africa behind. We need to be a very successful drug company worldwide and be partners with the people of Africa and the people who help the people of Africa like AMREF.*

On the distribution front GSK is working with Unicef, the Gates Foundation, Global Alliance for Vaccination and Immunisation (GAVI) and others on a pilot

---

19 See www.gsk.com/community/Andrew-Witty-Africa.htm

roll-out for their malaria vaccination programme through NGOs which has already involved almost 20,000 children. In June 2011 GSK announced a 95 per cent reduction in the price of their anti-diarrhoea vaccine. Witty's call for other pharmacists to do likewise made *The Times* newspaper's front page lead; diarrhoea is the second biggest killer of children under five years old in developing countries.

THE GLOBAL COMPANY

'Tomorrow's Global Company' was published by the think tank Tomorrow's Company in 2007.[20] It called, in general terms, for companies to break down barriers, espouse values and create frameworks which would enable business to become a true global citizen and fulfil its potential. Becoming an active global citizen, they argue, was not a choice business had to make but was essential for its very survival.

Sir Mark Moody-Stuart, Chairman of Anglo American, said:

> *Global businesses, operating in a market system, can be a tremendous force for good in the world – so long as the market is shaped and regulated in the right way. So it's up to us to work with governments, NGOs, academic experts and others to make sure we work within a system that delivers progress and helps to resolve the world's most difficult issues.*

Revisiting the report in 2011 Tomorrow's Company goes further: developing countries will not progress until collaborative cross-sector working becomes the norm, they say. Companies operating in the poorest states should not be thinking:

> *Here is a social problem which is in my company's interest to see resolved; which partners are available to do the necessary work together?*

But:

> *our partners are all around us. We will work together to prioritise what needs doing in our community in order to generate both the dignity of development and the opportunities of the market.*

Partnership, they will argue, should be the norm. Without the power of business the poorest will stay poor and markets will continue to function inadequately;

---

20 See www.tomorrowscompany.com/uploads/TGCpress180607.pdf

with the power of business harnessed to social progress not only will poorer countries develop but every community will thrive and the planet's future will be secured. Charities and NGOs are the vehicles through which that can happen.

One company that has taken the global citizen message to heart is the Virgin Group. Those 12 companies, some national, some international are operationally independent. Although all are forward- and outward-looking businesses in their own right and advocates of the triple bottom line a thirteenth organisation, Virgin Unite, provides all of them with an active, lively and global social responsibility programme covering UK, USA, Canada, Australia, South Africa, Nigeria and Kenya.

Virgin Unite has no commercial purpose or function. It describes itself as the glue that holds the Virgin Group's Corporate Social Responsibility (CSR) programme together, consulting, facilitating and engaging the other partners and enabling them to share best practice. The Virgin Group pays all Unite's administrative costs so that funds from the Virgin Foundation or Sir Richard Branson's own resources, or raised by or from 50,000 Virgin employees and other individuals and businesses, go directly to good causes. Unite's thesis echoes that of Tomorrow's Company:

> We unite people to tackle tough social and environmental problems with an entrepreneurial approach. Our aim is to help revolutionise the way businesses and the social sector work together – driving business as a force for good. This is based on the belief that this is the only way we can address the scale and urgency of the challenges facing the world today.[21]

In the UK alone 25 charity partners nominated by Virgin employees receive funding from people and activities in Unite's name, mostly working with children.

Their four global projects are:

The Elders: ten (former) world statesmen including Desmond Tutu, Kofi Annan, Gro Harlem Bruntland, Mary Robinson and Jimmy Carter working together on peace building, recovery from conflict, health and gender issues.

---

21 See www.virginunite.com/Templates/AboutVirginUnite.aspx?country=United+Kingdom&ni
d=96e9b78a-cc3b-4c6e-b4e4-bc0ba18184c1

The Carbon War Room: promoting entrepreneurial solutions to global warming.

The Branson Centre for Entrepreneurship: training, coaching, mentoring, supporting and financing young entrepreneurs in South Africa.

Bhubezi Community Health Centre, South Africa: a public–private–third sector enterprise providing health care especially around HIV/AIDS.

Each company in the Group and each country has its own causes as well. Virgin Unite works with them to devise strategies including partner selection and help them manage their campaigns. Participants can apply for a week's experience volunteering for 'Pride 'n' Purpose' in a South African village on Branson's own game reserve. In 2010 Virgin sponsored the London Marathon for the first time, when over 100 staff, including Sir Richard himself, ran to raise money for Mission:Possible, Virgin Unite's programme with charity partners to support disadvantaged young people in Britain.

Virgin combines success with social responsibility in a serious way.

AN INTERNATIONAL NON-GOVERNMENTAL ORGANISATION: CHRISTIAN AID

Despite being a major and respected name on the international development scene Christian Aid has few very large businesses on their list of corporate partners; until as recently as five years ago the organisation kept its distance from them. EMI is now there, as is Yell.com and the ubiquitous Co-operative Bank; others, like Christian Technology, Ecotricity and The Good Little Company are less well known. Traidcraft and Divine Chocolate are also there, lining up alongside insurance companies specialising in church property. The 15 corporate partners largely fund the charity through commission on product sales (including sausages), pro bono work and special events around Christian Aid Week rather than through complex common strategies.

Christian Aid is the development agency of 41 Christian churches in the UK and Ireland. Despite high levels of recognition for Christian Aid the organisation's branding is not a major focus either for most of its corporate partners or the local NGOs through which they work exclusively in developing countries. It is recognised that in non-Christian countries the brand could reduce their potential to deliver their development outcomes effectively.

Another International Non-Governmental Organisation (INGO), Oxfam, is discussed in Chapter 7.

OTHER PLAYERS

Many individuals set up charities for micro-causes for which they are passionate, having witnessed the need for development aid at first hand. Lisa Ashton visited Johannesburg in 2004 to make a film for the BBC. She met an elderly woman called Winnie Mabaso, who cooked meals for 1,700 children each week, many of whom were orphans. Winnie also volunteered to look after bed-ridden children in a suburb riddled by HIV/AIDS. Lisa promised to help by raising money in Britain. Within a year an orphanage had been built. Although Winnie died in 2007 the Zenzele Day Care Centre and Orphanage thrive, whilst very dependent on Lisa and her team. Meanwhile Lisa has established links between her local primary school and their opposite numbers in Zenzele.

In 2008, when MP for High Peak, I organised an Africa Day to celebrate not just the work of Lisa, one of my constituents, but of other small charities in the constituency and the excellent work being done on African development in primary and secondary schools locally. The Co-op donated fair trade refreshments, DfID gave us leaflets and information and an African drumming band brought entertainment. We had 300 visitors in three hours.

Every town and village, it seems, contains activists who seize upon something they have seen on holiday, on television or perhaps through their faith group. Setting up a charity with trustees, a web site, a bank account and a purpose is not difficult: keeping it going can be a real test. 'My village would be very pleased to be twinned with a British village', a Palestinian woman once told me. 'But if it's going to peter out inside two years, forget it'.

Few of these micro-charities enjoy business sponsorship or support; either because the business considered them too small or too insufficiently strategic or (perhaps more likely) because they weren't asked.

Conclusion

Just as we share our communities in the UK as individual, collective and corporate citizens, so we share our world.

The power of business to bring about change is huge but largely untested. With half of the world's biggest economies being corporate entities and not national ones, the potential for using that power for good is awe-inspiring. Charities and NGOs are the medium through which that good can be created.

This is not true for international companies alone: ISO26000, which we met in Chapter 3, calls upon all businesses to integrate the MDGs into their supply chain management systems and this must happen for development to be sustainable.

I am not calling for businesses to run countries. Government accountability through the ballot box is in the interests of both business and communities. But poorer countries tend to have weaker democracies and so external benevolence – not altruism – has a place. The third sector has the experience and expertise to be partners in delivering development outcomes, as governments already appreciate. They contribute subtleties and nuances that commercially-orientated souls may not possess and, harnessed to the economic power that business can bring or lend, they should be invincible. In building capacities in local NGOs we are building capacities in the people of developing countries themselves.

Call it social responsibility, enlightened self-interest, what you will, development is good for business and business is good for development.

7

Partnerships and Challenges in the Big Society

Whatever it is, the Big Society is here to stay. It has actually been with us a long time already. It is not the only factor that will influence cross-sector relations in the future but it is an important one, especially as there is an assumption that the corporate citizen should have parallel roles and responsibilities to those of other players within that Big Society.

> *If I had a plan, it would be the wrong plan.*

These were the words of Francis Maude, the Cabinet Office Minister responsible for the Office of Civil Society (OCS), describing the Big Society to a fringe meeting at the Conservative Party Conference in Birmingham in October 2010 (Wiggins, 2010). 'The Big Society', he went on, 'will look a bit chaotic and disorderly'.

On 12 January 2011 he told BBC Radio 4's PM programme:

> *It [Big Society] won't be uniform, it won't be perfect, it won't be tidy and there will be gaps.*

This was not the reassurance that the voluntary sector wanted to hear. Years of growth, optimism, relative financial security and the nearest thing to political certainty for the sector had come juddering to a halt as the Coalition Government made reducing the deficit generated by the global financial crisis its over-riding and urgent priority. Within weeks of the May 2010 general election it became clear that there would be big public spending cuts at national and local level from 2011 which would inevitably be concentrated on discretionary (non-statutory) spending. This was the very spending which provided much of the

£13 billion the sector received from the taxpayer each year through grants and increasingly through the contractual procurement of services.

The galling thing to many was that this same Government was looking to the third sector, rebranded 'civil society' overnight, to help get the country through its difficulties and out into an era of small government, personal emancipation, community empowerment, motherhood and apple pie.

'No one ordains what will happen in a capitalist economy', Maude continued. 'The same should happen in the Big Society'.

The David Cameron vision of the Big Society had emerged very late in the day, shortly before the election, as the 'big idea' that would shape the social policy of the Government that he was then offering to Britain's electors. Few outside those close to the future Prime Minister could define exactly what the Big Society was for some months. Even by October, Francis Maude's explanation was hardly the epitome of clarity.

Asked whether he meant that capitalist principles should underpin the provision of public services, Maude said:

> We won't just do nothing if 100 flowers don't bloom in 100 places. The 100 flowers will bloom, but we'll have to do some gardening and sow some seeds. It won't be universal.

This vaguely Maoist approach does not find favour with Jesse Norman, a Conservative MP first elected in May 2010, who had previously written a book called *The Big Society*. It described a vision subtly different from the Cabinet Office line (Norman, 2010), continuing themes Norman had developed in his previous works *Compassionate Conservatism* and *Compassionate Economics*.

Whilst Norman should be praised for rejecting both right wing libertarianism and traditional Tory paternalism, by accepting that there is an emancipatory role for the state to play in society, he shows little grasp of how the Big Society might function in practice. He talks of 'untapped capacity' within individuals without evidence that it exists or giving proper weight to collective actions, other than co-operatives which he claims are essentially conservative in origin. Most co-operators I know would argue that employee power, holding bosses to account and collective decision-making are left-leaning.

His portrayal of Labour as universally statist Fabians ignores the blending of traditions that New Labour intended to achieve. In a brief passage on practical actions in his final pages he overlooks the fact that many of the legislative tools that will support the Big Society, like community ownership of assets, owe their legislative origins to Hazel Blears and Ruth Kelly.

Jesse Norman's book is helpful in setting an intellectual and philosophical framework for the Big Society and calling for open minds on all sides in establishing a new settlement between state, individual and society.

In January 2011, about a year after it burst onto the political agenda, a YouGov poll[1] found that 63 per cent of British people did not know what 'Big Society' meant, 68 per cent thought it would not work and 59 per cent described it as either 'hot air' or cover for the Government's policy of public spending cuts. Eight per cent thought they did know what it was and 11 per cent thought it was practicable. Delving further, however, 46 per cent agreed with diverting power away from central government and towards local communities.

Three out of every five people who worked in the third sector or local government also denied having a good knowledge of what the Big Society was[2] although a similar proportion were prepared to accept that it might be a 'good thing'. 'More social action amongst citizens' was the only quality of the Big Society that over half those surveyed could identify and there was cynicism amongst the qualitative responses. A majority believed that it could not deliver better outcomes for society at lower cost; only one in six thought that it could.

Both voluntary groups and councils saw public spending cuts as the greatest barrier to achieving the Big Society (64 and 53 per cent respectively) whilst lack of agreement between (potential) partners, lack of appetite in communities and lack of capacity in the voluntary sector and smaller councils were all regarded as significant barriers.

In another poll, by Ipsos-MORI for the Hansard Society in March 2011, over half felt that 'getting involved' in their local community could make a difference, yet only one in ten were intending to do so (over and above the one in seven who said they were already involved). A third said they were

---

1   See http://today.yougov.co.uk/politics/Brits-baffled-by-Big-Society
2   See www.thirdsector.co.uk/news/archive/1035159/big-society-Well-go-it/?DCMP=ILC-
     SEARCH

'unenthusiastic' and a quarter 'alienated' by the 'Big Society mood'.[3] The Hansard Society also reveals that a major hurdle that the Big Society needs to cross to achieve acceptance is its association with one political party.[4]

In Sunderland, the Governance Foundation interviewed 1,200 people on a social housing estate. One in six said that they were not properly involved in the running of the estate but only one in 14 wanted to be more involved. One in 20 said they wanted to be consulted better but only five of the 1,200 individuals wanted the chance to be on the housing management board (Middleton, 2010). By comparing this run down estate with others, they found a direct correlation: the wealthier the neighbourhood, the greater the desire to be personally involved in running it.

So What is the Big Society?

It is not fair to describe the Big Society as completely featureless and vague. Nor, it transpires, will it 'take power away from politicians and give it to people', which is how the 10 Downing Street web site's first bite at the Big Society cherry described it in May 2010.[5] Strategists soon realised that any process which set out to deliberately keep MPs and councillors 'out of the loop' would alienate them and create battles best avoided, not least with some senior figures on the Government's own back benches.

Pat Samuel CBE is, like me, a former schoolteacher. But she became better known as the passionate and authoritative Deputy Director for Public Services at the (now) OCS before retiring. Speaking to an Inside Government conference in January 2011 she outlined the clearest vision I had yet heard of what the Big Society would actually look like.[6]

She described it as having three pillars: public sector reform, community empowerment and social action. Each would be supported by a raft of policies of which many had already been launched. As we are all, as corporates, charities and individuals, part of the Big Society that Government is trying to create it is worth looking in some detail at the pillars and what they contain.

---

3   See www.bbc.co.uk/news/uk-politics-12900961
4   See http://hansardsociety.org.uk/blogs/parliament_and_government/archive/2011/03/30/audit
     -of-political-engagement-8.aspx
5   See www.number10.gov.uk/news/topstorynews/2010/05/big-society-50248
6   See www.insidegovernment.co.uk/other/voluntary-sector/presentations/patsamuel.pdf

BIG SOCIETY PILLAR 1: PUBLIC SECTOR REFORM

At the heart of modernising public services was the 2010 Green Paper on Modernising Commissioning. A curiously bland White Paper followed in July 2011, 'Open Public Services', several months late and generally agreed to lack the momentum and incisiveness of its predecessor. The new approach was built on the assumption that any public service could be run better if outsourced to the right provider – whether private or voluntary sector – or even to a body which used to live elsewhere in the public sector.

Much was made of the Right to Provide which would essentially give public sector workers the right to say, 'We could provide our service in a better/ more client-focused/more cost effective manner if we set up a co-op and ran it ourselves'. It was in the best tradition of the old 'management buy-out' and a repudiation of the Aunt Sally that the man in Whitehall always knows best; and it was pioneered by Patricia Hewitt when Health Secretary up to 2007. However, such a challenge would only trigger a full tendering process so no 'Right to Provide' was actually guaranteed.

There are two interesting aspects to the policy: the Prime Minister has revealed a passion for co-operatives and mutuals which had hitherto been hidden and the Right to Provide already exists.

Employee takeovers have a proud history. Oldham Community Leisure is a trade union initiative created in 2002, when privatisation loomed, under the 1965 Industrial and Provident Societies Act; it has been a great success. Today it manages 14 facilities (sports centres, pools, pitches and a golf course) and has a £6 million turnover. The authority's leisure services subsidy has fallen from 60p in the pound to 30p whilst the number of employees has risen from 160 to 240. Mutualisation has brought reduced bureaucracy, faster decision-making, greater staff involvement, fewer disputes (only one employment tribunal in eight years) and a halving of absenteeism.[7]

Public sector reform in the Big Society would also include the ongoing National Training Programme for Commissioners (see Chapter 5) and Conservative backbencher Chris White's Public Services (Social Enterprise and Social Value) Bill. Under the Bill every successful tender for a public sector contract, from whatever sector, would have to demonstrate a positive social

---

7   See http://opmblog.co.uk/2010/11/12/employee-ownership-in-practice-oldham-community-
     leisure/

outcome. The Bill would require every local authority entering into a public procurement contract to consider economic, social and environmental well-being during the pre-procurement stage and consult accordingly.

Grateful for cross-party support, in his second reading speech[8] White thanked Labour's former Communities Secretary, Hazel Blears, for her encouragement. He went on to point out:

> *Sandwell Community Caring Trust ... started by taking over adult social care homes in the black country. It took over the failing homes, reformed the institutional structures, re-motivated staff and reinvested in buildings and equipment. It has driven down the cost of adult social care and kept people in the local community in work, and it has now won a contract to provide NHS and social services in Torbay. It is an excellent employer that is well supported by the communities it serves. In short, it is a fantastic example of what this sector can achieve, and it throws down a gauntlet to the rest of the country, even areas close to home, to follow its example.*

Sandwell Community Caring Trust was voted the second best public or third sector organisation to work for in the *Sunday Times* top 100 in 2011 and the eleventh best overall.

Although the Big Society thus brings little new to the field of public sector reform it encourages those who know public services well and are prepared to think out of the box to take risks in delivering them.

BIG SOCIETY PILLAR 2: COMMUNITY EMPOWERMENT

The Localism Bill, Pat Samuel argued, embodied the pillar of community empowerment. Most people would agree that councils should be more responsive to community need, more transparent, more accountable and less bureaucratic. There are contradictions inherent in the Bill such as reducing planning restrictions whilst giving communities more power to block unpopular planning applications; and requiring councils to get more information out to the public whilst stopping them from publishing in-house newspapers. Even the 'community right to challenge' in the Bill is but an extension of the 'community call to action' in Labour's last Local Government Act. The new right obliges

---

8   See www.publications.parliament.uk/pa/cm201011/cmhansrd/cm101119/debtext/101119-000
    1.htm#10111964000001

councils to consider bids from non-profits (including other councils) to run their services subject to approval by referendum – which could increase bureaucracy rather than reduce it.

The right of communities to buy threatened local assets and manage them independently is not new: the Labour Government introduced specific powers to subject both community halls and pubs to this right and funding was available to help the process along. A right in principle is not the same as an opportunity in practice as no new money is provided in the Bill to further this aim.

Indeed, funding is the elephant in the Big Society room. New Philanthropy Capital and Association of Chief Executives of Voluntary Organisations (ACEVO) estimate that the amount of money flowing into the third sector will fall by between £3–5 billion during 2011–14. Even if this were a gross overestimate, the Cabinet Office's £100 million emergency transition fund (generously appended by £7 million from the Department of Health) is a sticking plaster for the Titanic.

Local Strategic Partnerships (LSP), bringing together key players in all three sectors to co-ordinate local regeneration, were introduced in 2000. A few years later I overheard two councillors chatting. One said, 'Who do they think they are, these voluntary sector people? On our LSP they think they know everything. Don't they realise that we are elected and they're not?' The other replied, 'Oh, we don't have that problem. We don't have the voluntary sector on our LSP'. Some of the most successful LSPs have had 'voluntary sector people' in influential positions, even chairing them.

Councillors are the medium through which 'localism' has always been assumed to work. They are elected to represent the needs of their communities and be their advocates; a conscientious councillor appreciates that sub-communities make different and sometimes conflicting demands. He also knows that individuals have needs and that the ability to smooth the access to a responsive and caring service manager is one of his most valuable tools. Good councillors who listen as well as talk can be found in every political party and in every type of community.

Other councillors also exist: those that resent any voice in their community that is not their own; those that sit back on big majorities seemingly without the need to work for their voters' confidence, believing that democracy happens once every four years and not 24 hours per day; those that see themselves as providers and not facilitators. They can be found in every party, too.

The third strand of the community empowerment pillar is community budgeting. This recognises the considerable progress that conscientious local authorities have made in engaging people in budget-making over recent years. John Major had a useful philosophy called subsidiarity, the taking of all decisions in government at the lowest appropriate level. Subsidiarity in the twenty-first century includes giving local authorities a power of general competence,[9] allocating budgets to wards or communities and consulting on priorities at that level. 'Open Public Services' describes the strata of service provision as individual, neighbourhood and commissioned. This approach ought to reflect the best of Total Place, which broke down government silos to see how spending from different departments within a locality could be better integrated in terms of both cost and outcomes. Total Place was a very late Labour initiative and one of their best kept secrets, unfortunately.

My experience of such consultations is that they are useful even if the outcome is simply a better public understanding of what constrains councils in terms of policy and budgets, and even if the 'public' consists of a handful of activists of various hues plus the odd professional pedant. A problem shared is, after all, a problem halved and a rapidly contracting budget brings problems aplenty.

We will shortly see how two councils addressed these challenges.

BIG SOCIETY PILLAR 3: SOCIAL ACTION

The Big Society has been parodied as 'Why are you asking us to provide services? That's what we elected you to do!' Yet there is a long and noble tradition of social action in Britain: by some measures our volunteering rates are amongst the highest in the world and our voluntary organisations are impressive by international standards. One school of thought says that social action is hindered and held back by the state which is why we need to roll it back. Sweden, a country with even more of a welfare state mentality than Britain, has a small and immature third sector. This suggests that precisely the opposite has happened in UK – the state and the sector have actually stimulated each other.

---

9   'General competence' means that they can take action on any issue except those specifically excluded from their competence, rather than only on those specifically included.

Giving is often cited as the hallmark of a civilised society and the Giving White Paper[10] contains some good ideas. All are carrots rather than sticks and that is the way it should be: all voluntary action, the giving of time, money, goods and skills, must be without obligation other than that which is taken on voluntarily. Modest sums of money will be available to promote voluntary sector infrastructure, volunteering and philanthropy; from 2012 you can make a charitable donation from your local ATM. Blue Dot, a sort of Nectar point system for volunteering has been launched to encourage the donation of time. Missing from the White Paper is any push to explain to people why they might want to give in the first place.

With this welcome emphasis on the giving of time and money it is a pity that the 2011 Budget, which was heralded as reforming charity taxation, was not so encouraging.

We saw in Chapter 2 how Gift Aid works and how charities lost £100 million each year from April 2011 when three years of protecting Gift Aid against the impact of the 2008 penny fall in basic rate income tax ran out. In the 2011 Budget Chancellor Osborne made great play of having acceded to charities' requests on Gift Aid reform by allowing it to be claimed on certain anonymous donations. Any charity that had already been claiming Gift Aid for at least three years (why three years?) could henceforward claim the income tax back on the first £5,000 of cumulative income from collecting boxes and other anonymous sources. It would be officially assumed that this money had been donated by taxpayers.

The very smallest charities, which don't get £5,000 from any source let alone collection boxes, will not be able to claim the £5,000 back in full.

In order to promote giving by dead philanthropists, anyone who gave 10 per cent of their estate to charity could claim a reduction of 10 per cent on their inheritance tax payment. Only 3 per cent of estates pay inheritance tax and this reduction will be of little benefit in many of those cases. If it were attractive it could have the negative effect of encouraging people to delay making charitable donations until they die and thus reducing current funding to charities.

These measures, the Chancellor assured us on Budget day, would generate £540 million for the sector. Two-thirds of charity people taking part in an online poll for *Third Sector* magazine were sceptical even before, several days later, the Treasury added the rider 'between 2012 and 2016'.

---

10   See www.cabinetoffice.gov.uk/sites/default/files/resources/giving-white-paper.pdf [May 2011].

The National Citizens Service and Community Organisers initiatives have been no less controversial. Over recent years the young people's organisation v has done a good job in placing co-ordinators in local authority areas and recruiting young people to volunteer; in my own former constituency over 200 young people were recruited in the first year of the 'v-inspired' scheme.

V-Talent was also organised by v from 2009 with public money. Some 843 volunteers aged 16–25 took part. Over half were unemployed when they started a 30 hours per week, 44-week programme of volunteering and training with younger people outside school. In a not dissimilar scheme the City Year charity placed six teams of ten selected young people into London primary schools to provide one-to-one support for needy children and after school activities. Much of the funding for this comes from corporate sponsors like National Grid and Timberland, who also provide them with distinctive red and khaki uniforms as they do in USA where City Year started. v was one of City Year's initial funders.

Yet v's programme has been decimated as the Cabinet Office chopped their funding in 2010–11. During the impasse between this spending cut and the arrival of 'community organisers' on our streets great experience has been lost. v, along with 11 other partners such as the Prince's Trust, Catch 22 and the Football League, managed to get funding for a share of the National Citizen Service pilot in 2011 although the Prince's Trust subsequently withdrew from the 2012 round.

If social action is about volunteering then public funding for training volunteer managers – as essential for volunteers in the workplace as anywhere else – should not have been cut back and the pilot Access to Volunteering schemes, designed to help people with disabilities to volunteer, should not have been terminated.

A report on that two-year trial in three English regions was published by Fresh Minds, an independent consultancy engaged for that purpose, in spring 2011. It concluded that the fund had been cost effective and successful in raising the number of disabled volunteers (especially 'first timers') and had the makings of being sustainable. It had failed to attract the very smallest charities or widen the diversity of organisations utilising disabled volunteers (Fresh Minds, 2011). Although commissioned by Government the report is not on the Cabinet Office web site. In June 2011 the 'Access to Volunteering Fund' link from the Cabinet Office web site reported 'Server not found'.

THREATS AND OPPORTUNITIES

Falling public spending is not the background against which Big Society is being launched – it is very much at centre stage. Yet the drop in cash is not the greatest challenge Big Society faces; after all, funding levels to the third sector could be described as being taken back to where they were just half a dozen years ago. The greatest challenge will be the impact on the capacity of the voluntary sector to function where the local authority infrastructure framework has been taken away.

Purist Big Society advocates misunderstand the threats that the process contains, though they are right about the opportunities. They forget that the most disadvantaged communities with the greatest needs are also usually those with the least capacity – in terms of skills, cash, opportunity – to deliver the services they need for themselves: survey after survey reinforces this theme.[11] They also forget that local authorities are responsible for making sure services are delivered everywhere and that the third sector, because of its essentially informal nature, cannot deliver universal coverage by itself. Local authorities are essential partners in providing the hooks upon which third sector services hang; one of the saddest statistics as the tsunami of spending cuts hits councils is the fact that many third sector service providers no longer know who is responsible for their services because the commissioner is no longer in post.

Many critics of the Big Society misunderstand the opportunities that the process contains, though they are right about the threats. They see it as merely a cover for cuts and privatisation. That may indeed be an element in the thinking of some of our political leaders even if the wish to see wartime levels of good neighbourliness, pulling together and digging for victory is otherwise sincere.

However, you don't have to be a cynic to question the speed at which things are happening. Social enterprises and mutualisation both need time to come together, obtain working capital and build a business plan and time is simply not available. Cuts in services linked to opportunities for new providers are happening now; a 12-month delay in launching a new enterprise will see the window closed and an existing provider, probably from the well-financed private sector, stepping in.

---

11 This example reveals that young parents in social classes ABC1, and who tend to vote Liberal Democrat, are the people most likely to volunteer. See http://hansardsociety.org.uk/blogs/parliament_and_government/archive/2011/03/30/audit-of-political-engagement-8.aspx

The Big Society will have been seen to have failed and the private sector will take the low hanging and ripest fruit. A different type of cynic, found on the benches behind the Prime Minister in the Commons, will not be disappointed.

The Big Society in Lambeth and Suffolk

Two local authorities pre-empted the Big Society agenda by planning from 2009 how they were going to cope with the predicted funding downturn whilst maximising the engagement of their communities. The London Borough of Lambeth and Suffolk County Council could not have chosen two more different philosophies if they had sat down together and designed it that way; yet coming from different ends of the political spectrum the measures they proposed were remarkably similar.

Lambeth's 'Co-operative Council' is the brainchild of their Labour Leader, Steve Reed. The praying in aid of the Co-operative movement is no accident: Reed sees mutuals, with their origins in local communities or the council's own workforce, playing a major role in delivering future local services. But despite having to make cuts twice as deep as anticipated, he is not dumping the problem in the lap of local residents and walking away; far from it. Lambeth has approved a three-year programme of capacity-building linked to a pragmatic assessment of which services can be most readily devolved, with youth services and services for older and disabled people leading the way; and a greater say for services users in how they are run.[12]

Councillor Reed describes the process:[13]

> *The commissioning of public services currently provided by Lambeth Council needs to become a process where council staff and citizens co-operate together. This would mean that they work together to identify a problem, design a range of services that will tackle that problem and then commission the right organisation to provide these services, including the provision of appropriate support to help build community reliance.*

The process has three phases: one in which 'early adopters' are identified and incentivised and mutual and similar schemes are evaluated. In the second,

---

12 See www.lambeth.gov.uk/cooperativecouncil
13 Quoted in the Council's newspaper, *Lambeth Life*, February 2011.

more services will enter the fray and, in phase three, consideration will be given to larger scale takeover of services (such as council housing) by mutual trusts. Throughout the process the council will monitor and evaluate progress, learn lessons and plan further devolution.

Crucially, as part of the preparation for introducing the Co-operative Council model, Councillor Reed not only has his own Labour councillors on board but has political buy-in from other members of the council, too and more than a dozen other councils are thinking along the same lines.

In the 1980s I was represented in Parliament by Nicholas Ridley. He held several Cabinet posts and was renowned for his right wing, free market views. 'How many of your drivers own their own buses?' he was reputed to have asked the manager of a northern metropolitan bus service in the days before privatisation. His ministerial vision of local government was that councillors should meet once a year to hand out contracts to run the services and would have little other reason to exist.

Ridley's spirit appears to live on in Suffolk.[14] Although the County Council has denied adopting the 'Ridley model' they have been depicted as the 'Everything must go!' council.[15] Chief Executive Andrea Hill argued, not unreasonably, that 'salami-slicing' cuts create instability, insecurity and inability to plan for the future; hence her choice of radical front-loaded measures, such as the idea of letting the whole education department (two-thirds of the County Council's staff) be taken over by an in-house trust.

At a consultation event Conservative Leader of the Council Jeremy Pembroke was asked what mandate he had for the euphemistic process of 'divestment':

> *We are actually facing a gap of between £110m and £125m. We have a statutory duty, but much more importantly we have a moral duty, to look after the most vulnerable in our community and at the same time raise educational standards. That was the mandate. To keep to that pledge, we have to do things differently, because we don't have the money to go on with the traditional way of doing it. So, I believe the*

---

14 Suffolk is the seventeenth best public sector employer according to the *Sunday Times* top 100 companies list 2010.

15 The Leader and the Chief Executive were answering questions from the public at an event in November 2010. This was fully reported on the Council's web site at the time but is no longer available.

New Strategic Direction is the way we are best equipped to stick to that
mandate.

Divestment was not the same thing as outsourcing, Councillor Pembroke
subsequently told *C'llr*, the magazine of the Local Government Information
Unit (LGIU) (Pembroke, 2010). Rather it was:

> ... *creating a mixed economy of local service providers that are more*
> *flexible, more local and easier for customers to understand. It's a*
> *different model of delivering our services, working with town and*
> *parish councils, social enterprises, voluntary groups, mutualised staff*
> *buyouts, arms length bodies, trusts and other organisations to find the*
> *best way of delivering services.*

It sounds like outsourcing to me. The former Labour Leader of the Council
Bryony Rudkin, speaking at the 2010 Labour Party conference, called Suffolk's
plans, 'A circus act with no safety net'.

Councillor Pembroke then resigned, citing the need for new leadership to
prepare the county for the 2013 election. Two senior officials resigned on the
same day although any connection between the departures was denied. A few
weeks later, in May 2011, the controversial Andrea Hill (at £218,000 the second
highest paid Council Executive in the country)[16] was invited to stay at home
indefinitely on full pay as further plans for divestment were withdrawn; she
resigned a few weeks later.[17]

Suffolk listed the six outcomes it was seeking from its divestment process:
reducing overheads, changing the council's role from being provider to being
a community leader and advocate; more localised and joined up services; a
balance of responsibility between council, communities and the independent
and private sectors; unlocking staff creativity; and empowering service users.

I doubt whether Lambeth would demur from the content of this list although
the order of priorities would be different, perhaps even reversed. Suffolk wants
to outsource services quickly to a variety of competent providers to save a
third of its budget; Lambeth wants to empower communities and individuals

---

16 *The Sunday Telegraph*, reported at www.localgov.co.uk/index.cfm?method=news.detail&
    id=71708
17 See www.bbc.co.uk/news/uk-politics-13638495

through capacity-building measures, with a presumption against private sector takeover, in order to provide better services, phased in over a period.

A Role in Big Society for the Private Sector?

Jesse Norman's book is silent on the role of the private sector in the Big Society, with two exceptions: he says that the bailed-out banks should give to charity out of gratitude for being bailed out and that top slicing the annual fees paid to Private Finance Initiative (PFI) contractors could save half a billion pounds a year. That may be true, but why stop there?

Other than the occasional 'nudge' and promises to do more to encourage corporate citizenship the Big Society has so far been a closed book for companies.

Until now, perhaps. In May 2011 the promised Business Connector programme was announced. These are individuals seconded from the private sector to be ambassadors for corporate citizenry. In 19 pilot schemes running in 2011–12 their role is loosely defined, as *Retail Gazette* explained when reporting Sainsbury's early enthusiasm for lending staff to the scheme:

> The role will evolve as key stakeholders identify what works best, but they will ultimately promote and facilitate long-term, strategic partnerships between the commercial and voluntary communities.[18]

Any philosophy, Big or otherwise, that believes that society can function effectively with only the state and the citizen as partners is failing to see the big picture. In the same way as aid is but a small fraction of the wealth that exists even in the poorest countries, so taxation just scratches the surface of the wealth that is tied up in private and corporate Britain. The trick is to mobilise that wealth through carrots rather than sticks: Big Society may provide several ways to do this, by introducing a wider and deeper culture of corporate engagement and by encouraging greater investment in those companies, especially social enterprises, that bring about social change.

The private sector brings jobs to society. With employment comes purpose, self-fulfilment, skills, income, comradeship, a sense of the future, providing for the family, even happiness.

---

18 See www.retailgazette.co.uk/articles/33332-sainsburys-to-create-business-connector-jobs

Ed Davey, the then Business Minister, told the Associate Parliamentary Group on CSR in early 2011 that he wanted business to reduce carbon emissions, to care for the environment, promote skills, relate to communities, enhance the quality of life and support Small and Medium-sized Enterprises (SMEs) through the supply chain. Many leading businesses, as we have seen, already regard that agenda as a minimum.

Responsible employers value security and commitment in their workforce, treat them as a precious asset, recognise and celebrate their rights, share their successes and minimise their environmental impact.

Investment is usually seen as a way of making money by making money work. If you change the nature of the risk that money takes you change the nature of its impact. As we shall see, there is evidence that even here in the heart of what makes capitalism capitalism, attitudes may be starting to change with the evolution of a new breed of social investors prepared to earn less from their money in return for making the world a slightly better place.

True corporate citizens regard the traditional approach as a bare minimum and argue the business case for social responsibility and corporate citizenship. Yet there is not yet a robust framework to support such behaviour, no authoritative body of cross-sector good practice from which all can learn nor cohesive academic authentication of what is being done.

Twenty-first Century Partnerships

Throughout this book the reader will have come across examples of modern and innovative partnerships between companies and charities. Yet companies engaging in long-term, strategic, dynamic and effective partnerships and charities abandoning prejudices, creating capacity and making full, long-term and strategic commitments to a business partner are still rare.

One reason for this scarcity is that of over a million registered companies in Britain:[19]

- just 850 are members of Business in the Community (BITC);[20]

---

19 2.16 million businesses of which 56 per cent are companies, according to ONS in 2008, others are sole traders.
20 BITC's 850 members employ a quarter of Britain's private sector workforce.

- fewer than 100 are in the Corporate Responsibility Group;

- 100 are in the International Business Leaders Forum (IBLF);

- 120 in the London Benchmarking Group (LBG); and

- 600 are in Directory of Social Change's (DSC) Guide to Company Giving (Lillya, 2011).

On the other hand, CAF has given advice to 3,000 businesses. Many companies are members of several of these lists and larger companies dominate all of the groups. Most of this advice is on payroll giving or tax implications although Charities Aid Foundation (CAF) is developing a wider brief on corporate citizenship consultancy.

LBG exists to improve, share and evaluate the corporate community involvement of its members, which is effectively the community involvement strand of ISO26000. Although it ought to be possible to measure cash inputs easily, questions arise which need to have agreed and consistent forms of answer:

- Do cash contributions list overseas and UK contributions separately?

- When does a cash donation count? When it is given by the company to an in-house foundation or trust this year or when it is dispersed to the community next year?

- Should pro bono work such as a lawyer might give be assessed at its commercial rate per hour or at cost?

- Should donations in kind be costed at replacement value, catalogue value, market value, scrap value, second-hand value or at cost?

- Is there a simple way of measuring the value of employee volunteering time other than taking every person's pay into account individually?

LBG calculates the value of pro bono professional work as the market rate minus the profit element; the value of other volunteering is the full salary cost (not just pay) of the employees involved divided by their full time equivalent number. Charitable cash donations should be counted when they are spent and not when they are transferred from company to in-house foundation. By this measure the number one company on DSC's big donors list, BHP Billiton, might not have appeared in 2010s top 20 donors.

LBG's 2011 annual report states that its 120 members donated £1.4 billion-worth of benefit to the community in 2010, of which 57 per cent was cash whilst the share of in-kind donations was up from 19 per cent (in 2008 and 2009) to 31 per cent. Health (39 per cent of the total) was the biggest area of gifts in kind, particularly influenced by high-value donations by pharmaceutical companies, several of whom have recently joined the group. Education and young people each attracted 21 per cent. Donations were equally divided between UK and abroad. 350,000 employees contributed 2.9 million hours of volunteering and only about 1 per cent of the cash; customers and the general public each contributed about three times as much cash as employees.

Like for like, these figures indicate a 4 per cent rise in LBG members' contributions, exceeding the contribution target of 1 per cent of pre-tax profit for the first time since 2006. Falling profits may have exaggerated this figure.

This pattern may look different to that found by DSC (see Chapter 5) in that their expected switch from cash to kind was not apparent whereas here it was. The reason? LBG members use an established, agreed and therefore reliable mode of reporting whilst DSC's larger number of sources are inconsistent in their reporting behaviour.

FTSE4Good and the Dow Jones Sustainability Index are other measures of corporate environmental and social sustainability, designed to help investors identify good corporate citizens amongst those quoted on the stock exchange.

CORPORATE REPORTING

Under the 2006 Companies Act businesses must report on environmental and social aspects of their work. Friends of the Earth, the Trade Justice Movement and the Corporate Responsibility Coalition campaigned to achieve this and yet there is still no statutory or even recommended form in which the data should be classified and presented. This absence of official guidance makes it impossible to get an accurate picture of who is doing what relative to whom.

It is not much to ask that the same expectation of consistency and relevance should apply to the social and environmental aspects of the triple bottom line as applies to the financial one. Again, Tomorrow's Company and others support the Global Reporting Initiative[21] or GRI, an international campaign to achieve consistency on triple bottom line reporting. On the GRI web site comprehensive coverage of the recently released G3.1 guidelines can be found, including copious examples of sector-specific issues.

As Tomorrow's Company's report 'Tomorrow's Corporate Reporting'[22] states:

> *The purpose of corporate reporting is to assist in the effective functioning of the market economy by enabling shareholders, investors and other stakeholders to assess the overall performance of a business and establish its present and future value. In addition, the dynamic of the corporate reporting system in part determines the ability of regulators, auditors and other parties to provide the necessary checks and balances over the business ecosystem needed to ensure its health and sustainability.*

This is no less true of social and environmental impact reporting than of basic financial reporting.

Let us look in detail at one umbrella organisation, one charity and one company who are at the cutting edge of corporate citizenship: BITC, Oxfam and Aviva.

BUSINESS IN THE COMMUNITY

BITC[23] is one of a suite of charities established by the Prince of Wales to foster community values following the alarming riots of Brixton and Toxteth in 1981. It is chaired by Mark Price of Waitrose who recently succeeded Sir Stuart Rose, under whose leadership Marks & Spencer became one of our most effective corporate citizens.

There is a strong business case for corporate citizenship and community engagement, BITC argues, as their 'people and planet' tag line echoes the triple bottom line. Sustainability is not just an environmental concept, they

---

21 See www.globalreporting.org
22 See http://tomorrowscorporatereporting.com/
23 See www.bitc.org.uk

say, although that poses challenges enough; it requires business models and practices which are supportive of communities whilst globalisation demands that business manages the world's depleting resources sustainably.

Launching BITC's Visioning the Future – Transforming Business campaign in March 2011, Kingfisher plc's CEO Ian Cheshire said:

> *The changes we are likely to see to our society and environment over the next two decades and beyond will require a paradigm shift in the economy and society. The companies that recognise and plan for it now will be the winners of the future. We need to think now about how business services will evolve in the next two decades and beyond. The opportunities are real for those who help create a sustainable future.*

On the *Guardian*'s Professional Network web site a few days later, Cheshire called – in *The Guardian*'s words – for a 'radical reappraisal of capitalism':

> *The wellbeing challenge also forces us to think about our total impact as a business rather than the narrow shareholder value lens, since businesses that do not create broader social value will again not survive the longer term.*

Extolling Kingfisher's leading example on environmental matters, such as B&Q now only selling certified sustainable timber, he concluded:

> *Along with the wellbeing of our customers and colleagues, communities will be central to our future.*

Amen to that.

BITC works on many fronts. The CommunityMark standard recognises companies which:

- identify pressing social issues relevant to local communities and their businesses;

- work in partnership with communities;

- properly plan and manage community investment;

- inspire and engage stakeholders;

- measure and evaluate outcomes and strive for improvement.

The benefits of being recognised as a CommunityMark company are claimed to be exactly those of corporate engagement with communities generally and the standard is respected as 'robust' by practitioners. The group which drew up its demanding criteria included LBG, National Council for Voluntary Organisations (NCVO), CAF, OTS (now OCS) and Volunteering England. The CommunityMark was launched in 2007 with 20 applicants acknowledged as compliant in year one and over 40 today; every award is re-checked 15 months after being made. The CommunityMark can be achieved by companies of any size. The five principles are recognised as the best practice framework to aide companies in further development of their strategic community investment.

For a wider audience a Community Footprint Tool is in preparation to help companies understand, manage and measure local socio-economic impacts, both positive and negative; in terms of employment, supply chain, location, community investment and products and services.

BITC works on two fronts to help make employee volunteering culturally normal: Cares and ProHelp. Cares is a suite of employee volunteering opportunities centred around economic renewal and engagement with schools or people facing multiple barriers to employment. Its activities in 35 locations have so far involved 350 companies.

ProHelp, which involves 400 professional firms, offered over £1.3 million-worth of pro bono advice and support to 600 community groups in 2010. ProHelp includes surveyors, architects, consulting engineers, accountants, solicitors, managers, marketing and design agencies. BITC also runs the only national day for employee volunteering in which teams of company volunteers (not just BITC members) undertake one-off community-based projects. These are often then followed up with more sustained activity. Even though the 205 employers involved in 2009 were clearly well disposed towards volunteering before engaging in 'Give & Gain Day' the level of support, engagement and impact was impressive with 40 per cent of the 4,300 volunteers doing so for the first time. In 2011, the Day saw over 24,000 volunteers around the world volunteering which equates to almost £3 million of support. In the UK alone 8,451 volunteers impacted on the lives of more than 273,332 people within communities most in need. Outside 'Give & Gain' patterns of employee volunteering vary significantly.

BITC is clearly committed to delving ever deeper into the potential that corporate engagement in communities offers. It is a coalition of the willing, many of whom are large enough to have their own chains or national networks and to make significant community impacts themselves. The organisation is led by 24 'premier members', half of whom are also members of the Corporate Responsibility Group, a parallel good practice umbrella body, 19 are members of the LBG and a third are clients of Pilotlight. Only four of the group are in the top 25 corporate donors to charity in cash terms although ten are in the top 25 for non-cash donations in 2010 as listed by the Directory of Social Change (Lillya, 2011). One member of the group, HMRC, is from the public sector. The 24 are clearly exemplars of business being positively engaged in the community.

The challenge to BITC and corporate citizens generally is to spread their wings and get their message more widely heard and acted upon. Hopefully BITC's new Community Footprint tool will support this push as it is inexpensive to use, reflective rather than preaching, contains an implicit business case for engagement and is clearly in line with the political priorities of the day.

Another challenge BITC faces is how to record and encourage the achievements of organisations that consistently score over 95 per cent on their Corporate Responsibility Index, as National Grid has done for eight consecutive years. The answer has been to create a Platinum Plus category of achiever.

National Grid's activity deserves a book of its own. Whilst it concentrates on key areas of its commercial mission for much of its community focus – energy, the environment, safer homes, education and skills – its other activities are manifold. They include sponsorship of the Special Olympics, matched funding of employee fundraising, employee-led community grants, literacy, a sponsored Cub Scout badge (on home and gas safety) and the City Year scheme. National Grid is one of Stonewall's 'Top 100' employers for gay and lesbian equality at work. Their partnerships with charities are long term: they regard the 'Charity of the Year' approach as ineffective.

National Grid's takeover of an American company with a culture of volunteering and an established charitable foundation has helped it develop its positive ethos. Enthusiastic buy-in from senior management and direct reporting of its Corporate Social Responsibility (CSR) activity into the Chief Executive also help and commercial benefits from Corporate Responsibility activity are acknowledged. One challenge it faces is that its level of employee volunteering is higher in its office-based staff than in its peripatetic workforce, though new volunteering experiences through a partnership working with young people through the Ellen MacArthur Foundation may address this.

OXFAM

No charity can quite rival Oxfam when it comes to engagement with business in Britain. Their highly profitable and mutually advantageous partnership with Marks & Spencer's customers has been described elsewhere (Chapter 4) yet it is but the tip of the iceberg. As their web site says:

> ... *whether you're a smaller company wanting to support a specific project, or a larger company looking for a more strategic relationship, we can arrange a suitable partnership for you.*

Oxfam UK is one of 14 bearing the name around the world working with 17 million poor people in over 60 countries. Oxfam UK is by far the largest partner in this international organisation, the first among equals, but although their willingness to embrace business is supported by Oxfam USA it has not been universally welcomed in the family. In many countries traditional scepticism of corporate motives still pervades. A story which explains how Oxfam UK's anti-corporate complacency of the past started to melt has become part of the organisation's folklore. Apparently their leaders were stunned into silence at a private meeting with the directors of a large company with whom they had previously clashed: 'This is a new problem we face', explained the directors. 'We wanted to know how you would handle it'.

Out in the developing world, Oxfam then realised, who were their clients? They were small farmers: SMEs, the private sector.

What were they doing with them? They were trying to help them grow to scale and farm more efficiently – to gain market access both locally and more widely, the very philosophical territory which the private sector inhabits.

And where will the international private sector find its markets of the future, create most jobs and still add value to its products? In developing countries.

On the ground not all programme managers are as pragmatic as their national leaders in their home country. The lead director for Africa for an international manufacturing company told me that Oxfam's leadership talked a very good talk when discussing partnerships in Africa, but on the ground 'they don't want to know us'. That meant there was no co-operation. He named another UK-based development charity as being 'even worse' which explained why his company's blossoming African partnerships were with local, American or United Nations (UN) organisations.

Having different attitudes to engagement with the private sector by different Oxfam national groups operating within a single developing country may appear perverse though their UK leadership has been working on a positive strategy of local private sector engagement in host countries for some time.

Oxfam's UK income alone in 2010 was approaching £318 million,[24] up 9.7 per cent on the previous year despite the global recession. Direct fundraising accounted for £222 million, mostly from regular donations by individuals rather than corporates, and the cost of undertaking fundraising was significantly down.

Oxfam UK takes a practical but sophisticated approach to dealing with partners, not simply as sources of funding but as potential allies in working for the world's poorest; they will not be bought off from the policies they choose to pursue:

> Oxfam works in partnership with companies that show a commitment to developing policies, strategies and practices that work in favour of poor people where we are convinced that this relationship will deliver real and lasting benefits. Oxfam's partnerships are not an endorsement of a company. They are based on mutual respect and transparency, and Oxfam's right to question and criticise.[25]

That right to question and criticise extends to filtering potential partners so that arms, tobacco and other potentially controversial applicants will not be chosen, though fewer questions are asked of one-off, no strings donations. Although the granting of partnership status is not an endorsement of a business it is clear that in partnering Marks & Spencer, which has a policy of ethical sourcing of

---

24 See www.oxfam.org.uk/resources/downloads/reports/report_accounts09_10.pdf
25 See www.oxfam.org.uk/resources/issues/privatesector/corporate_engagement.html

clothing, the charity is expressing a preference over other clothing retailers whose supply chains may not be as transparent.

Oxfam 365 is an alliance of companies and other donors on alert for emergencies throughout the globe. It maintains experts and warehouses in a state of alert for earthquakes, tsunamis, drought and other humanitarian catastrophes. In return for corporate donations there is a comprehensive offer:

> *Oxfam 365 partners receive the highest level of brand association and relationship management from Oxfam. We will also provide you with a bespoke communication plan so you can let staff, clients and suppliers know about your partnership with Oxfam.*

With 800,000 registered UK supporters and 750 shops in UK as well as an incredible 99 per cent brand recognition Oxfam is a valuable partner for any business, with something concrete to offer to any relationship in terms of reputation, access to markets and a workforce 'feel good factor'.

In April 2011 the Oxfam web site listed over 20 corporate partners, including several whose names crop up regularly in such contexts: Aviva, Marks & Spencer, Pizza Express, Vodafone, Accenture, Taylors of Harrogate and the Co-operative Group, from whom a top slice on their branded credit card contributes nearly half a million pounds a year. Some partners arrange for Oxfam people to educate their employees about development issues.

AVIVA

To say that Aviva, the insurance giant, has a comprehensive approach to social responsibility is a gross understatement. The strategy covers five headings: Trust and integrity, Climate change and environment, Financial capability, Attracting and retaining talent and Developing communities.[26]

Its main community engagement element is a partnership called Street to School which stands out from the crowd for a number of reasons:

- it is a long-term commitment of five years;

- it is ambitious, aiming to help 500,000 street children engage in education or training in 28 countries;

---

26 See www.aviva.com/reports/cr10/overview/cr-strategy/

- it is big, accounting for at least half of the company's £11.4 million community investment budget;

- UK employee volunteers work with vulnerable children after Aviva has paid for any vetting by the Criminal Records Bureau;

- it will expand to involve customers and supply chain partners;

- by focusing on children it supports this insurer's purpose of protecting families;

- 29 per cent of employees use payroll giving (a staggering figure) largely to the UK partner, Railway Children;

- the UK charity partner is not a well-known brand;

- it has different delivery partners in different parts of the world including Save the Children in several developing countries.

In 2010, the first full year of Street to School, 128,000 children were helped by the charity partners with Aviva money. Three-quarters of them are now accessing education or training where they were not doing so previously.

Aviva claims to be the first company to ask its shareholders to approve its CR report alongside its more conventional annual report. Their staff surveys confirm that employees believe that it is sincere and genuine in its commitment.

Every year in Britain 100,000 children run away from home; three in ten are under 12 years old and one in six sleeps rough. Across the globe trafficking of children, exploitation for sexual or employment reasons and family breakdown are rife. Even though Tanzania has not had a war since the Second World War it has five million orphans. 11 million children live on the streets in India.

Hearing that there are only five designated refuge beds available for homeless runaway children in Britain stimulated Aviva to form its partnership with Railway Children. As the charity says of its partner on its own web site:

> Their customers buy insurance, savings and investments to look after themselves and their families. But sadly, many street children have no-one to protect and care for them.

Together the partnership provides immediate support for young runaways; preventative education programmes in schools and colleges, sometimes delivered by Aviva employees; education outreach in partnership with local authorities; fundraising, volunteering and campaigning support.

This is a holistic, values-driven, engaged, long-term and appropriate partnership of the very best kind with definable inputs, outputs and outcomes.

Business/Charity Partnerships in the Big Society

Many of the partnerships we have considered point to a positive future for co-working on a shared value agenda. Remember:

- one-third of the turnover of award-winning charity READ International is donations in kind;

- Serco and Turning Point will be running a prison together;

- Marks & Spencer and Oxfam are ubiquitous partners of many (and of each other).

But we have also seen that a tiny fraction of companies have signed up to alliances and organisations that see community engagement as a necessary or essential element of their corporate being – and that most smaller ones, who make up the vast majority of employers, are still on the starting blocks.

Within the large ones there is little coherence as to which department should take the lead. Although the best have an organisational arrangement which works, the lack of a common approach makes sharing and learning difficult outside groups like BITC, LBG and CRG – and outside those groups is where most companies are.

We have heard warm words from the Government about the role of business in the Big Society; of cross-sector partnerships being the future as non-traditional providers are invited into local authority networks to do what they do best. And yet those networks are suffering from severe cutbacks and warm words are diluted by tepid actions. Who would have thought that when the Department for Work and Pensions (DWP) announced time and again that the third sector would benefit from great opportunities provided by its welfare to work contracts the sector would win so few prime contractor roles?

Of 40 outcomes announced by DWP in April 2011 just one prime contract went to a third sector provider. Bidders included experienced contractors like Groundwork, Business Trust for Conservation Volunteers (BTCV) and the Shaw Trust. The successful third sector bid was from the Careers Development Group, a new self-styled Big Society initiative in the South East involving a former chair of Volunteering England. This together with one other contract where an Irish charity partnered a private company cannot justify the DWP press office claim that the outcome is a 'Massive boost for the Big Society'. 36 of the 40 contracts went to big corporates.

Writing in *The Guardian*, Patrick Butler revealed that 289 charities were named as subcontractors in the supply chains for the above contracts (Butler, 2011). At the same time, he reported, the Centre for Economic and Social Inclusion had surveyed 217 charities with experience of subcontracting: over half said they had been offered take-it-or-leave-it deals by potential prime contractor partners. One in eight felt they had been forced to sign up to 'unreasonable' deals. Just over half described the deals as 'the best we could get', 'unreasonable' or 'very negative' and most unsuccessful bidders felt that the future of their organisation was threatened as a result.

Sir Stephen Bubb, the outspoken Chief Executive of ACEVO, is normally up for a gamble on the Big Society but he described the outcome of DWP's process as 'disappointing'. Merlin will have to weave much magic if this situation is to lead to sustainable outcomes for unemployed people and the charities that work with them.

One private sector group whose contribution to third sector partnerships and good causes we have not so far considered is investors.

CONSCIENCE MONEY: ETHICAL AND SOCIAL INVESTMENT

Many conscientious people taking out life assurance or a private pension in recent years will have considered an 'ethical' policy. These come in different shapes and sizes but generally they avoid investing in the arms trade, tobacco or products tested on animals. Others will avoid politically sensitive markets such as Burma for fear of appearing to prop up a military regime. These are all causes upon which charities and third sector bodies campaign. The size of this market has grown in recent years but it is still small and it is generally populated by smaller investors.

In 2005 the UN invited the world's largest institutional investors to develop a code entitled 'Principles of Responsible Investment (UNPRI)'.[27] The group of 20 bodies has since grown to 800 investment community members from 45 countries. Of the 227 asset owners who have signed up the majority are public sector pension funds although they include foundations such as the Joseph Rowntree Trust, a trade union pension fund (Unison) and the investment body of the Church of England.[28] Around 60 UK asset managers and 25 other professional partners provide PRI-compatible investment products and services.

The six Principles of Responsible Investment (PRI) refer to environmental, social and (corporate) governance (ESG) issues, a measure reminiscent of the GRI and of ISO26000 itself. They are:

- we will incorporate ESG issues into investment analysis and decision-making processes;

- we will be active owners and incorporate ESG issues into our ownership policies and practices;

- we will seek appropriate disclosure on ESG issues by the entities in which we invest;

- we will promote acceptance and implementation of the Principles within the investment industry;

- we will work together to enhance our effectiveness in implementing the Principles;

- we will each report on our activities and progress towards implementing the Principles.

The Principles are not enforceable but aspirational, work in progress, a direction to head in rather than a checklist with which to comply. The minimum requirement to remain a signatory is participation in an annual survey to demonstrate continued improvement.

---

27 See www.unpri.org/
28 The Church of England reported a high (15 per cent) return on its ethical investments in 2011.

Eight hundred signatories may not sound a lot; but in the year up to summer 2010 the list grew by more than 30 per cent and the total assets represented by the membership, at $22 trillion, is a tenth of the world's capital markets. In that same period just two organisations were de-listed for non-compliance and a further eight left the register voluntarily.[29]

If UNPRI represents a passive approach of voluntary compliance then Bridges Ventures is at the cutting edge of socially responsible investment (SRI). Bridges Ventures was set up in 2002 by the Egyptian-born entrepreneur Sir Ronald Cohen to invest in deprived areas of Britain. It applies a 'social screen' to all investments from a particular venture capital fund, requiring three-quarters of its value to be invested in the most deprived 25 per cent of council wards in the UK or to produce 'strong educational, healthcare or environmental benefits' for a local community.

Multimillionaire Cohen chaired Gordon Brown's Social Investment Task Force from 2000. A Labour Party donor, the father of 'venture philanthropy' was recruited by the Coalition Government to advise on the operation of its Big Society Bank (now renamed Big Society Capital for legal reasons) and is its first chairman.

Social Investment is defined as that which accepts a rate of return (including sometimes nil) that is lower than the market might otherwise provide, in return for effecting a social change. I am a social investor: I hold shares in Torrs Hydro, a community hydropower project in Derbyshire, from which I receive no return except for the warm knowledge that if it was not for us few hundred souls the project would not now be producing zero carbon electricity for the local Co-op store and the national grid.

But we are small fry. Proper social investors these days are venture capitalists with a conscience, investing where commercial investors fear to tread as returns might be both delayed and reduced compared to a commercial investment. The reduced financial return is justified by the creation of a desirable social change.

Social enterprises, the hybrids which range from businesses with a charitable purpose to charities with a business method, are the natural home for such investments and seen by many as the big growth area of the future for both the

---

29   See www.unpri.org/files/2010_Report-on-progress-press-release.pdf

economy and for Big Society. The Social Investment Consultancy reports (2011) that the market in investment in social enterprises in Britain is currently just £190 million, a drop in the ocean compared to charitable income. However, the global market is expected to reach £300 billion in the next decade, with much of that growth being in Africa. Perhaps Social Investment could provide a home for the millions of pounds of assets of foundations and charities who are not currently using them to the full?

Two-thirds of all UK investments in social enterprise are under £5,000 – again, not really venture capitalist territory. The constitutions of very few social enterprises offer the investor an equity share. There are more than a dozen social investment funds which operate in the zone above £100,000 with a handful of UK funders in the £1 million to £10 million bracket: Social Finance, Bridges Ventures (two funds), the Social Investment Business (three funds), the Charity Bank and the Dutch Triodos Bank.

The non-executive board of Social Finance reads like a Who's Who of the banking and charity worlds: the organisation's role since 2007 has been to develop a market for Social Impact Bonds (SIB) (see below), a task on which they are working alongside the Big Lottery Fund and others.

In February 2011 National Endowment for Science, Technology and the Arts (NESTA) reported that one in three social enterprises were under five years old, that two in five were dependent upon government directly or indirectly for over half of their income and that the average social enterprise had a turnover of just £175,000 per year (NESTA/Young Foundation, 2011).

Even though advice is available to those contemplating establishing employee mutuals as social enterprises, such as from Social Enterprise London's 'Transitions' guide, there is not yet a sound basis upon which to build a new social architecture on the scale required in response to either the positive stimulus of the Big Society nor the negative and urgent one of 'the cuts'.

INPUTS, OUTPUTS, OUTCOMES AND IMPACTS

Wherever investment is involved you can be sure that someone will be there measuring something. Inputs, outputs, outcomes and impacts are essential ways of demonstrating that an intervention works and is therefore worthwhile; but counting is not always easy.

Companies that count everything on their balance sheets for their shareholders are often lax when it comes to demonstrating their engagement with communities: NatWest's high-profile advertising campaign of 2010–11 trumpeted: 'We will give 15,000 days of employee volunteering time to local communities'. This is a measure of input: it tells you nothing about what will change in those communities as a result of this intervention – if anything.

If 'six employees spent a day volunteering' is a measure of input then so is 'six cans of paint'. The output might be: 'They painted the interior walls of the Youth Centre'. The outcome might be: 'The atmosphere became less stressful and people took a greater pride in their meeting place'. And the long-term impact caused at least in part by this process might be: 'Crime levels in the community fell and people lived together more harmoniously'.

If only it were so simple! Inputs are the easiest to measure, outputs can be readily observed and often measured. Outcomes are less tangible but directly related to outputs whilst impacts are complex, very rarely the result of a single intervention. They represent the ultimate goal, the aspiration which prompted the input, and it will often be difficult to explain exactly how any particular outcome has contributed. As impacts are of strategic importance their management is traditionally the remit of those who are publicly accountable for their actions: government.

Not all outcomes are positive. Negative outcomes may be caused by a known or unknown risk going bad; a particular positive outcome might not have been expected due to low or incomplete expectations – or serendipity.

Every organisation involved in social change – charity, voluntary organisation, social enterprise, government agency or conscientious corporate citizen – should know what it is doing in its community and why, as well as how effective it is being. Anything less than this is irresponsible and cannot lead to things being done better.

Difficulties in measurement are well understood and proxy assessments are often used. Asking a group of disaffected young people how they felt in terms of confidence and capability before a day of organised white water rafting and comparing it to how they felt immediately afterwards, and again three months later, will give an indication of direction of travel but it will not produce objective data. An outcome of 'six in ten said the experience improved their self-belief on the day and three months later two in ten said it had had a lasting effect' may be sufficient to justify repeating the exercise.

'Investment in social change' in terms of cash, hours, gifts in kind and skills given voluntarily by members of the public or employees is nonetheless investment. But if it does not produce a net positive change or at least counter a net negative trend then it is not worth doing.

I recall a local charity which used to work on behalf of a council, delivering meals to housebound people. When the authority said, 'We have found a more efficient way of delivering the meals. We'd like you to provide a befriending service instead' the volunteers said 'no'. 'We deliver meals, that's what we do'. Another charity was soon found, which was just as well; a charity whose outcomes were measured in acres of tin foil and gallons of shepherd's pie would likely not have the same social impact as one which measured them in smiles per hour.

The American giant, Walmart, has had a change of heart on sustainability recently. A Norwegian pension fund withdrew its investment from them in protest at the absence of a code of conduct for a sustainable supply chain. Walmart developed one, the investment returned and the company hasn't looked back. Traditionally conservative institutional investors must realise that they have the power to bring about positive social change.

The Labour Government introduced Community Investment Tax Relief (CITR). This encourages investment in disadvantaged communities by giving back a quarter of the value of the investment over five years to investors who back businesses and other enterprises in those areas through investment in accredited Community Development Finance Institutions (CDFIs). Although an independent review on simplifying taxation recommended its abolition in the 2011 Budget George Osborne decided to keep CITR and promote it. So far it has been worth over £60 million to the CDFIs.

SOCIAL RETURN ON INVESTMENT (SROI)

The Cabinet Office together with the National Programme for Third Sector Commissioning has produced guidance on the thorny question of 'Social Return on Investment' (SROI).[30] The basic principles of SROI are suggested to be:

---

30 For example, see www.neweconomics.org/sites/neweconomics.org/files/A_guide_to_Social_Return_on_Investment_1.pdf [2009 guide].

1. Involve stakeholders: Inform what gets measured and how it is measured and valued by involving relevant stakeholders, especially people directly affected.

2. Understand what changes: Describe how change is created and evaluate this through evidence gathered, recognising positive and negative changes as well as those that are intended and unintended.

3. Value the things that matter: Use financial proxies to recognise the value of outcomes. Many outcomes are not traded in markets and as a result their value is not recognised.

4. Only include what is material: Decide what information and evidence must be included to give a true and fair picture, so that stakeholders can draw reasonable conclusions about impact.

5. Do not over-claim: Only claim the value that organisations are responsible for creating.

6. Be transparent: Demonstrate the basis on which the analysis may be considered accurate and honest and show that it will be reported to and discussed with stakeholders.

7. Verify the result: It is important to consider appropriate independent assurance of the process in order to be able to present findings that decision-makers will find credible.

This approach has informed that of the LBG in advocating a common approach to measuring community engagement by business.

SROI can therefore be seen as contributing to a business model, a means to an end and a way of evaluating work done. It does not always reflect a direct cause and effect relationship but it does carry values of sustainability, innovation, beneficiary involvement, effective outcomes, replicability, scalability and the often overlooked exit strategy. Companies, not just 'traditional' investors, should consider making even modest investments as part of their community involvement strategy under ISO26000.

The New Economics Foundation, a think tank on philanthropy and economics for good, markets a tool for calculating the cash value of SROI.[31]

We have seen that companies are giving more to charities nowadays, with a recent trend for more of this to be in kind, hours and skills and less in cash. Investing in employee volunteering may be advantageous to the HR department but if its social return is minimal, is it worth doing?

Traditional charitable giving waves goodbye to cash and asks no questions after the gift has been made. People claim to be impressed if a pound spent on a charity Christmas card generates 95p to help donkeys but they don't seem to mind that only 28p of their National Lottery pound ends up with 'good causes'.

Corporate citizenship demands that inputs, outputs, outcomes and impacts are accounted for when donations (or investments) are made in the same way that councils must account for them to their voters and charities to their trustees and regulators. You wouldn't find professional investors just giving money away, would you?

SOCIAL IMPACT BONDS

It was Jack Straw, as Justice Secretary, who planted the seed for the first SIB in 2009 and Ken Clarke who celebrated its germination at Peterborough jail in autumn 2010. But what sort of plant is it? Who will harvest its fruits and are they good to eat?

Essentially, a group of investors says to the Government 'We will purchase the services of voluntary organisations to create an agreed, desirable, achievable and quantifiable social change over a defined period of time. In doing so we will save you money. If we are successful, you will pay us a return which makes the investment worth our while, but which is less than the cost to you of maintaining the status quo'.

In that first SIB a consortium of charities is being funded to reduce by at least 7.5 per cent over six years the re-offending rate of male prisoners who serve less than a year inside Peterborough jail. The degree of success will be measured by comparison with a control group who will not get the mentoring and support that these men will enjoy. A principal organisation

---

31 See www.neweconomics.org/projects/social-return-investment

delivering the programme is the St Giles Trust, whose 'Through the Gates' programme of intensive personal support for ex-offenders re-integrating into their communities has already been demonstrated as effective by the professionals at Pro Bono Economics.

The savings to the taxpayer are clear: fewer people going to prison, reduced burden on police and courts, less social cost. If the reduction is more than 7.5 per cent the return to the investors is greater. If the target is not reached it is the investors, including the Big Lottery Fund and 17 others co-ordinated by the group Social Finance, who take the hit. Unlike other 'payment by results' schemes SIBs do not offload the financial risk of outsourcing onto the third sector: the risk remains with the investors.

What is remarkable about SIBs is that the commissioner sets the agenda; the SIB funds public services from sources not previously utilised; it diversifies the voluntary sector's funding base; it breaks down the silos of traditional service provision and it gives all parties, government, investor and service provider, an incentive to succeed.

Critics say that SIBs will target the lowest hanging fruit. But does not every organisation choose which contracts it bids for? They say that SIBs favour schemes with quick results, but six years in the Peterborough case is much better than the annual or three-year commitments which the state normally awards.

Scalability is a challenge. The first SIB targets one group of prisoners in one prison. The highest financial returns will accrue if re-conviction rates rise at other prisons, so exaggerating the comparator. If SIBs were universal, what comparator could be used?

We are told that early intervention with socially challenged families raises aspirations, achievement and health outcomes and reduces offending rates in the next generation. Sure Start's outputs are complex, often intangible and very long term; they cater for local rather than national need; and they face the same funding crisis as everyone else.

As early intervention takes root, so long advocated by Graham Allen MP and now endorsed by ministers, will the professional risk takers – the investment community – show their true community spirit by getting their hands dirty in the Sure Start garden? Inputs will be readily measured and outputs less so, but outcomes and impacts will be increasingly difficult

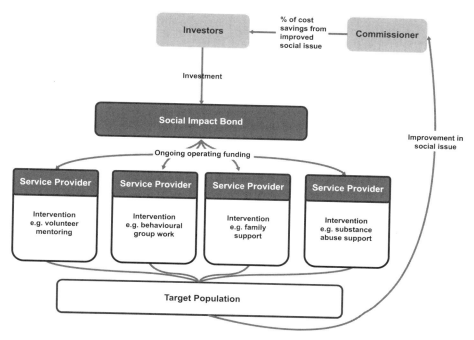

Figure 7.1   The structure of a typical Social Impact Bond
Source: www.socialfinance.org.uk/work/sibs

to measure. SIBs are not beds of roses so much as essential tools to have in the shed. Whatever challenges they raise, the potential benefits from SIBs in localities around the country are immense.

Where to Now?

David Robinson was sceptical about the Big Society when he first heard about it in the run-up to the 2010 general election. He thought it was a flash in the pan, a 'speech-writer's flourish', but six months later he admitted he had been wrong. He had been 'surprised and impressed' by the energy, consistency and insight Prime Minister Cameron had shown. He went on:

> There is scarcely any corner of the public domain that isn't looking to embrace new forms of participation, ownership and management.

And:

> *The idea that we should all have the opportunity and the encouragement to play a part in the communities we share is not a new one but it is a good one. I admire your big hearted vision and I respect your clear sighted perseverance in pursuing it …*

But:

> *… I am worried. Next year [2011] those who need our services – many amongst the most vulnerable in the country – will need them more. The expenditure cuts are a double whammy in communities like ours, increasing unemployment (the public sector is the biggest local employer) and closing services at the same time.*

Robinson is the co-founder of Community Links, a 30-year-old charity based in the London's East End where 1,500 volunteers serve 30,000 people each year in the most disadvantaged communities through a variety of projects. The Community Links portfolio includes some sophisticated and effective pro bono volunteering.

David Cameron has praised Community Links for its drive, focus and Big Society qualities on more than one occasion; he has called it 'one of Britain's most inspiring community organisations'.

In Robinson's letter to *The Guardian* published on 30 December 2010, from which the above quotes are taken,[32] he gives substance to his concerns:

> *… Organisations like us are surely the bedrock of the Big Society, and we are wobbling.*

> *Without buildings, leadership, training and support we can't grow our 'little platoons' quickly enough to fill the gaps. Indeed we won't even be able to sustain them at their current level. Cuts in public expenditure in many areas of our work, coupled with major changes in Legal Aid and New Deal mean most of our budget for 2011/2012 is at risk. Ultimately this will diminish our community not make it stronger.*

He called on the Prime Minister to slow down the cuts programme, do a proper impact study and inject £5 billion into the Big Society to make it happen. The £5 billion was the size of the funding cuts some claimed were being inflicted on the

---

32 See www.community-links.org/linksuk/?p=2225&cpage=1#

third sector. The Prime Minister's response is not, as far as I know, recorded. As another Chief Executive of a major charity told me:

A 25 per cent cut is not a cut; it's a major realignment.

No one will argue that the Big Society does not embody values and activities well worth having. Some will argue that there is little new in the idea and that many of the opportunities it presents already exist along with much of the necessary legal framework. I have argued that it is not the cutting of the money that will have the biggest impact although that will be profound. It will be the loss of networks, experience and expertise in the previously comprehensive and ubiquitous local authority framework. Those losses will make it impossible for a third sector-based Big Society to function in a co-ordinated manner which is universally accessible and fair to those who need those services. Where those networks and intra-community bonds are the weakest is where they are most likely to disappear and leave people, communities and voluntary sector groups floundering.

Many parody the Big Society idea as dumping responsibility for delivering services on communities and volunteers and being driven by the traditional 'small government' Conservative ideal. As David Robinson says, the sheer speed of what is happening makes it difficult to avoid that conclusion. But even with the new vanguard of neighbourhood and community co-ordinators, another round of wheels being reinvented, if communities do not have the capacity to pick up the pieces of what David Cameron used to call 'Broken Britain', who does? Who else has the networks, the funds, the manpower to deliver the Big Society? Step forward business, the private sector.

Logistics, supply chains and networking are meat and drink to the business community – look how Coca-Cola's distribution mechanism is being used to supply medicines and other commodities in Africa. The private sector cannot say it does not have the funds – what capital assets are sitting in business bank accounts, just waiting to be put to good use, if only on loan? One estimate says £146 billion.[33] As for manpower, in America the voluntary sector as a whole is far more workplace-based than it is here, so might employee volunteering – perhaps accompanied by a form of national voluntary service – be the future?

---

33 Senior partner Stephen Lloyd, speaking to an event organised by charity lawyers Bates, Wells and Braithwaite on Regulating Social Finance, June 2011.

In a fair trade café in a London church cum charity centre I saw 30 young people scrubbing, polishing, planting and sweeping, their green teeshirts bearing the words 'Starbucks Community Service'. On April 5 2011 Starbucks mobilised its workforce across nine UK cities in partnership with the charity UK Youth for eight hours of community-based volunteering. Starbucks' web site informs us that: 'Community service projects will focus on literacy, refurbishing schools, neighbourhood renovations, as well as technology, gardening and painting projects'.

During the year Starbucks' employees globally will give 200,000 hours of community service to 2,000 projects on top of their longstanding and comprehensive ten-year UK partnerships with the National Literacy Trust and the Prince's Trust. At the same time the company has a profound commitment to ethical sourcing of coffee and tea which acknowledges that they are produced by real people in real communities. Starbucks' global goal for all acts of employee volunteering is a five-fold increase by 2015.

This particular group of 16 to 18-year-olds came from Youth Cymru in Cardiff to give the centre a makeover. Co-ordinated by the Starbucks' employees, many had been released from sixth form for the day – the Welsh baccalaureate includes community service (if not specifically missionary work in England).

The programme includes 'masterclasses' to share experiences and celebrate the work of the volunteers. One outcome is for the young people to use the experience to design and execute similar community projects in their home towns.

'We've been a partner of Starbucks for around two years', UK Youth's young Ambassador Josh Cope told me. 'We found out about the project online, responded to Starbucks' tender and were chosen as their partner'.

He went on to explain that UK Youth is also involved with programmes such as Think Big (with Telephonica O_2 as a partner throughout most of Europe), Roadsafe (with the transport company UPS) and Bike Club (Asda) and that they get an office in Canary Wharf and much of their legal advice for free.

'Business is the future for charity partnerships', he says, 'but charities have to grow up. It looks bad if they're just after the money and nothing else from these partners, it's a missed opportunity'.

He praises O$_2$ for bringing together different charities with different viewpoints: 'No Government scheme would ever have got Youth Cymru and Women's Royal Voluntary Service (WRVS) working on the same project', he told me.

Josh is very down to earth and practical for one so young. I calm my enthusiasm and remember the statistics: only 850 UK companies are members of the biggest group which fosters CR. There is a new international standard on social responsibility, ISO26000, which cannot be accredited and is therefore not enforceable. Just 10 per cent of all the world's financial investments are classed as 'responsible'.

Michael Porter, the guru of Creating Shared Value, told the Nestlé Global Forum on Shared Value in May 2011:

> *Business has been thinking that its role in society is to do CSR. CSR is fundamentally about philanthropy, it's about giving back, it's about compliance with rules and I think what I have concluded anyway is that CSR just hasn't worked.*

I agree that CSR risks being seen in simplistic terms and becoming compliance-led; both would be unfortunate. But as the sustainability guru, John Elkington, like Porter an advisor to Nestlé, says in response to him (Elkington, 2011):

> *CSR pioneers were revolutionary precisely because they went way beyond compliance regimes – and their work in areas like stakeholder engagement and non-financial reporting pushed the envelope.*

Let us not worry about which acronym, CSR, SR, CR or CSV best describes the holistic approach that corporate citizens need to make to be part of the Big Society – or whatever that ends up being called.

Let us strip 'Big Society' of its political connotations and treat it at face value. Whether Britain is broken today or not, great stresses are in the pipeline from funding, framework and service cuts. Communities are going to have to cope. No doubt many will rise to the occasion and their voluntary bodies will be at the fore whilst others will stumble and fall.

At the same time corporate citizenship has become a more legitimate and widespread public expectation of business and people can tell when a corporate's commitment is less than total. It is widely accepted that people are more likely to buy from companies they trust, work productively for organisations they respect and recommend businesses they admire. It is not only the companies that deliver quasi-public services that can benefit from the boost that trust, reputation and community engagement can bring. No longer is money the only currency of such exchanges; cash, goods and time move in one direction and reputation and image in the other, with the cross-fertilisation of skills and expertise.

To date there has been little coherent leadership from Government in Britain's path to corporate citizenship or from the corporate world's own ranks, though excellent exemplars exist. It has taken years for the business case for environmentally sound practices to be established as mainstream; community-based practices are not there yet and there is no equivalent to the climate change imperative breathing down boardroom necks on the social agenda.

When they are good, community-focused companies are very, very good; but when they are bad they are neglectful to the point of irresponsibility.

The good get together but they are talking to themselves; charities outside the premier league still too often regard business as the enemy or at least having nothing meaningful to offer them.

We are all missing several tricks.

Predictions and Bottom Lines

An author of a recent 'how to …' book on business–charity partnerships was speaking at a working breakfast under Chatham House rules. I asked the group what additional measures would be needed to encourage business to adopt the community involvement agenda under the sixth strand of ISO26000 and the author replied, 'Tax incentives'.

It ain't going to happen.

As drastic cuts are made in local and national services; as the third sector faces cuts which will close groups down; and as the Coalition's long-term strategy is for spending to bounce back (but not yet) whilst the tax bill will not rise, there will be no such give away.

The sixth strand of ISO26000 (Community involvement and development) will not be made statutory and nor will the Government adopt an explicit 'do community involvement of your own accord or we will oblige you to do it' approach. There will be no further legislation in this Parliament on its first five strands.

The best corporate citizens will 'do' CSR ever better, adopt more holistic and medium-term approaches and develop multiple parallel mission-specific partnerships with charities rather than link with big names for the sake of big names. Cash will represent a smaller proportion of a growing market for corporate giving and common standards of measurement will slowly gain currency.

Investment by the financial market in social enterprises large and small will blossom as the number of investors willing to sacrifice a few percentage points of profit in the interests of social change grows; but as an organising force it will lack the global coherence that only accountable government can bring. Ethical investment more generally will grow.

The time scale of the Government's public spending cuts (principally the spending period 2011–14) will prove too demanding a target for community, social enterprise and third sector providers to pick up the pieces. On the day Lord Nat Wei announced he was no longer advising the Government on Big Society he said that achieving it required a culture change that could take two Parliaments to achieve.[34]

The private sector, admonished by Francis Maude for seeking too big a share of outsourced services early in 2011, will quietly step in.

Major donor philanthropy, philanthrocapitalist or otherwise, will continue but become more varied. Outcomes will become more important to donors but integration of philanthropic targeting into mainstream social investment will be slow. Part of the health of the philanthropic sector will come from the new rich: witness, for example, rock stars such as Annie Lennox OBE (AIDS in Africa), Pixie Lott (Beatbullying), Kellie Holmes (young people through v). Robbie Williams has been a patron of his local children's hospice in Stoke on Trent since 2002, helping them raise £2 million each year to keep going. The veteran journalist Sandy Gall has been honoured for his work in funding artificial limbs in Afghanistan and footballers such as Chelsea's Didier Drogba

---

34 See www.bbc.co.uk/news/uk-politics-13529808 [May 2011].

have their own foundations up and running. Drogba funds education and health services in his native Ivory Coast including building a hospital.[35]

The Companies Act 2006 requires companies to report on their environmental and community investment. The Government will bring forward regulations that will ensure that this is integrated into mainstream reporting and its criteria will allow comparison and progress to be measured, hopefully based on GRI principles.

Charities will continue to become more professional at the top but many smaller ones will disappear due to either closure or a long anticipated wave of mergers. Progress on charities becoming prime contractors will be more marked at local authority level than at regional or national levels, not least because of the evolution of professional third sector hubs.

Thought leaders in business, frustrated by the lack of buy-in on community engagement, will become even more focused on their own company's excellence. More people within the private sector will say the right things and the best will continue to lead the pack, with some pulling further ahead before the bulk starts to edge forward gradually. Some fortunate communities will gain real benefit from those social enterprises which receive investment from sponsoring companies but they will be piecemeal.

Disadvantaged communities will make the slowest progress towards creating a Big Society. This was anticipated in the Young Foundation report 'Sinking and Swimming' in 2009, which suggested that increased investment in conventional and traditional forms of service provision by the Labour Government from 1997 onwards had been subject to the law of diminishing returns (Young Foundation, 2009). Every initiative to tackle disadvantage – dedicated zones, Tax Credits, Sure Start, the half-hearted Total Place – had made progress but only so far.

The End of the Road for Big Government?

Almost every measure of disadvantage – homelessness, unemployment, child poverty, teen pregnancy – diminished under Labour but then stalled. Some measures of failure – like the writing of prescriptions to treat depression or the gap between richest and poorest in society – had continued to rise almost

---

35 See www.thedidierdrogbafoundation.com/

unabated over the period. Had a limit been reached to what the state could achieve? Had the wholesale provision of services reached the end of the road? Was the personalisation of services, which had started with domiciliary care and was at the heart of the Social Impact Bond on reoffending in Peterborough, the only way forward? How could that model be applied to children, housing, sustainable job creation?

Has state provision of universally accessible services reached the end of its useful life? Abandoning the deprived and disadvantaged is neither a moral nor a long-term economic option, so a conclusion that is politically uncomfortable to some has to be confronted: that the community-based Big Society model of provision, the true heir of Tony Blair's legacy that 'it's how services are provided that matters, not who provides them' is starting to look like the way forward.

The Clinton/Blair Third Way was revolutionary because it said: 'Hang on guys, not everything the other lot says is necessarily wrong, no tradition has a monopoly on good ideas'. It said that pragmatism was better than dogmatism, that 'what works' trumped all and that the balance between market forces

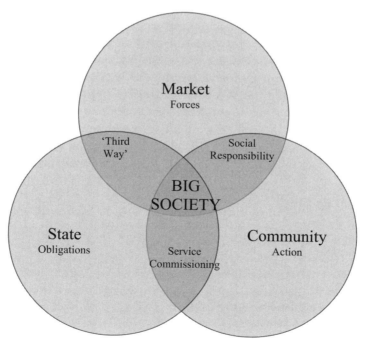

Figure 7.2   The Big Society

and state provision would be different in different circumstances for different services. If the third way was about the proper balance between markets and the state then Big Society ought to be about the three-way balance with community too.

Had the 'third way' been of the third millennium rather than the 1990s no doubt more credit for the potential of the third sector and communities would have been explicitly given. 'What works' is another way of saying 'a worthwhile alignment of inputs, outputs and outcomes'. This is echoed too in Maurice Glasman's 'Blue Labour' and Will Hutton's 'good capitalism' (Hutton, 2011). Bill Clinton recognised this in an article for the *Financial Times* in January 2012.[36]

David Cameron has already distanced himself from Margaret Thatcher's adage that 'there is no such thing as society'; and he has tried with various degrees of success to distance himself and his style from the 'heir of Blair' label.

Yet his Big Society does have its origins in the Tory ideological tradition of the small state; in a radical reinterpretation of John Major's subsidiarity theory; in the leftist Co-operative and mutuals movement and in the social democratic Blairite Third Way. Together these traditions do indeed describe a Big Society.

Patrick Diamond, a former advisor in Tony Blair's Downing Street, points out that neither Bevan nor Beveridge saw the National Health Service (NHS) as a rigid and monolithic exclusive provider of health care (Diamond, 2011). In calling for a programme of affiliative welfare (helping each other), new mutualism (variations on a co-operative theme), local democratic empowerment and a civil economy (developing pluralistic local markets) he is asserting exactly the need to recognise the limits of the state and the weaknesses of both the Big Society and the Third Way and move forward thus enlightened.

He has it absolutely right.

With such a plethora of traditions behind it, properly funded and with appropriate and motivated partners in the private sector, the public sector and the third sector how can a multidimensional Big Society possibly fail?

Well, you wouldn't want to start from here.

---

36   See http://www.ft.com/cms/s/0/544c317a-42a2-11e1-93ea-00144feab49a.html#axzz1o5XCVFos

Bibliography

Ainsworth, D. 2011. Social Investment Business will Launch Consortia to Bid for Public Sector Contracts, *Third Sector*, 15 March 2011. Available at www.thirdsector.co.uk/news/rss/article/1060132/Social-Investment-Business-will-launch-consortia-bid-public-sector-contracts/ [accessed June 2011].

Anderson, M. and Escher, P. 2010. *The MBA Oath: Setting a Higher Standard for Business Leaders*, Portfolio, New York.

Archambault, E. 2000. The Third Sector in France, *German Policy Studies*, Volume 1. Available at www.questia.com/googleScholar.qst;jsessionid=84C38F13B35 634B2C750A7BE6262AF44.inst1_1b?docId=5002380114 [accessed June 2011].

Baksi, C. 2011. Pro Bono Thrives in Private Practice, *Law Society Gazette*, 10 February 2011. Available at www.lawgazette.co.uk/news/pro-bono-thrives-private-practice [accessed June 2011].

Ball, J. 2011. Innocent Smoothie Maker says Charity Cash Bottled for Best Interest Rate, *The Guardian*, 26 May 2011. Available at www.guardian.co.uk/uk/2011/may/26/innocent-smoothies-charity-cash [accessed June 2011].

Benjamin, A. 2007. Loan Star (interview with Richard Gutch), *The Guardian*, 4 July 2007. Available at www.guardian.co.uk/society/2007/jul/04/voluntary sector.guardiansocietysupplement [accessed June 2011].

Bishop, M. and Green, M. 2008. *Philanthrocapitalism: How the Rich can Save the World*, Bloomsbury, London

BITC and Little, A.D. 2003. *The Business Case for Corporate Responsibility*, BITC, London

Boffey, D. 2011. Council Sell-off of Clothing Banks 'Threatens Survival' of Charity Shops, *The Guardian*, 29 May 2011. Available at www.guardian.co.uk/society/2011/may/29/charities-clothing-banks-privatisation [accessed June 2011].

Brandsma, P., Moratis, L. and Cochius, T. 2009. *Motivations for and Potential Barriers of ISO26000 Uptake in the Netherlands*, CSR Institute, Rotterdam; quoted in Moratis and Cochius (2011)

Brindle, D. 2011. Charities Shine in Reputation Chart, *The Guardian*, 2 June 2010. Available at www.guardian.co.uk/society/2010/jun/02/charities-shine-reputation-chart [accessed June 2011].

Butler, P. 2011. Cuts: Are Charities Getting a Fair Share of the 'Back to Work' Business? *The Guardian*, 1 April 2011. Available at www.guardian.co.uk/voluntary-sector [accessed June 2011].

C&E Advisory. 2011. *Corporate–NGO Partnerships Barometer*. Available at www.candeadvisory.com/projects/report [accessed June 2011].

CAF (Charities Aid Foundation). 2011. *The World Giving Index 2011*.

Clinton, B. 2012. Charity Needs Capitalism to Solve the World's Problems, *Financial Times*, 20 January 2012. Available at http://www.ft.com/cms/s/0/544c3 17a-42a2-11e1-93ea-00144feab49a.html#axzz1o5XCVFos [accessed June 2011].

Cohen, E. 2010. *CSR for HR, A Necessary Partnership for Advancing Responsible Business Practices*, Greenleaf Publishing, Sheffield.

Co-operative Group. 2010. *The Co-operative Sustainability Report: Focus on Sustainability*, 2010. Available at www.co-operative.coop/Corporate/sustainability/2010/downloads/FINAL_Sustainability_Report_2009.pdf [accessed June 2011].

Cowie, I. 2011. 10 DIY Tips to Avoid Breaking the Bribery Act, *The Daily Telegraph*, 1 July 2011. Available at http://blogs.telegraph.co.uk/finance/ianmcowie/100010710/10-diy-tips-to-avoid-breaking-the-bribery-act/ [accessed June 2011].

Curtis, P. 2011. MPs Condemn Coalition's Bonfire of the Quangos as Botched, *The Guardian*, 7 January 2011. Available at www.guardian.co.uk/politics/2011/jan/07/mps-committee-bonfire-quangos-botched [accessed June 2011].

Diamond, P. 2011. From the Big Society to the Good Society, *Civitas Review*, Volume 8, Issue 1, February 2011. Available at www.civitas.org.uk/pdf/CivitasReviewFebruary2011.pdf [accessed June 2011].

Department for Trade and Industry (DTI). 2004. *Corporate Social Responsibility: A Government Update*. Available at http://webarchive.nationalarchives.gov.uk/+/http://www.bis.gov.uk/files/file48771.pdf [accessed June 2011].

Elkington, J. 1997. *Cannibals with Forks: The Triple Bottom Line of 21st Century Business*, Capstone, Minnesota.

Elkington, J. 2011. Don't Abandon CSR for Creating Shared Value Just Yet, *The Guardian*, 25 May 2011. Available at www.guardian.co.uk/sustainable-business/sustainability-with-john-elkington/corporate-social-resposibility-creating-shared-value?& [accessed June 2011].

Ellis, T. 2010. A New Dawn? *Charities Direct*, November 2010. Available at www.charitiesdirect.com/caritas-magazine/a-new-dawn-836.html [accessed June 2011].

Federation of Small Businesses. 2007. *Social and Environmental Responsibility and the Small Business Owner*. Available at www.fsb.org.uk/policy/assets/ CSR%20Dec%202008.pdf [accessed June 2011].

Fresh Minds. 2011. Access to Volunteering Evaluation, Fresh Minds. Available at www.freshmindsresearch.co.uk/latest-thinking/ [accessed June 2011].

Funding Commission. 2010. *Funding the Future*, NCVO, December 2010. Available at www.ncvo-vol.org.uk/sites/default/files/A4_Summary.pdf [accessed June 2011].

Gammon, A. and Ellison, G. 2010. *Volunteering is the Business*, v and YouGov, London. Available at http://vinspired.com/uploads/admin_assets/datas/1541 /original/Volunteering_is_the_Business_FINAL.pdf [accessed June 2011].

Harrington, S. 2011. HR/CSR, *Human Resources*, January 2011. Available at http://www.hrmagazine.co.uk/hr/news/1015217/time-hr-csr [accessed June 2011].

Hodgson, R., Berry, L., Hind, A., Melmoth, G., Thompson, D. and Tyler, D., and the secretariat – Anderton, E., Gray, C., Hale, D. and Wallace, S. 2011. *Unshackling Good Neighbours, Report of the Task Force Established to Consider how to cut Red Tape for Small Charities, Voluntary Organisations and Social Enterprises*. Available at www.cabinetoffice.gov.uk/sites/default/files/resources /unshackling-good-neighbours.pdf [accessed June 2011].

Hutton, W. 2011. Liberal Social Democracy, Fairness and Good Capitalism, *Policy Network*, 9 May 2011. Available at www.policy-network.net/articles/ 3999/Liberal-social-democracy-fairness-and-good-capitalism-- [accessed June 2011].

Jones, G. 2010. BTCV makes Big Property Saving after Enlisting Pro Bono Support, *Civil Society Finance*, March 2010. Available at www.civilsociety. co.uk/finance/news/content/6164/btcv_makes_big_property_saving_after_ enlisting_pro_bono_support [accessed June 2011].

Jump, P. 2009. France Warned on Cross-border Donations, *Third Sector*, 1 December 2009. Available at www.thirdsector.co.uk/news/Article/970410/ france-warned-cross-border-donations/ [accessed June 2011].

King, I. 2011. Mapping British Business: Public Service, *The Times*, 27 April 2011. Available at www.mappingbritishbusiness.co.uk/public-services/ Introduction/ [accessed June 2011].

Lillya, D. 2011. *The Guide to UK Company Giving 2010–11*. Directory of Social Change, London.

Little, M. 2007. Mutuals Must Have Bigger Role in Services – Co-operative Party, *Third Sector*, 17 January 2007. Available at www.thirdsector.co.uk/ news/Article/628694/mutuals-bigger-role-services-co-operative-party/ [accessed June 2011].

Macleod, S. 2010. CSR is no Longer a 'Bolt-on' Activity, *The Guardian*, 10 December 2010. Available at www.guardian.co.uk/sustainable-business/blog/csr-corporate-social-responsibility?intcmp=122 [accessed June 2011].

Mason, T. 2011. Rising Pressure, *Charity Finance*, April 2011.

Middleton, A. 2010. *Evidence, Ideology and the Big Society*, The Governance Foundation. Available at www.governancefoundation.org/documents/Evidence_Ideology_and_the_Big_Society.pdf [accessed June 2011].

Moore, S. 1977. *Essential Handbook of Voluntary Work: Working for Free*, Pan, London.

Moratis, L. and Cochius, T. 2011. *ISO26000: The Business Guide to the New Standard on Social Responsibility*, Greenleaf, Sheffield.

National Audit Office (NAO). 2012. *Central Government's Implementation of the National Compact*. Available at www.nao.org.uk/publications/1012/national_compact.aspx [accessed June 2011].

NESTA/Young Foundation. 2011. *Growing Social Enterprises*, NESTA, London.

Neuberger, J. et al. 2008. *Manifesto for Change*, Volunteering England, London.

Norman, J. 2010. *Big Society*, University of Buckingham Press, Buckingham.

Osman, M. 2011. In-kind Donations: Who Benefits? *Humanitarian Exchange*, Issue 49, January 2011.

Pembroke, J. 2010. The Shape of Things to Come, *C'llr*, December 2010, LGIU. Available at https://member.lgiu.org.uk/SiteCollectionDocuments/Cllr/Cllr%20Dec%202010.pdf [accessed June 2011].

Pharaoh, C. 2011. Swings and Roundabouts, *Fundraising*, Issue 49, July 2011.

Pharaoh, C. and Keidan, C. 2010. *Family Foundation Giving Trends, 2010*, Centre for Charitable Giving and Philanthropy/Alliance Publishing Trust, 2010. Available at www.cgap.org.uk/news/72/76/Family-Foundation-Giving-Trends-2010.html [accessed June 2011].

Plummer, J. 2011. Office for Civil Society 'Consistently Fails to Comply with the Compact', *Third Sector*, 11 March 2011. Available at www.thirdsector.co.uk/news/archive/1059510/Office-Civil-Society-consistently-fails-comply-Compact/?DCMP=ILC-SEARCH [accessed June 2011].

Prospect. 2008. *Negotiator's Guide: Corporate Social Responsibility*, Prospect Trade Union, London. Available at www.prospect.org.uk/resources_and_publications/negotiatorguides?_ts=1 [accessed June 2011].

Quirke, D. 1998. *Corporate Volunteering: The Potential and the Way Forward*, Australian Volunteer Programme Management. Available at www.ozvpm.com/resourcebank/resource_corporate.php [accessed June 2011].

Saxton, J. 2011. Payroll Giving: Loved by Government, Loathed by Fundraisers, *The Guardian Voluntary Sector Blog*, 29 June 2011. Available at www.guardian.co.uk/voluntary-sector-network/2011/jun/29/payroll-giving-downsides-for-fundraisers [accessed June 2011].

Serco. 2010. *Corporate Responsibility Review 2009*. Available at www.serco.com/ Images/Corporate_Responsibiilty_Report_2009_tcm3-34265.pdf [accessed June 2011].

Shared Intelligence. 2008. *Evaluation of the National Programme for Third Sector Commissioning*, Cabinet Office and IDeA, 2008. Available at www.idea.gov. uk/idk/aio/8024335www.idea.gov.uk/idk/aio/8024335 [accessed June 2011].

Smouha, B. 2011. *The Trustee's Dilemma: to Spend or to Save?*, Coalition for Efficiency. Available at www.cfefficiency.org.uk/THE%20TRUSTEE'S%20 DILEMMA%20-%20TO%20SPEND%20OR%20TO%20SAVE.pdf [accessed June 2011].

Stanford, P. 2002. Campaigning: Sounds Like a Revolution, *Third Sector*, 31 July 2002. Available at www.thirdsector.co.uk/news/archive/615281/ CAMPAIGNING-Sounds-Revolution---RNID-engaged-classic-campaigning-persuade-Government-provide-digital-hearing-aids-free-NHS-prepared-stuck-dirty-work/?DCMP=ILC-SEARCH [accessed June 2011].

Tennyson, R. 1998. *Managing Partnerships: Tools for Mobilising the Public Sector, Business and Civil Society as Partners in Development*, Prince of Wales Business Leaders' Forum, London (out of print).

Tennyson, R. 2004. *The Brokering Guidebook – Tools for Navigating Cross Sector Partnerships*, IBLF, London.

The Social Investment Consultancy. 2011. *Q1 briefing: Financing Small Enterprises in the UK*. TSIC, quoting JP Morgan Global Research, 2010, *Impact Investments: an Emerging Asset Class*. Available at www.tsiconsultancy.com/wp-content/ uploads/tsic-2011-q1-briefing-financing-social-enterprises-in-the-uk.pdf [accessed June 2011].

Thornton, G. and Jenkins, R. 2010. *Social and Economic Benefits of the Compact, Commission for the Compact*, September 2010. No longer available on the Commission's web site but available at, for example: www.raise-networks. org.uk/media/documents/socialandeconomicbenefitsreportfinal.pdf [accessed June 2011].

Tomorrow's Company. 2011. *Tomorrow's Force for Good*, Tomorrow's Company. Available at www.forceforgood.com/Uploaded_Content/tool/11102011173 550829.pdf [accessed June 2011].

UN Global Compact. 2010. *A Guide to Engagement in the Global Compact*, UNGC, New York.

Wiggins, K. 2010. Minister Admits Big Society will be 'Chaotic', *Third Sector*, 5 October 2010. Available at www.thirdsector.co.uk/news/Article/1033203/ minister-admits-big-society-will-chaotic/ [accessed June 2011].

Wiggins, K. and Cook, S. 2011. Interview: Dame Suzi Leather, *Third Sector*, 22 February 2011. Available at www.thirdsector.co.uk/news/Article/1055835/Interview-Dame-Suzi-Leather [accessed June 2011].

Young Foundation. 2009. *Sinking and Swimming: Understanding Britain's Unmet Needs*, Young Foundation. Available at www.youngfoundation.org/general-/-all/news/sinking-and-swimming-understanding-britains-unmet-needs [accessed June 2011].

Zemmeck, M. et al. 2011. *Use it or Lose it: A Summative Evaluation of the Compact*, Commission for the Compact, 2011. No longer available on the Commission web site but available at, for example, www.baringfoundation.org.uk/CompactUIOLI.pdf [accessed June 2011].

Zurich Municipal and Ipsos-MORI. 2010. *Tough Choices*. Zurich. Available at www.ipsos-mori.com/researchpublications/publications/publication.aspx?oItemId=1393 [accessed June 2011].

Index

The use of **bold** indicates entries of particular importance on a given subject.

If you have found this book useful you may be interested in other titles from Gower

Human Resources or Human Capital?
Managing People as Assets
Andrew Mayo
Hardback: 978-1-4094-2285-3
e-book: 978-1-4094-2286-0

Hyperthinking
Creating a New Mindset for the Digital Age
Philip Weiss
Paperback: 978-1-4094-2845-9
e-book: 978-1-4094-2846-6

The Culture Builders
Leadership Strategies for Employee Performance
Jane Sparrow
Paperback: 978-1-4094-3724-6
e-book: 978-1-4094-3725-3

Managing Sustainable Development Programmes
A Learning Approach to Change
Göran Brulin and Lennart Svensson
Hardback: 978-1-4094-3719-2
e-book: 978-1-4094-3720-8

Leading Complex Projects and Tools for Complex Projects
Two Volume Set
Kaye Remington
Hardback: 978-1-4094-4143-4

GOWER

Change Leadership
Developing a Change-Adept Organization
Martin Orridge
Paperback: 978-0-566-08935-0
e-book: 978-0-566-09243-5

Project Psychology
Using Psychological Models and Techniques to Create
a Successful Project
Sharon De Mascia
Hardback: 978-0-566-08942-8
e-book: 978-1-4094-3829-8

Project-Based Organizations
A Guide
Michel Thiry
Paperback: 978-0-566-08880-3

Program Management
Michel Thiry
Paperback: 978-0-566-08882-7
e-book: 978-1-4094-0716-4

Visit **www.gowerpublishing.com** and

- search the entire catalogue of Gower books in print
- order titles online at 10% discount
- take advantage of special offers
- sign up for our monthly e-mail update service
- download free sample chapters from all recent titles
- download or order our catalogue